NARRATIVES OF

NARRATIVES OF CHILDHOOD

VU University Press is an imprint of:
VU Boekhandel/Uitgeverij bv
De Boelelaan 1105
1081 HV Amsterdam
The Netherlands
e-mail: vu-uitgeverij@vuboekhandel.nl

ISBN 90 5383 846 5
NUR 847

Design cover: De Ontwerperij (Marcel Bakker), Amsterdam
Lay out: Studio Brouwer, Haarlem
Printer: Wilco, Amersfoort

contents

I
REFLECTIONS

[1]

Multiple narratives of childhood: Tools for the improvement of early childhood education

Bert van Oers

> *Better than larger values,*
> *However true their show;*
> *This timid life of evidence*
> *Keeps pleading, "I don't know"*
> Emily Dickinson (1891), COLLECTED POEMS

The ecology of child development

One of the great advancements of developmental studies is the acknowledgement of the contextual nature of child development. Nowadays child development is generally conceived of as a process that is driven by a multiplicity of forces of biological and sociocultural nature. A great deal of the academic efforts concerning the study of development is spent in teasing out the nature of these forces, their relative weight, and their interactions for the explanation of child development.

Definitely, it is an important objective for the human sciences to understand the impact of bio-neurological characteristics for human psychological development, but it is also a field that can easily lead us astray. The establishment of the bio-neurological facts by itself can never satisfyingly explain human development, for it is the interpretation and the resulting meanings of those facts for the educators (parents, teacher, care-takers, doctors) that determine to a great extent how these facts will influence the development of individual humans. Vygotsky addressed this issue in his study of the fundamental problems of anomalous developments. He distinguished *primary causes*, related to the specific biological or neurological conditions of a child, and *secondary causes*, which consist of the typical ways of interacting of the educator with the child that are assumed to be appropriate for this child given its special characteristics (Vygotsky, 1929/1983, p. 52). These interaction styles (as secondary causes) are basically dependent on the sociocultural valuations of the child's habitus and the cultural insights into the nature of the primary causes. Vygotsky often refers to the development of blind or hearing-impaired people as an example. It is evident that their psychological development is not primarily or exclusively determined by their physical handicaps but depends on the society's success in finding alternative ways of interacting (especially: communicating) with the blind (or hearing impaired), for instance by the invention of Braille or sign language.

Vygotsky's theory of compensation is evident for these clear cases of blindness or deafness, but the thesis is probably also plausible for all other human characteristics that allegedly have an impact on human development. Important conclusions follow from this theoretical starting point. First of all, it emphasises the relevance of the study and careful organisation of appropriate ways of interactions with the developing child, taking into account his or her special characteristics, and finding ways of sensitive interaction and communication. Secondly, it makes sense, from a pedagogical point of view, to focus attention exclusively on the qualities of the educational context and interactions (like we will do in this book), without denying the existence and influence of genetic predispositions (through biological – neurological factors).

Likewise, Bronfenbrenner's bio-ecological theory of human development starts out from a similar assumption and argues that the explanation of human development needs both a profound study of the direct interactions with the child and a deeper understanding of the institutional contexts of these developmental processes (see Bronfenbrenner & Cecci, 1994). The direct interactions (or 'proximal processes' as Bronfenbrenner calls them) exert decisive influences on the child's course of development, especially when these interactions are sensitively tuned to the specific developmental qualities of the child. These processes operate over time and can have different effects on development: significantly furthering the development of children's and adults' competences, while at the same time buffering dysfunctional states and behaviours.

But as Bronfenbrenner points out, the style of interacting with children in itself is not located in a cultural vacuum, but depends on the imagination and permissiveness of the cultural environment (including its different institutions). Or to put it differently: the style of interacting with children depends on what the cultural community can imagine as an acceptable and developmentally productive environment, and on what this community on the basis of its conventions and norms permits the members to do with their children. In his seminal work on the ecology of human development Bronfenbrenner (1979) already elaborates the concept of human belief systems as forces that induce and sustain human development. Bronfenbrenner argues that the beliefs (and developmental theories) of parents, peers, teachers, and mentors exert a powerful influence on the direction and effectiveness of educational interactions (proximal processes). And as these beliefs are subject to change as a function of education, training, intervention, mass media, research etc., development is a function of the cultural understandings (belief systems) of a community regarding child development.

The view on child development as dependent on the direct environment of the child has evolved into a contextual conception of child development. Super & Harkness (1986) developed a framework for thinking about contextualised development with the notion of developmental niche. The term 'niche' is borrowed from biological ecology and refers to the special features of the environment an organism inhabits. In a psychological sense, a developmental niche refers to the direct and specific sociocultural environment in which a person acts and interacts. Basic constituents of the niche, according to Super & Harkness, are the (1) *physical and social settings of everyday life*, (2) the *customs of child rearing* and (3) the *psychology of the caretakers.*

Gauvain (1996, 2001) elaborates her theory of contextualised development along simi- lar lines, but emphasises the role of cultural activities as the direct context for deve- lopment. From her activity theoretical perspective Gauvain (2001, p. 45) argues:

> "The sociocultural context of development –that is its values, goals, and practices of the community- is instantiated in local social situations via the ways in which people interact and the areas of mental functioning that are stressed and rewarded in these settings and transactions".

The contextual view of human development is an attempt to explain human develop- ment in terms of social interactions within the direct environment of the developing individual. As I argued elsewhere, a powerful way of conceptualising this direct envi- ronment is to interpret it in terms of activities and especially of activities that are bound up with a particular cultural community (see also van Oers, 1998). Basically, such sociocultural activities are historically evolving systems. The activities in a fami- ly, in a school, in a particular intervention program, a church, sport clubs, court house, shopping centres etc are all cultural products. These are evolving systems that influ- ence their members' actions differently and that, consequently, have different deve- lopmental effects.

Vygotsky and El'konin also acknowledged this historical evolution of developmental contexts. The permanent transformation of cultural activity systems, due to changing cultural situations and conditions that result from the new cultural products (inclu- ding understandings!) and tools, regulate people's actions in new ways. These new actions provoke new courses of individual development. But Vygotsky and El'konin not only referred to the sociogenetic changes of activity systems. According to Vygotsky (1984, p. 258 – 260) the dynamics of individual development are to a great extent also dependent upon the special way the person relates to his or her environ- ment and this depends on the developmental stage or, to put it more precisely, on the leading activity of the person. The leading activity of a person is based on the dominant motivation of the person and manifests itself in his/her way of relating to the situation. Every developmental stage can be characterised by a particular leading activity (like 'play' for the young child, 'learning activity' for the older child and for the young ado- lescent, or 'labour' for the adult). This specific and unique relationship of a person with his or her social environment is called *'the social situation of development'* (Vygotsky, 1984, p. 258). Activities in context not only have a sociogenetic dimension, but also an ontogenetic dimension. Both dimensions are relevant for the understan- ding of child behaviour. They are related in a profound way, as every ontogenetic stage is partly an offspring of a particular stage in sociogenesis.

The formation of such developmental contexts depends on the *understandings* in the community of the basic elements of that social context (like goals, values, tools, iden- tity, childhood, conventions, knowledge etc). The interactions that influence child development (as proximal processes) are guided by the structure of the activity, the understandings and practices of the interacting members, and by their mutual understandings of each others' meanings and intentions.

A deeper understanding of the process and the organisation of contexts and interactions is a basic task for pedagogical psychology. A huge number of studies concerning the promotion of development in context is already carried out and still under way. One of the remarkable characteristics of many of these studies is that they deal in one way or another with the genesis, transformation, and transaction of meanings. Meanings are involved when people are engaged in (proximal) interactions, but meanings are also involved when educators discuss possible ways of intervention or interactions for the benefit of the children. All those meanings are by themselves contextualised constructions: they fit into a more or less coherent whole. They systematise individual utterances, point to referents and trigger anticipations. In short: the language-based processes that constitute or guide interactions seem to be of a narrative nature. Narrativity seems to be an essential element in the ecology of human development. In order to gain a more profound understanding of contextualised developmental processes it is fruitful to engage in a deeper study of narratives.

On the nature of narratives

One of the first attempts at defining the essence of human narratives can be found in Aristotle's "*Poetics*". In his view any narrative is a recounting of a *whole*, which has a beginning, a middle part and an ending. The beginning presents the occasion that calls for a certain act or story (it can be a cause, provocation, pretext, or an unexpected event, etc). It is not necessarily a result of a previous event, but it always has a follow up. The middle part describes the course of events and incidents, and the ending gives an account of how the tensions were solved and often refers to the future (like in: 'they lived happily ever after'). The ending, according to Aristotle, follows naturally after something, either as its necessary or usual consequent, and with nothing necessarily after it (Aristotle, *Poetics*, 7, 1450^b: 25 – 31). So we can say that a narrative is a structured, clearly identifiable and delineated whole.

Any narrative is an extended verbal exposition that unfolds in real time and that represents an act (or succession of events). Aristotle related the narrative to imitation ("not of persons, but of action and life", Aristotle, *Poetics*, 6, 1450^a: 16) and tried to identify its basic means. In his view it is the *plot* that is the essence of any narrative (1450^a: 37-38). The plot is the combination of incidents or things done in a story (6, 1450^a: 5) that are ordered on a consequential basis (*propter hoc*, the one necessarily follows the other; to be distinguished from a mere succession *post hoc*, 10, 1452^a: 20 – 21).

The plot notion has aroused a lot of discussion in philosophy and literary criticism. Nobody denies the importance of the plot in a narrative, but the definition of the plot itself is still contested. Ricoeur (1981) generalises the Aristotelian concept of tragedy to all kinds of narrative by conceiving of it as a sort of language game that aims at emplotment (plot construction – Ricoeur, 1981, p. 288). Emplotment is the tentative and historically informed process of combining time and configuration. Any narrative can be characterised by a certain configuration of events and actions that are put in a sequential order (which shouldn't necessarily coincide with real time!).

Hence, the plot of a narrative works as its organising scheme and configures the story as a typical and coherent constellation of incidents and actions. Ochs & Capps (2001), however, argue that the plot shouldn't be seen as a necessarily pre-given and fixed entity. Quoting the literary critic Thomas Leitch they write:

> "The constitutive feature of narrative development is the sequence of the audience's perceptions, projections, and reintegrations of the story, typically following a line of development from illusion to disillusionment, and for this purpose plot in the sense of a temporal or causal sequence of events is clearly not necessary…Story is possible without a plot" (Ochs & Capps, 2001, p. 19).

Ochs & Capps do not deny the existence and relevance of the plot for a narrative. They argue, however, that in many cases plots are constructed in the course of the narration through the collaborative efforts and exchanges of different participants of a conversation or story-telling activity. In most forms of everyday conversations and storytelling, a narration is triggered by a circumstantial cause, an unexpected event for instance, and the storytelling – with the help of interlocutors – often produces its own plot in the ongoing narrative process. Although there is no real plot from the beginning, Ochs & Capps still take these conversational exchanges as genuine forms of narratives. In order to capture such living narratives in a conceptualisation, they conceive of narrative as a host genre that can encompass a huge variety of different specific appearances. In their view, the narrative can be understood in terms of a set of dimensions that it displays in differing degrees: "Each narrative dimension establishes a *range* of possibilities, which are realized in particular narrative performances. We use these dimensions and their fields of possibilities to analyse how different interlocutors shape the telling of a narrative and how life events are structured through narrative form" (Ochs & Capps, 2001, p. 19).

The dimensions on which narratives can be distinguished, according to Ochs & Capps are:

- *Tellership:* this dimension refers to the participants involved in the recounting of the narrative; the dimension ranges from one active teller to multiple active tellers. Actually, this dimension identifies the agent of the narration;
- *Tellability:* this dimension refers to the fact that the relevance of a story may vary, which makes the narration for a potential audience more or less worthwhile to listen to. A story that explains an unexpected event, or that follows a breach of expectation is a highly tellable narrative (if told in a rhetorically effective manner), a report of relatively ordinary events, on the other hand, mostly has a low level of tellability. Ochs & Capps explain that the roots of high tellability in children probably are located in their awareness of unexpected events;
- *Embeddedness:* this dimension ranges from the story that may be detached or isolated from the things that engage the present audience, to a story that is closely con-

nected to the things that make sense to the audience at that moment; the latter type of stories are mostly embedded in the ongoing activities;

- *Linearity:* narratives can vary on the strictness of temporal or causal order; at the one end of the dimension there are narratives with a strictly closed temporal and causal order (like a recounting of a course of events or a logical argument), at the other extreme we have narratives with an open temporal and causal order; in the latter narratives the teller may express emotional outbursts that lead the story astray for a moment, but it can also occur that the teller inserts repetitions for rhetorical reasons, or explores alternative renderings of the story;
- *Moral stance:* the narration may vary in the ways it conveys morality and evaluations of the events in the narration: is there one explicit, absolute evaluation expressed or is the moral qualification open, uncertain or fluid?

Ochs & Capps' system gives us a powerful classification system of different types of narration without having to assume a plot from the beginning. A narration with one teller, reporting a highly boring story in a detached way, following a strictly temporal or logical ordering of events, with a hidden moral evaluation may be a theoretical description of the monologues of some teachers in an expository teaching style. On the other hand: the child telling and evaluating what happens at school, often distracted by sideways, and therefore guided by the questions of her mother, is also involved in a narrative activity.

As Ochs & Capps point out, every narration can be characterised as an attempt at balancing authenticity and coherence. 'Human beings', as they express it, 'are caught between the desire for coherence and the desire for authenticity of life experience' (p. 278- 279). In their view the ability to strike a balance between coherence and authenticity is a hallmark of narrative competence (p. 279). In the understanding of different types of narration and their functions in everyday life this balancing is a crucial process. In narrations that try to air understandings or recountings from memory, the coherence often dominates authenticity. The school system also overvalues coherent narrations in spite of a loss of authenticity. Many narrations are schema-driven expositions in order to guarantee coherence. Bartlet (1932) already pointed out the importance of schemas for the functioning of human memory. That is not to say that every report of an event is always exactly the same, but that the core meaning of the report –despite its accidental and situational variations, remains more or less the same. The same is true for narrations that express theoretical understanding: they can vary with the situation or the audience, but in essence they pretend to express the same core meaning. In schools many of the narrations are schema-driven, based on stereotype and conventional plot configurations. In the teaching of theoretical understanding at school, we try to assist children in appropriating the conceptual core from which a theory can be reconstructed, but in practice this often results in mastering a specific narration of the theory that is basically just one of the realisations of the conceptual core. A theory cannot exist without its narrations, but the theory is not identical to only one of its narrations. School-knowledge is theory driven narration, but unfortunately it is often presented as a one-teller-narration, with minimal tellability ("information"), detached, logically ordered, and morally indifferent, rather than a theory driven narrative activity of a community of tellers involved in a joint problem solving process, that is relevant for them all, embedded in their daily activities and related to their personal questions and interests, collaboratively constructing coherence in the narration that makes sense for them, and aware of the value-laden nature of their positions and choices.

Although it doesn't make much sense to call a specific theoretical point of view a narrative, it is evident that such a theory can only exist and be negotiated trough the narratives that are constructed from it. A theory is a cultural instrument for bringing a particular style and coherence into a narrative. As such, theories are important cultural tools for narrative competence that fosters participation in cultural communities. This point of view may reminds us of the way Bruner (1986) explained human thought in terms of two radically different modes of thinking: a paradigmatic mode and a narrative mode. The paradigmatic (or logico-scientific) mode, according to Bruner, describes a way of thinking that strives for logical systematicity in thinking, and that aims at categorization, conceptualisation, and explanation on the basis of predefined concepts and definitions, rigid rules, deductions, argumentation and research. Its language is regulated by requirements of consistency and noncontradiction (Bruner, 1986, p 12- 13). The narrative mode, according to Bruner, tries to convince an audience of the life-likeness of the narrated events. It deals with human interests, intention, or the vicissitudes of human life. The rules for the narrative mode of thought are not logical rules, but are rooted in aesthetics and in beliefs about speech genres that suggest trustworthiness.

In his further analysis, Bruner admits that stories that exemplify the narrative mode, are based on themes ("deep-structures"), and the same is true for the course of paradigmatic thought. With the help of Ochs & Capps' dimensions of narratives we can now see that the so-called paradigmatic thought is better understood as a special kind of narrative that takes special positions on the dimensions of narratives. Paradigmatic thought can be characterised as a narrative with one teller that tries to construe its explanation of unexpected events in a detached way from an allegedly value-free position. The context of the explanation is embedded in the theory itself, from which the narrative draws its relevance. The audience is assumed to have adopted the same theoretical context, so that the tellability for this audience is assumed to be high (though it can be otherwise for people with a different mind set).

So in my view, both the narrative and the paradigmatic mode of thought are driven by deep structures (meaningful themes or theories), and are basically exemplars of narrative activity. The nature of the deep structures may be radically different, as well as the rules for redescription of the deep structure into the unfolding narration. On the surface level –that is the level that interlocutors have to cope with- they are both of the same kind: narratives that try to communicate points of view on a state of affairs in an authenticated and coherent way.

Narratives of childhood

How can we apply these findings regarding narratives to our attempt at understanding childhood, child development, and early education practices? Therefore we have to understand the role of narratives in the life forms in which the children are involved. In these life forms narratives play important roles: we tell children stories and we listen to children's stories or account of events. From the first section of this chapter we know, however, that the things that people (mostly adults) say and think about children are also strong determinants of the life forms of children. So in a broad sense we can distinguish at least three types of narratives of childhood: narratives *for* children, narratives *of* children, and narratives *about* children. In the following paragraphs I will dwell a bit longer on each one of these narrative types and their functions in early childhood education.

Narratives FOR children

The most well-know type of narrations in childhood is without doubt the stories and narratives that children hear around them. Some of them are made on the spot as accounts of events in the children's everyday life. In this section I will, however, focus mainly on the narratives that are especially made *for* children, but it must be stipulated that there exist a lot of narratives around children that are not especially made for them (such as the things parents tell to each other, what the mother says to a doctor, what the older brother tells his girlfriend etc). There is little doubt that such narratives might be very influential for children's development, as they also give a window onto the child's direct life experiences and present models for cultural narrative frameworks. There is, however, not much research concerning the impact of this type of narratives on children's development.

In this section, I will focus on narratives that are especially made for and addressed to children, such as the stories that adults make for children and are read to them. These narratives are also saturated with cultural meanings and provide the children with a window onto their culture. Engel (1995) points out that a distinction should be made between a narrative and a story. A story is intentionally told and experienced as a delineated whole that has a particular meaning, order, and casting. Mostly it also has got a name (like 'Alice in Wonderland'). A narrative is also an account of experiences but, unlike a story, can be embedded in a conversation or interaction and need not be experienced as a story by the speaker' (Engel, 1995, p. 19). Although this distinction can indeed meaningfully be made, I regard stories as a special sub-type of narratives. Children have to deal with narratives of all kinds (including stories).

Stories for children often have a clear pedagogical function. For a long time, children depend on others for getting engaged in such stories, and they depend on adult selections and valuations with regard to the stories that are told to them or not. But the same applies when children start reading stories for themselves. Stories for children are used to make them feel at ease, to create a feeling of togetherness and attachment, to give them a feeling of excitement or other types of emotions. But children stories often also contain an implicit or explicit moral stance, exhibit conventional rules and values of the community, and exemplify literacy tools (like printing, text, narrative frameworks, genres, utterance, intonation etc) to them. The story for children is obviously a social tool for acculturation of children into the existing (dominant) cultural of their community. It is the stories that are told to children that express part of a culture's collective memory and that lay a basis for their cultural socialisation and identity (see Wertsch, 2002).

It is not very difficult to classify children stories in terms of Ochs & Capps' dimensions. The written stories are generally used as a one-teller narration, but it is also clear that this depends on how the story is used by the adult. In settings with interactive reading/telling children also have a role in (re)construing the story. Especially with picture books, this collaborative story telling (co-narration) is common practice in educational settings. These stories are presumed to have a high tellability, to be related to the children's lives, and most of them have a strict linear organisation following a succession of events in time. *Alice in Wonderland* can be taken as an example here of a story to be told, that employs the technique of unexpected events in order to draw children into the story. When telling the story interactively, it is obvious how many parallel readings and sidesteps can be made. Many stories entice the children to act as co-tellers, triggering narratives of all sorts. It is their way of striking a balance between the coherence of the original narrative (the story) and their authentic renderings of it.

Considering the crucial role of narratives for children in their early life, it is amazing that so little effort has been made to study in detail the mechanisms of the influence of these stories on the children's development towards full participation in their community's activities. As a result, many elements of the story as a cultural tool are left implicit and can have an indoctrinating result (especially with regard to the moral stance taken in a particular story).

A significant contribution to the understanding of how stories for children are constructed can be found in the work of Kieran Egan (1986, 1997; see also chapter 2). In his view the cultural history of the human race, has produced tools for construing experience and inscripting these experiences in stories, first as orally transmittable culture, later in as products of a literate culture. The tools for construing, inscripting, and communicating experiences are evolving during cultural history, and they can be found in the stories that are made in a culture for the transaction of culture to new generations. These tools are essential for the cultural development of children. They help shaping our understanding of our community's culture.

For that reason it is important to get children involved in the act of story telling and give them a window on these meaning making tools of their culture. One of the essential mechanisms of story making, analysed by Egan, is the use of binary opposites (rich-poor, big-small, brave-cowardly etc). These opposites have the potential to draw children into a story, engage them, and entice them to become co-tellers. In our culture, however, authors of stories for children often decide to transform the binary opposite into a continuous dimension that allows intermediate positions that can bridge the gap between the opposites. That is how these talking rabbits and ghosts etc. come into being and populate the child's world. They are assumed to bridge the gap between life and death, or between animal and man, and make both worlds accessible at once (see chapter 2 for a further explanation). Narratives for children often create a new world assuming that it makes the conventions and morals of the adult world more easily accessible for children.

Egan focuses primarily on the affective and meaning making mechanism of story telling activities. Early education practices have developed different ways of getting children involved in narrative activity, by making them co-tellers of stories, or by encouraging them to remake the story in their own way, for example by playing the story out or by constructing a miniature set-up of a scene from the story on a table ('story table' – a common practice in the Dutch early childhood curriculum 'Basisontwikkeling', see part II of this book). Reconstruction of stories helps children getting access into the world described in these stories and stimulates them at the same time to practice with tools for construing and inscripting experiences.

But engaging stories can also have a positive influence on the children's social position and moral outlook on their social world. Nussbaum (1997, ch. 3) aptly points out how narrative imagination is an essential preparation for moral interaction. Through getting engaged in a narrative the child can move her or himself into someone else. By exploring stories with the help of others, they can be led to notice the sufferings of others with a new keenness. Narratives for children can give them access to new experiences that may contribute to their abilities of empathy, according to Nussbaum. 'Habits of empathy and conjecture conduce to a certain type of citizenship and a certain form of community' (Nussbaum, 1997, p. 90). Therefore she concludes: '[P]ut the study of literature at the heart of a curriculum for citizenship, because it develops arts of interpretation that are essential for civic participation and awareness' (p. 97). Narratives made for children often intend to have that effect. It is not sure if they do for all children under all circumstances, and how it works. But even if the stories themselves cannot explain the development of empathy and open citizenship, they do support the adults' attempts to socialize children in their community's culture. In that sense too narratives for children are definitely an important dynamic factor in children's education.

Narratives OF children

Through getting involved in conversation since their birth, and through story telling and co-narration, children become storytellers themselves. Children make narratives –often with the help of others- in order to express their life experiences or to retell stories that had been read to them. Narratives of children are primarily constructed for satisfying the child's need of being understood. In their narratives children solve cognitive puzzles in their world and make emotional sense of themselves and the people around them (Engel, 1995, p. 37-38).

The way how children make these narratives and fulfil these functions is to a great extent dependent on their direct community. By the adults' particular way of responding to the children, or by modelling narrating in particular way, children adopt special ways of narrating themselves, wherein cognitive and emotional problems are solved in ways that are congruent with their community's. This was one of the findings of Shirley Brice Heath (1983) in her seminal book *Ways with words*. In this study she portrays the narrative styles of two small communities (only a few miles apart): a white working-class community (Roadville) and a community of black working class families (Trackton). The narratives of Roadville children more often express a religious or moral undertone (a more or less explicit moral stance) and manifest more school-like characteristics. Moreover, children in Roadville are not allowed to tell stories unless an adult invites the child to do so. Heath furthermore points out: 'When children are asked to retell an event they are expected to tell non-fictive stories, which " stick to the truth"' (Heath, 1983, p. 160). Children from the Trackton community, on the other hand, learn to tell stories through participation. Heath pictures them as 'talking junks' (p. 166). They make narratives for entertainment, are more free in their telling and use more fiction.

In her detailed analysis Heath demonstrates that narratives of children are strongly influenced by the style of story telling that dominates in their culture. From a pedagogical point of view we can say that narratives of children have a function of expression, but for the educator the narratives also function as a window to the child's mind and culture. When an educator wants to be appropriately responsive to the child, it is necessary to know the child's inner life and view on the world. Carefully listening to the child's narratives is essential for this (see Engel, chapter 3 of this book). Burton (1999, see also chapter 4 of this book) endorses this point of view in her studies on the development of mathematical thinking in young children. The mathematical narratives of young children are crucial for understanding their emerging conceptions of mathematical objects. The educator needs this information if he/she wants to respond appropriately to the children's thinking. Only through understanding of these narratives, as Burton points out, we can begin to understand children's unconventionally expressed meanings in a profound way, and prevent ourselves from underestimating children's actual abilities.

Both the studies of Engel (1995) and of Ochs & Capps (2001) give detailed descriptions of the strategies, which children use for their narratives, and explain some of the dynamics of the process. It turns out that children's narratives are never randomly construed and if we don't understand them it is mostly a matter of the adult's lack of knowledge of the dynamics of the children's way of narrative construction. As we can learn from the studies of Singer (see chapter 5 in this book), children often follow their own logic in construing their living narratives. Adults have to discover the children's logic by carefully listening to their narratives in the light of these children's apparent intentions.

Children's narratives create opportunities for development and for practicing the meaning making mechanisms that are so essential for their participation in their communities. Observational studies of young children's interactions have demonstrated that children possess a number of abilities for construing narrative-like messages already from an early age (see for example Bruner, 1983). In our own studies (van Oers, 1997) we found that young children's drawings often also have a narrative character, but for the completion of their narrative they want to use language as well as a kind of supplement of their drawing in order to make sure that the meaning of their narrative is well understood. As a matter of fact, children often use their drawings as a kind of inscription that helps them to remember the narrative they have in mind. Like a name, a picture or a photograph is a helpful means for reconstructing a narrative. Especially photographs and drawings can have a strong narrative content (see Harrison, 2002). As demonstrated in part II of this book, photographs and drawings can play an important role in early education in order to enhance children's narrative abilities.

But children don't just use these developing narrative abilities only for communication of events from their daily lives. With their – socially constructed – narrative abilities they also construe narratives about themselves, about childhood and their position in the world. It is through such self-narratives and the responses of the sociocultural environment to them, that the child builds a self-image (identity) and a conception of childhood (see for example Holland et al., 1998; Cook-Gumperz, 1991). Identity is also an authored construction, based on the ongoing narrative of the person about him or herself or about the human in general. The construction of all self-narratives is essentially a dialogical process of narrating that starts very early in life, with the help of the narrative tools they have appropriated from their significant adults and peers. Evidently, such self-narratives are deeply cultural and finally turn out to be one of the most pervasive narratives of children.

Narratives ABOUT children
As we have argued above, adults have a strong influence on the stories for and of children. In the way they speak about children or react to children's actions, utterances and narratives, adults express clear-cut opinions about children and their positions. When adults, for instance, argue that a young child must learn from hand-on activities, they apparently have a general conception of young children's development that indicates concrete actions at the given age level (they might even call it the concrete-operational stage). Most of such utterances and narratives are informed by developmental theories (folk theories or scientific theories). As we have seen before, theories are often a basis for a particular kind of narratives. The precise wordings may vary, but the ideas expressed are often predictable for anyone who knows the theory.

Narratives about children probably are the most frequently occurring narratives around children. Most narratives about children are theory-based. Theories configure people's narratives and enhance the narrative's coherence. But as Ochs & Capps (2001) already have pointed out, there exists an essential tension between the pursuit of coherence in a narrative and the need for authenticity. In addition to that, theories also have truth pretensions: they make themselves out to be true descriptions of reality and require people (due to that quality) to act accordingly. Post-modern epistemology toned down the singularity of truth and the strictness of theoretical knowledge for practical actions, by defining truth in relation to local settings and collaborating communities. But nevertheless, it is still the theory that configures the narrative in that situation and in that community. And it is the collaboratively arrived at theory that still gives an outstanding value to that particular narrated conception of the situation. Theory, due to its nature, always imposes structured coherence to a situation, and reduces the authenticity of the interpretations initially involved.

The same is valid about theory-based narratives about children. Developmental theories construct pictures about how children are and how their developmental course will be. As long as we are ready to assume the truth of those theories, there seems to be nothing wrong. Morss (1996; see also chapter 6 in the present book), however, aptly scrutinized developmental theories and criticised their pretension of describing the only true way the developmental path of a human being unfolds. According to him there are no lawful underlying patterns that configure development as a causal process. Development is configured on the basis of collaboratively construed narratives, essentially contestable narratives that is. Educators always should be aware of the dominating and potentially restricting nature of their narratives about children, and must look for ways of getting children themselves involved in the construction of the narratives about them. Whatever, the outcome of the developmentalism debate, critically thinking about developmental theories will produce new developmental narratives that will tend to configure children's development, probably at the cost of its authenticity. The basic function of all narratives about children, then, is the provocation of new narratives about children and fuelling the never-ending debate about the life-form of our future citizens.

Exploring the narrative of the playing child

The history of early childhood education is dominated by a huge number of images of the child, and related suggestions of how to deal with children in a way that is true to their nature (see Morgan, 1999 for an interesting but overly Americanised overview). Every child's life is populated with narratives of different types. For the innovation of education it is important to understand how these narratives of childhood influence the child's development.

One of the narratives about children that is gaining popularity nowadays is the narrative that conceives of the child as a human being with a playful relationship with reality. Under the influence of Fröbel this narrative of childhood portrays the child as a human being that needs to develop its true god-given nature by a spontaneous unfolding of its naturally given qualities. The adults' task is to create safe opportunities for the child for selecting its own projects and subjects. For Fröbel, play is essential to the living organism, because play involves a natural interaction between children and their objects of action.

Fröbel's narrative on young children's play activity is utterly naturalistic. It has gained much influence on many early education teachers and thinkers about child development (for example Dewey). The notion of child's play as a nature-based kind of behaviour is, however, contestable for several reasons. First of all, it is clear that not only children play, but all people play under particular conditions. According to Huizinga (1938), play is the basis of all culture. For him this was a purely cultural-historical statement and not a naturalistic one. Play does not emerge naturally but comes up in situations where people can't or don't want to be dominated by external rules or structures. According to Caillois (1958), play even has been sublimated into cultural practices, like speculation on the stock exchange business. Secondly, not all children play, and children do not always play. Instead of assuming that children sometimes (under some social or cultural conditions) act against their nature, it seems more plausible to see play as a *cultural format* of human activities, rather than as an activity in itself. It was El'konin (1976) who explicitly explained play as a cultural phenomenon that originates as an answer to the social need to give children access to the cultural activities that surround them. In his view, children's role-playing, for example, was a result of the changing position of the child in the human society (El'konin, 1976, p. 67). In play children can participate in sociocultural activities of their wish, as long as it is accepted that they may make personalised versions of that activity (van Oers, 1999, 2000). Through play children can fulfil their desires because of the relative freedom that they get in the realisation of the sociocultural activities (see Vygotsky, 1978).

Basically, in our view, play is a format of human sociocultural activities that accepts diversity of realisations of the activity, and allows the participants some degrees of freedom of actions. Being basically a sociocultural activity, play always follows some rules, but does not uniformly prescribe the enactment of the activity. Moreover, play is based on voluntary participation. So in essence we can say that play is only a special way of accomplishing an activity, i.e. a format that is laid over sociocultural activities under special circumstances. It gives children access to such activities, but it can also give adults creative ways of accomplishing cultural activities according to their wish, abilities and moods.

The narrative of the playing child, basically, is a narrative of the potentials of the human being in general, especially with regard to the abilities of accomplishing creative intellectual labour (borrowing an expression from Hegel). Using this narrative as a guide for education is an attempt to establish a humanistic form of education that both takes the agencies of the participants seriously and holds on to the cultural responsibilities of the educators. Every educational system should provide its pupils with the cultural heritage of the community, but never at the expense of the individual dignity of the agents involved. A play-based curriculum takes the interests of the players seriously, but also aims at improving their abilities for participation in that sociocultural activity by holding out the cultural tools that may support their proficiency in accomplishing that activity in an innovative and critical way.

The play-based curriculum that we are currently developing and implementing in the Netherlands, took up the challenge of establishing an educational organisation at school that organises cultural learning processes in the context of playful activities with both pupils and teachers as their players. It is an organisation that allows the pupils some degrees of freedom in the realisation of the activities, that assumes certain cultural rules, and tries to develop the interests of the children so that they develop the wish to be informed, or the wish to improve their participatory abilities.

In the second part of this book we collected a number of chapters that illustrate how the narrative *about* the playing child is conceived and implemented in the early education in the Netherlands. Starting out from this narrative about children, a strategy of interacting with young children is constructed in a special program for early years teachers in preschool and primary school sessions ("Startblokken" and "Basisontwikkeling", see Janssen-Vos, chapter 7). This narrative portrays the child as a participant in sociocultural activities who is being assisted in (re)constructing its own version of the culture that it encounters. The outcomes of this process can be described as a new collection of narratives *of* the children regarding the parts of culture that they encountered.

The implementation of this approach in practice is a process of negotiating this narrative of the playing child with the teachers and examining with them how this narrative can be made a useful tool for their own teaching practices. As Wertsch (1998) already pointed out, there exists an essential and irreducible tension between the tool and the agent. Tools and agents must mutually adapt to each other, which implies development on either side of their relationship. In chapter 8 (van Oers, Pompert & Schiferli) we illustrate how the playing child narrative can be negotiated with the teachers and what kind of developments this may provoke in the teacher.

Some of the chapters in part II of this book demonstrate how the narratives *of* the children are taken seriously for the guidance and promotion of their literacy learning processes (Pompert & Janssen-Vos, chapter 9) and mathematical learning (Fijma, chapter 10). The narratives that children construe about remarkable events in their play are used by the teacher to get a window into the child's thinking and inner life, but also as material for further development and enculturation. In this play-based curriculum children are not supposed to learn reading by first technically mastering the literacy codes. Learning to read is based on narrating, becoming a writer with the assistance of the teacher, and finally trying to make sense of the written codification of their own narratives. In the mean time they will hear also narratives for children in the stories that teachers tell. These stories fulfil the function of socialisation that I described above, and help creating a collective culture of childhood. Motivated by the excitement of reading their own stories the children build up an interest in reading others' narratives and want to improve their abilities of technical reading for that purpose.

But there is also another type of narratives for children that the children in this play-based curriculum have to deal with. In the accomplishment of this approach in a classroom, the teacher cannot interact in one standard way with the children. Instead she must take the diversity among the children into account and construct – with the help of the children – little narratives about each of them and for each of them. In these developmental narratives about and for the children, children can see themselves and reconstruct the picture about themselves. At the same time such narratives also inform the teacher's way of interacting with these children, provide information for hypothesising a provisional learning trajectory of the pupils' future learning course, and even prompt new actions as a zone of proximal development. How teachers deal with the special characteristics of the individual children is described in chapters 10 (Fijma) and 12 (Peters).

The category of narratives for children not only includes developmental narratives about the children or children story books. A particularly important type of narratives for children consists of the more or less conventional narratives that characterise the children's developmental niches (e.g. the school's, the classroom's, or the family's culture). It contains the descriptions of the institutional morals, conventions and typical ways of interacting ("This is how we work in our school" or "Don't bully other children").

Of particular importance here are, for instance, the often implicit narratives about how to conduct conversations and discourses. Grice (1975) already pointed out that every conversation also transmits implicit messages about how conversations *should* be conducted. According to Grice (1975), in conversations people also learn to observe so-called conversational maxims that define what counts as an appropriate narrative in that context (maxims like: "Avoid obscurity"or "Be consistent" etc). In terms of our own view we could say, that through being involved in narrative activities children also learn a particular narrative about narratives.

In a school context it is evident that such implicit agreements are operative in a variety of ways. We could refer for example to the 'implicit didactical contract' that regulates the participants' behaviour and division of labour in a particular classroom. Chapter 11 (Dijk) shows that such hidden conventions can influence the child's narrative strategies in a significant way. This author proposes some evidence that suggests that it is not enough to treat the narratives of children seriously when we want to promote children's development through conversations. It is evident from this that narratives are always a part of a complex intertextual system, including both the different narratives of childhood and the (institutionalised and fossilised) narratives around children.

It seems we are only at the beginning of teasing out all the complexities of the education of young children in the context of schools or early care institutions. The different narratives of childhood do seem to be helpful tools for the improvement for early education, but our understanding of how precisely they work, still requires a lot of thought, debate and research.

References

Aristotle. Poetics. In J. Barnes (ed.), *The complete works of Aristotle*. Vol. 2 (pp. 2316-2340). Princeton, NJ: Princeton University Press.

Bartlet, F.C. (1932). *Remembering. A study in experimental and social psychology*. Cambridge: Cambridge University Press.

Bronfenbrenner, U. (1979). *The ecology of human development, Experiments by nature and design*. Cambridge: Harvard University Press.

Bronfenbrenner, U. & Ceci, S.J. (1994). Nature – Nurture reconceptualized in developmental perspective: a bio-ecological model. *Psychological review, 101*, 568-586.

Bruner, J. S. (1983). *Child's talk. Learning to use language*. Oxford: Oxford University Press.

Bruner, J. (1986). *Actual minds, possible worlds*. Cambridge: Harvard University Press.

Burton, L. (1999). The implications of the narrative approach to the learning of mathematics.

In L Burton (Ed.), *Learning mathematics. From hierarchies to networks* (pp. 21-35). London: Falmer Press.

Caillois, R. (1958). *Les jeux et les hommes. Le masque et le vertige.* Paris: Gallimard.

Cook-Gumperz, J (1991). Children's construction of "childness". In: B. Scales, M. Almy, A. Nicolopoulou,, & S. Ervin-Tripp (Eds.), *Play and the social context of development in early education and care* (pp. 207-218).New York: Teacher College, Columbia University Press.

Egan, K. (1986). *Teaching as story telling.* London, Ontario: Althouse press.

Egan, K. (1997). *The educated mind. How cognitive tools shape our understanding.* Chicago: University of Chicago Press.

El'konin, D.B. (1972/1989). K probleme periodizacii psichičeskogo razvitija v detskom vozraste [The problem of stages in the psychological development of young children]. D.B. Elkonin, *Izbrannye psichologičeskie trudy* (pp. 60-77). Moscow: Pedagogika.

Engel, S. (1995). *The stories children tell. Making sense of the narratives of childhood.* New York: Freeman.

Gauvain, M. (1996). Thinking in niches: sociocultural influences on cognitive development. In D. Faulkner, K. Littleton, & M. Woodhead (Eds.), *Learning relationships in the classroom* (pp. 67-90). London: Routledge.

Gauvain, M. (2001). *The social context of cognitive development.* New York: Guilford Press.

Grice, H.P. (1975). Logic and conversation. In: P. Cole & J.L. Morgan (Eds.), *Syntax and semantics* Vol. 3: Speech acts. (pp. 41-58). New York: Academic Press.

Harrison, B. (2002). Photographic Visions and Narrative Inquiry. *Narrative Inquiry,* Volume 12(1), pp. 87-111.

Heath, S.B. (1983). *Ways with words. Language, life, and work in communities and classrooms.* Cambridge: Cambridge University Press.

Huizinga, J. (1938). *Homo ludens.Proeve ener bepaling van het spelelement der cultuur* [Homo Ludens. Attemp at defining the element of play in cultures]. Groningen: Tjeenk Willink.

Holland, D., Lachicotte, W., Skinner, D., & Cain, C. (1998). *Identity and agency in cultural worlds.* Cambridge: Harvard University Press.

Morgan, H. (1999). *The imagination of early childhood education.* London: Bergin & Garvey.

Morss, J.R. (1996). *Growing critical. Alternatives to developmental psychology.* London: Routledge.

Nussbaum, M.C. (1997). *Cultivating humanity. A classical defense of reform in liberal education.* Cambridge: Harvard University Press.

Ochs, E. & Capps, L. (2001). *Living narrative. Creating lives in everyday storytelling.* Cambridge: Harvard University Press.

Oers, B. van (1997). The narrative nature of young children's iconic representations: some evidence and implications. *International Journal of Early Years Education.* 1997, vol. 5, nr 3, 237-246

Oers, B. van (1998). From context to contextualizing. In E. Forman & B. van Oers (eds.), Mathematics learning in sociocultural contexts. Special issue of *Learning and Instruction,* vol. 8, nr 6, 473-488.

Oers, B. van (1999). Education for the improvement of cultural participation. In G. Brougère & S. Rayna (Eds.), *Culture, childhood, and preschool education /Culture, enfance et éducation préscolaire.* (pp 217-238). Paris: UNESCO, 1999.

Oers, B. van. (2000). Rehabilitatie van de homo ludens? [Rehabilitation of the homo ludens?]. In H. de Frankrijker, H-J. Kuipers, J. Scholtens, & R. van der Veer (red.), *Gezin, morele opvoeding en anti-sociaal gedrag. Thema's uit de empirische, wijsgerige en historische pedagogiek* (pp. 94-103). Amsterdam: SWP.

Super, C.M. & Harkness, S. (1986). The developmental niche: a conceptualization at the interface of child and culture. *International Journal of behavioural development, 9,* 545-569.

Vygotsky, L.S. (1929/1983). Osnovnye problemy defektologii [Fundamental problems of defectology]. In L.S. Vygotsky, *Sobranie sočinenij,* Tom 5. [Collected works.Volume 5]. Moscow: Pedagogika.

Vygotsky, L.S. (1978). *Mind in society.* Cambridge: Harvard University Press

Vygotsky, L.S. (1984). Problema vozrasta [The problem of age]. In L.S. Vygotsky, *Sobranie sočinenij, Tom 4.* [Collected works.Volume 54]. Moscow: Pedagogika.

Wertsch, J.V. (1998). *Mind as action.* New York: Oxford University Press.

Wertsch, J. V. (2002). *Voices of collective remembering.* Cambridge: Cambridge University Press.

[2]

The cognitive tools
of children's imagination

Kieran Egan

Introduction

Having outlined this chapter, I considered how best to introduce its main themes, especially as I had given it a suspicious title. I came up with three different introductions, and spent some time deciding which would be best. Each seemed to help bring to the fore a particular dimension of the general argument. After some indecisive time I decided that I might as well give all three introductions – as long as I keep them brief enough.

Introduction 1 takes us back about 300,000 years. According to our current knowledge of the evolutionary story, it seems that our hominid ancestors around that time experienced the last major spurt in brain size. Clearly these larger brains were proving of significant competitive advantage to their possessors, and so the size of brain was increasing rapidly. But this created a major problem for our ancestors, especially for the women. The problem concerned the architecture of the female pelvis; to what degree could the pelvis be widened to enable birth of these larger brained babies while also allowing the women to be able to walk fast? There would clearly come a point at which widening the pelvis would prevent women also being swiftly moving bipedal creatures.

The evolutionary solution to this problem was for humans to give birth to their babies with immature brains and to let the babies' brains grow outside the womb. Our chimpanzee cousins have, at birth, brains of about 350 c.c. and during the rest of their lives their brains grow by about 100 c.c. Human babies are born with much the same sized brains as chimpanzees', but the normal human brain grows by well over 1,000 c.c., most of that growth occurring by age five.

During those five years, human infants learn some remarkable things. Most of that rapidly growing brain seems to be associated with our quick facility in recognizing and using symbols, most elaborately and plainly evident in our learning and using language. But learning language is only a part of our oddity in the natural world. Indeed, our learning of language and symbol-use in general is so powerfully over-determined in our early years that we cannot not learn a language if we are brought up in a normal language-using environment. We are, as Terrence Deacon has put it "idiots savants" of symbol use (1998). We cannot, or can with only immense effort, evade the shaping of our consciousness that language forces on us. As the Chinese sage, Chuang Tzu, jokingly put it: "How I wish that I could meet a man who has got beyond words, so that I might have a word with him" (1996).

One of my central themes, then, is the nature of this shaping of our early consciousness that language forces on us, and some of its implications for how we might better educate our young.

Introduction 2 begins with an observation of Plato's. He tells the story of the Egyptian god Thot trying to persuade the greater god Thamus that the latter should give some research and development money to Thot so that he might develop his great invention of writing. He outlined all the advantages of writing, but Thamus was adamant that writing would be a disaster for humankind. He argued that:

> The discovery of the alphabet will create forgetfulness in the learners' souls, because they will not use their memories; they will trust to the external written characters and not remember of themselves. Your invention is not an aid to memory...you give your disciples not truth, but only the semblance of truth; they will be the hearers of many things and they will learn nothing. (Plato: *Phaedrus*).

In education today we tend to think of literacy as an unquestionable good. But Thamus makes a point that I think we should pay more attention to. That is, that literacy has psychological costs as well as the more obvious benefits. We are so attuned to the benefits, and how hard it is to ensure that children get them adequately, that we tend to ignore the costs.

In this chapter I will be attending to some of the cognitive tools that come along with the development and use of oral language. They are cognitive tools that are often somewhat suppressed with the development of literacy. I will be arguing for their independent importance in the cognitive tool-kit of humankind, and will also give a warning about how we can easily introduce literacy in ways that suppress some of these oral capacities and, as a result, diminish children's imaginations.

Introduction 3 invites you to imagine that you are in a completely dark cave. In your hand you have a walking stick. You are having to move forward, and are feeling your way with the stick. You poke the ground and feel that there is something soft over there, perhaps moss, or perhaps it is more crumbly, so more likely mushrooms, and over here you feel hard, uneven flinty rock, and so on. This is an example used by Michael Polanyi (1967) to illustrate how remarkable humans are in their use of tools. We extend, as it were, our senses through our tools, and, reciprocally, incorporate our tools into our bodies. We imagine that we feel the cluster of mushrooms or flinty rock, but, of course, what we feel is simply the impress of the stick against our hand.

What we may see in this very crude example is just a small index of the way our minds incorporate our cognitive tools. We incorporate language, for example, so completely that we find it hard to imagine what it might be like to be human and conscious of the world without language. Such efforts of the imagination ensure that we are fascinated by cases of feral children, such as that of Victor, the Wild Boy of Aveyron, as described by J.-M.-G. Itard (1801).

This strange incorporation of cognitive tools has also, incidentally, left us a little bewildered about how to describe the growth of the human mind in its process of education. We have had two very general ways, or traditions, of trying to describe it. One of these ways derives from Plato's astonishingly original account, largely given in his Republic. To simplify not a little, he argues that the mind is essentially made up of the knowledge that it learns; that is, the mind is primarily an epistemological organ. If you want to educate someone, then, you must attend carefully to the kind of knowledge that shapes the mind to perceive what is real and true about the world. The amount and quality of what the individual learns determines how well educated the person is. Certain forms of knowledge can carry the mind to rich understanding of the world and of human experience, and these forms of knowledge should determine the curriculum for the young whom we want to educate.

The second general way of trying to describe the development of the mind derives in significant part from the work of Jean-Jacques Rousseau. He tended to see the mind as somewhat like the body; that is, as the body grows through regular stages, so too the mind has its own spontaneous developmental process. So he conceived of the mind as a psychological organ, much in the manner that we most commonly think of it today. To educate someone adequately, it is necessary to understand the mind's spontaneous developmental process, and build our curriculum to support that.

Now, needless to say, these are simplistic caricatures, but not, I think, false for that. We can see these two competing ideas at the center of continuing arguments between the groups we call "progressivist" or "modern" educators and "liberal" or "traditional" educators; between "subject-centered" and "child-centered". These are tired old terms, but we can't get too bored with them until we have worked out a way to get beyond the dilemma they have posed for us for more than two hundred years now. It is not a matter of finding a balance between them, because they are fundamentally incompatible ideas – a topic I won't pursue here (but see Egan, 1997). Neither of these traditions, I will argue, has been adequate in helping us educate children. Both have provided useful guidance to the educator, of course, but both have also misled educators somewhat about children's minds. Neither, for example, has been good at helping us understand such prominent features of children's thinking as are evident in their imaginative activities and fantasy lives.

This dilemma forms an introduction to this chapter because I want to show how we might transcend it by focusing neither on knowledge nor on the child's mind. Rather, following Vygotsky's lead, I will focus instead on the cognitive tools that children pick up as they grow up in society. That is, we will think of the mind as a socio-cultural organ, and see what the results can be for early education.

So, there are the three introductions. The first one leads into the theme of the chapter that recognizes the complexity and oddity of early human learning, especially in the way in which language so powerfully shapes how and what we learn. The second introduction focuses us on some of the potential problems of that shaping, and particularly the degree to which the cognitive tools that come along with oral language can be at risk in the process of becoming literate. That is, because we tend to be quite unaware of these risks – because we tend to think of achieving literacy as simply an unquestionable benefit to each child – we tend also to be unaware of the importance of the cognitive tools of orality that can be damaged or lost in the process of becoming literate.

The third introduction emphasizes further the uncertainty at the heart of early education. By looking at the two most prominent and competing theories of how children learn the cognitive tools of their culture, and considering how neither is particularly good at accounting for the child's imaginative grasp of knowledge, I open the way into the body of the chapter in which I will try to offer a somewhat Vygotskian answer that seems to me more adequate. The work these three introductions is supposed to do is prepare you for a discussion of some central themes of early learning that will be a little unconventional, but, I hope you will conclude, none the worse for that.

Kinds of understanding

My work, for a while, has involved exploring how we might reconceive education if we look closely at the main cultural tools that children pick up as they grow within modern societies. I have focused particularly on the main linguistic tools, and then tried to analyze the sets of sub-tools that come along with them. These sets of tools give us, I argue (1997), somewhat distinctive kinds of understanding. I have suggested we might distinguish five such kinds of understanding. The first I call Somatic. This is pre-linguistic and determined by the kind of body and senses we have. These deliver a distinctively human "take" on the world prior to, and subsequently underlying, later language developments. That is, for all our later cognitive tools development, we remain creatures whose understanding of the world is profoundly shaped by our particular kind of bodies and senses.

The second kind of understanding I call Mythic, and it is a product of learning to use an oral language. A sub-set of the cognitive tools that come along with oral language is the main subject of this chapter. Universally, in all human cultures, the development of oral language involves a set of cognitive tools, such as the use of stories to give shape and affective meaning to events, the use of binary oppositions to provide an initial grasp on phenomena, an engagement with fantasy, and the use of rhyme, rhythm, and meter for increasing the memorability and impact of utterances. So I will consider what stories are and why they engage children so powerfully, why children are so attracted to fantasy, why they enjoy rhythmic language, why forming their own images from words is so important, why emotionally charged binary oppositions are so prominent in their imaginative lives (security/anxiety, courage/cowardice, love/hate, etc.), and then go on to show how these cognitive tools of oral language can be used in designing lessons and units of study in the everyday classroom.

The remaining kinds of understanding need not detain us here. The Romantic is a product of learning literacy within a western cultural context, the Philosophic is a product of learning the fluent use of theoretic abstractions, and the Ironic is a product of learning how to use languages' reflexiveness for complex communicational purposes.

The oral culture of childhood and the poetics of memory

If you live in an oral culture, you know only what you can remember. Languaged people without writing need to preserve their store of knowledge, feelings, hopes, and fears in living memories. To do this most effectively – oral cultures discovered long ago – people learned to deploy a set of techniques that were a part of language itself. So rhyme and rhythm could help the process of remembering: "Thirty days hath September/ April, June, and November ..." is one hold-over in English that compactly contains a lot of information about how many days there are in each month in an easily memorable form. If one does not have writing, the preservation of lore in the living memory leads to a mind that re-sounds with a store of rhymes and rhythms.

The need to preserve lore in the memory also led to the discovery that language could be used to stimulate vivid images in the mind, and lore coded into such images was more easily remembered and so reliably preserved across generations. Generating images from words seems invariably to involve some emotional component (Warnock, 1976) – which helps to account for the greater richness we typically experience from generating our own images from text or listening to an oral story than from seeing images presented to us on film or television.

I will explore these and some other characteristic cognitive tools of oral-language thinking below. I will focus particularly on the nature and uses of stories, fantasy, metaphor formation, and binary oppositions.

What is a story?

Stories are unique kinds of narratives in that they have, in their basic forms, ends that satisfy some tension generated by their beginnings. They can thus fix the hearer's affective orientation to the events, characters, ideas, or whatever, that make them up. They allow us the satisfaction that life and history – which are, without the stories we try to lay on them, just one damn thing after another – deny us. The story was perhaps the most important of all social inventions, in that it provided the bond for languaged people to tie themselves into more complex societies than extended kin-groupings, emotionally committed to shared social and cosmic stories. Stories, basically, are little tools for orienting our emotions.

So a compact answer to the question about the nature of stories is to say that they are narrative units that can fix the affective meaning of the elements that compose them. That is, a story is a unit of some particular kind; it has a beginning that sets up a conflict or expectation, a middle that complicates it, and an end that resolves it. The defining feature of stories, as distinct from other kinds of narratives – like arguments, histories, scientific reports – is that they orient our feelings about their contents. The stories that most engage young children have some characteristics that are commonly different from those that engage adults, but the form of the story seems to be a cultural universal. The engaging quality of stories seems tied up with the fact that they end. Unlike history or our lives, in which succeeding events compel us constantly to reassess our feelings about earlier events, the story fixes how we should feel, and this provides us with a rare security and satisfaction. Particularly for young children, it seems, this security of knowing how to feel about what is being learned is an important component in making things meaningful; what is learned within a story is "affectively meaningful."

The structure of children's fantasy

If we consider the kinds of fantasy stories young children are most powerfully engaged by – and it is a rare adult who does not recall in detail, say, Cinderella, while the same adult may remember nothing of the more "relevant", "issues-oriented" stories read to them as children – we may see that their underlying structure is usually a simple binary conflict based on security/fear, courage/cowardice, good/evil, and so on. Now so much has been written lately about binary opposites, critical of their pernicious influence, that we need to be careful in pointing out that the generation of opposites and mediating between them seems to be basic to human thinking when shaped by language (though possibly more pronounced in some languages than in others. (For a discussion of this issue, see Egan, 1997, Chs. 2 and 6.) Three simple observations might be made about these binary structures; first, they are abstract, second, they are affective, and, third, they can "expand" understanding to anything in the universe that can be organized in terms of their basic affective concepts.

Their abstractness perhaps merits emphasis in the face of the near-ubiquitous assertion in education that young children are "concrete thinkers". That young children do not commonly use abstract terms explicitly does not mean that they do not constantly use abstractions in their thinking. Indeed, one might reasonably make a case for "the primacy of the abstract" (Hayek, 1970) and for children's ability to make sense of the concrete only to the degree that the concrete elements are tied to some affective abstraction (Egan, 1989).

The point about the binary oppositions and mediation is that once you grasp from experience such oppositions as solitude/company, for example, you can make sense of a solitary like Obi-Wan Kenobi in *Star Wars*. That is, you don't need to "expand" the child's horizons gradually from something familiar till you can make star warriors, monks, or witches meaningful; they can be grasped directly in terms of such abstract binary terms.

Children themselves support the claim that fantasy has a special attraction for them. When asked what kinds of stories they like best, typical groups of first-graders name a wide variety of stories. But the top preferences, recorded in a wide survey of some years ago, were for "an animal who could talk," "a prince and a princess," and "a magic ring." Least favorite were real-life stories about "what an astronaut does," "a person on TV.," and "building a bridge" (Favat, 1977).

Fantasy just comes along with language. That is, fantasy is primarily a product of the languaged mind, and so we might look at early language development for clues as to where fantasy originates.

Consider how young children begin to gain a languaged grasp over the world. The toddler is sitting in a high-chair and touches a cup of milk directly from the refrigerator. Fingers are withdrawn with a frown. "Cold," says the mother. Attracted by an open fire, the toddler walks towards it until the father puts out a protective arm. "Hot," says the father. Children first notice, necessarily, temperatures that are hotter and colder than their bodies, and typically begin their languaged grasp over temperature with words like "hot" and "cold." The child can then learn a word like "warm" – that comfortable temperature about the same as the body's own. Putting a cautious toe or finger towards the bath water, the child can announce "hot!" if it is too hot or "cold!" if it is too cold, and the parent can encourage the child with assurances that it is just beautifully "warm." Further temperature terms, such as "cool' or "pretty hot" can be learned to fit along the continuum from hot to cold.

This way of learning to grasp the world in language and concepts is clearly very common. Young children first learn opposites based on their bodies – "hot" is hotter than the body, "cold" is colder; "big" is bigger than their body, "small" is smaller; "hard" is harder than the body, "soft" is softer; and so on. Young children learn a great deal about the world using this procedure – wet/dry, rough/smooth, fast/slow, and so on. Once they have formed an opposition, they can learn other terms along the continuum between such opposites.

While they are very young, most children learn that some things are alive, like us and the cat and birds, and other things are dead. Perhaps it might be the death of a pet, or a dead bird brought into the house by a cat, or perhaps the idea of death might be learned through a story or by the experience of their own or a friends' grandparent or great-grandparent dying. Most of us learned the opposition life/death long before we can remember.

What do you get when you apply to those opposites the same procedure that has been so successful in gaining a conceptual grasp over the physical world? What fits between "life" and "death," as "warm" fits between "hot" and "cold"? Well, ghosts, for example. Ghosts are to life and death as warm is to hot and cold. A ghost is a mediation between life and death; ghosts are in some sense alive and in some sense dead.

When children are three or four years old, they might tell their cat or pet rabbit all their secrets. But the animal will not tell them its secrets back. Or, at least, it will not tell them in the language the child uses. Some cultures would put this differently, of course. Some cultures do claim that animals communicate with humans. But all cultures recognize a fundamental distinction between human and animal. Human/animal, like life/death, are opposites that do not have a mediating category; they are not ends of a continuum, but discrete concepts. So what do we get if we try to mediate between them, if we treat them as though they are not discrete and are ends of a continuum? Well, we get creatures like mermaids, Yetis, Big Foot – those half-human, half-animal creatures that are so familiar to the Western imagination and that are common in the mythologies of all oral cultures.

A two-year-old may stub a toe against a chair and, in pain, hit the chair, only to be in more pain. It becomes clear very early that chairs don't have intentions or feelings like the child's. If we take a toddler for a stroll in the woods, the child comes to recognize that a tree that has fallen over and has saplings growing out of it is a natural object. But the tree that has had a bench carved into it so that weary toddlers and their grandparents can sit and rest for a few minutes has been culturally transformed. Before we can remember, we distinguish at a profound level between nature and culture. Typical three-year-olds will not use terms like "nature" and "culture," of course, but "made" or "real" or some other terms will reflect their recognition of the distinction. So what do you get when you mediate between this further discrete opposition, nature/culture? For one thing, you get Peter Rabbit. That is, you get all those talking, dressed, middle-class animals of children's fantasy stories – natural animals mixed with the archetypal cultural capacity of language-use. Peter Rabbit is to nature and culture as a ghost is to life and death or warm is to hot and cold.

If we listen to toddlers' stunningly rapid language development – from eighteen months to adolescence the average child learns a new word every few waking hours – we may notice a common, powerful, and very successful procedure in use for elaborating a conceptual grasp over the world around them. Oppositions are created from continua of size, speed, temperature, texture, and also, of course, of morality – so we get good/bad, love/hate, fear/security, and so on. The world is inconvenient in facing us with such discrete categories as life/death, human/animal, nature/culture, and, in the modern world, human/machine. What one finds in the invented mediations between these categories are the stuff of all the fantasy stories and myths of the world, from zombies to werewolves to talking ravens, and from Frankenstein's monster to Mr. Data of Star Trek.

Metaphor and Image

A further element of young children's oral cultural life is their easy use and understanding of metaphor: "I wanted to play after dinner but mom killed that idea." Gardner et al. (1979) report that nursery school children are much more likely than older children to complete with a metaphor a sentence of the form "He looks as gigantic as ..." This ready and early grasp of metaphor, and punning, is prerequisite to, and an essential part of, understanding the kinds of jokes that are a vivid part of young children's oral culture: "What did the dentist say when his wife baked a pie?" "Can I do the filling?" "Why was the farmer cross?" "Because someone trod on his corn." "How do you make a potato puff?" "Chase it around the garden" "Where do you find chili beans?" "At the North Pole." "Knock, Knock." "Who's there?" "Beets." "Beets who?" "Beats me, I just forgot the joke." "What colors would you paint the sun and the wind?" "The sun rose and the wind blew."

It seems important to recognize the centrality of metaphor in children's intellectual lives because so much research on children's thinking deals only with those logical tasks which are more easily grasped by currently dominant research methods. It is those logical tasks that children deal with least well, but early on they show remarkable ease, facility, and flexibility in dealing with the more complex logic of metaphor. We can program computers to deal with the most sophisticated logical operations, but cannot make much progress at all in programming them to recognize or deal with metaphors. This ease with metaphor is also important because it seems tied to the active, generative, imaginative core of human intellectual life. There is in metaphor a logic that eludes our analytic grasp. Metaphor does not reflect the world, but is crucial to generating novel conceptions of it. In Max Black's words, "it would be more illuminating . . . to say that metaphor creates the similarity than to say it formulates some similarity antecedently existing" (Black, 1962, p. 83).

Gradual expansion from the known to the unknown?

It is commonly claimed that we must start teaching with what is already well known by the student, and build new knowledge on that basis. "If I had to reduce all of educational psychology to just one principle, I would say this: The most important single factor influencing learning is what the learner already knows. Ascertain this and teach him accordingly" (Ausubel, 1968, p. 18). I think there are four reasons why we might be wary of accepting this principle. Here are four things that might cause us to worry about it:

First, if this is a fundamental principle of human learning, there is no way the process can begin.

Second, if novelty is the problem for human learners – i.e., things unconnected with what is already known – reducing the amount of the novelty doesn't solve the problem. And if we can manage some novelty, why can't we manage more?

The third objection is less directed at the principle than at the way it has been, as far as I can see, invariably interpreted in education. It is assumed that what children know first and best is the details of their everyday social lives. That is, it is assumed that children's thinking is simple, concrete, and engaged with their local experience. But children also have imaginations and emotions and these, too, connect with the world. If children's minds are supposed to be restricted to the everyday details of their social lives why are they full of monsters, talking middle-class rabbits, and titanic emotions? We cannot sensibly explain Peter Rabbit's appeal in terms of its "familiar family setting" (Applebee, 1978, p. 75), when it involves a safe forest and a dangerous cultivated garden, and death so close, and so on.

Fourth, and this appeals to old-fashioned intuition, a few moments' reflection should make clear that no-one's understanding of the world expanded and expands according to this principle of gradual content association.

Implications for teaching

By focusing on cognitive tools development rather than knowledge or psychological development, the principles of children's learning I have sketched above seem quite a little different from those one most commonly sees recommended to us by educational psychology textbooks. Just to sketch quite casually some of alternative principles so far indicated, we might prefer to accept the following:

1. children are abstract as well as concrete thinkers;

2. children's thinking is powerfully affective;

3. children readily understand content organized into story forms;

4. children are readily engaged by forming images from words;

5. children are prodigal producers and consumers of metaphors;

6. children's learning is stimulated by rhyme and rhythm;

7. children's learning can proceed by forming binary oppositions and mediating them. There seem to be significant implications for teaching that follow from these alternative principles. The first implication is that one might begin to think of "teaching as story telling." This is not to suggest that we should spend our time telling children lots of fictional stories, though more emphasis on such stories may be one result of this alternative approach, but rather that we think of the content of the curriculum more as great stories to tell than as objectives to attain. We might, then, think of "story" much in the sense a newspaper editor asks a reporter "What's the story on this?" That is, we will not look for a fiction related to the content but rather seek out the affective meaning – the emotional resonance – within the content.

So, instead of using a planning model derived from Ralph Tyler's (1949) useful, but industry-influenced (Callaghan, 1962), objectives-content-methods-evaluation scheme, we might construct an alternative model derived from some of the principles sketched above.

Table: *The story form planning framework*

The story form planning framework

1. *Identifying importance*

    What is emotionally important about this topic? What is affectively engaging about it?

2. *Finding binary opposites*

    What binary concepts best capture the affective importance of the topic?

3. *Organizing the content into a story form*

    3.1 First teaching event:

    What content most dramatically embodies the binary concepts, in order to provide access to the topic? What image best captures that content and its dramatic contrast?

    3.2 Structuring the body of the lesson or unit:

    What content best articulates the topic into a clear story form?

    What vivid metaphors does it suggest?

4. *Conclusion*

    What is the best way of resolving the conflict inherent in the binary concepts? What degree of mediation is it appropriate to seek? How far is it appropriate to make the binary concepts explicit?

5. *Evaluation*

    How can one know whether the topic has been understood, its importance grasped, and the content learned?

Let me give a quick example of how this model might be used, taking an example from a book written by three Australian teachers who have been using the model for a few years (Armstrong, Connolly, & Saville, 1994). Among the units of study they outline in the book is one on the environment.

They identified the importance – the emotional importance to them and to the children – in the sense that what the individual does make a difference to the environment, and that the environment they influence is the one they will grow old in and the one they will pass on to their children.

The binary opposites they identified, based on their exploration of their feelings about the environment, were despair and hope.

They began organizing the content into a story structure by choosing something that provided a dramatic exemplification of those binary opposites. They used the book and video The Man Who Planted Trees by Jean Giono. It tells the story of Elzéar Bouffier, who, over a lifetime, filled a whole region with hope by his solitary efforts to reforest a desolate area of the French Alps. From this beginning they built activities and knowledge that conveyed an understanding of the environment by constantly contrasting hope with despair. They included in the process a project designed to improve a local area of despoiled scrubland.

As they regenerated the wasteland, the students felt the hope that working along with nature can give, and recognized that over the years what they had done would have significant beneficial consequences. Their purpose was less mediation than the confirming of hope. The unit of study also involved personal development activities, science and mathematics, language, and other arts, all integrated into the single extended story about human hopes and despairs concerning the environment.

Evaluation was based on the students' grasp of the story of regeneration they played a part in, the clarity and accuracy of their predictions for the results of their work, discussion of their emotions and thoughts about their work, their enthusiasm, commitment, and involvement, their ability to extract relevant information that would have practical beneficial effects, their ability to present this in confident and competent oral and written forms, and their ability to cooperate in a group to achieve agreed on goals. The trouble with this model, without more examples than I can give here (but see Egan, 1988, 1989), is that it is difficult to begin by locating within oneself something affectively engaging, something emotionally moving, about the content. Yet it is only by connecting with that emotional association that the content can be made meaningful and engaging to children. The affective engagement with content does not go away as we grow older. The model draws attention to those characteristics that we share with young children – even if our emotional and imaginative grasp on content will often be less vivid. The model tries to make these elements central for us to focus on when planning. It also, far from incidentally, suggests that the beginning of our own thinking about planning teaching be tied up with our affective life and imagination.

Conclusion

I have tried to move from very general theory to an example of practice showing how early education might be influenced by our thinking in terms of the oral cultural cognitive tools that young children pick up as they grow into modern societies. Those tools are closely tied up with what we call, rather vaguely, the imagination. If we think of early education as primarily concerned with the development of these cognitive tools, we will, I think, enrich for many children the experience of being human.

References

Applebee, A. N. (1978). *The child's concept of story*. Chicago: University of Chicago Press.

Armstrong, M., Connolly, A., & Saville, K. (1994). *Journeys of discovery*. Melbourne: Oxford University Press.

Ausubel, D. P. (1968). *Educational Psychology: A cognitive view*. London: Holt, Reinhart, & Winston.

Black, M.(1962). *Models and metaphors*. Ithaca, NY: Cornell University Press.

Callahan, R. (1962). *Education and the cult of efficiency*. Chicago: University of Chicago Press.

Chuang Tzu. (1996). *Basic writings*. Burton Watson, trans. New York: Columbia University Press. First printing of this edition, 1964.

Deacon, T. (1998). *The Symbolic species: The coevolution of language and the brain*. New York: W.W. Norton.

Egan, K. (1989). *Teaching as story telling*. Chicago: University of Chicago Press, 1988.

Egan, K. (1988). *Primary understanding*. New York: Routledge.

Egan, K. (1997). *The educated mind: How cognitive tools shape our understanding*. Chicago: University of Chicago Press.

Favat, A. (1977). *Child and tale: The origins of interest*. Washington, DC: National Council of Teachers of English.

Gardner, H., & Winner, E. (1979). The development of metaphoric competence: Implications for humanistic disciplines. In Sheldon Sacks (Ed.), *On metaphor*. Chicago: University of Chicago Press.

Hayek, F.A. von (1970). The primacy of the abstract. In A. Koestler & J.R. Smythies (Eds.), *Beyond reductionism*. New York: Macmillan.

Itard, Jean-Marc-Gaspard. (1962). *The wild boy of Aveyron* (George & Muriel Humphrey, Trans.). Englewood Cliffs, NJ: Prentice Hall. Compiled from two reports, first printed in 1801 and 1807.

Polanyi, Ml. (1967). *The Tacit Dimension*. New York: Anchor Books.

Tyler, R. (1949). *Basic principles of curriculum and instruction*. Chicago: University of Chicago Press.

Warnock, M. (1976). *Imagination*. London: Faber.

[3]

My harmless inside heart turned green: Children's narratives and their inner lives

Susan Engel

Children's stories

S ome stories fit our models of narrative development, but many of the most interesting ones do not. I want to begin with an example of the kind of spoken narrative that keeps me fascinated with young children's stories, and that has led me to think that we don't yet really understand how it is that children use narrative as a means of construing their worlds.

The following was spoken by a little boy as he stood in his kitchen, looking at the vegetables lying on the kitchen counter. What he said was not in response to anything anyone else had said or done, but just seemed to appear:

> *My harmless inside heart turned green. I stabbed myself by accident*
> *And my heart rotted*
> *Because it could no longer*
> *Live*
> *Without being in me.*

I hope this illustrates how interesting and how specific each child's narrative, or narrative-like utterance can be. Many of the stories children spontaneously tell or write look very little like the ones investigated in good experiments.

This story for instance is enigmatic, confusing, idiosyncratic, and whimsical. Like many of the narratives and narrative fragments spoken by young children, it does not fit logical models (even the models created to capture the thinking of young children). But it does suggest that children's stories are brimming with different levels of meaning. They can tell us a lot about what a child is thinking but also how he is thinking. Our task is to find some general principles that describe or explain narratives, (or tell us what narratives reveal about a child's mind) without losing sight of the specificity and originality – the meaning that makes narratives so interesting and important to study in the first place.

The last twenty years have seen an explosion of information and insight about the ways in which young children become adept storytellers. We know that children become more independent as storytellers (more able to tell a complete story without the support and contributions of an adult conversational partner). We know that early on their stories are often only fragments or germs of stories (they may not have a beginning or an end, they may lack a problem or high point, and/or its resolutions, they may lack a commentary that directs the audience's interpretation, etc).

We also know that as children develop, their stories become more "regular", that is, more like the stories of adults in their community. Older children create stories that are less idiosyncratic, revealing, dynamic, and expressive of a specific view of the world. It may also be that those levels of meaning become harder to dig out of the story.

Contrast for instance the two following stories, one dictated by a five year old, and one written by a 9 year old.

Ex. A: Autobiographical story written by a five-year-old

My best memory is a tropical fish. I caught it at a lake. We ate it. I caught it with a worm. It tasted good.

Ex. B: Autobiographical story written by a nine-year-old

I remember we were going to get a deck on our house. Soon the carpenters came with the wood. First they had to cut down the wall and put the sliding glass door in. The next day they started digging four big holes. They were five feet deep. Next they put big posts in the holes and cemented them in. The next day they started putting the deck floor together. The boards were put together. Like a zigzag. It's called baringbone *(this was the child's spelling of "herringbone" - SE)*. Soon it was finished. It was a pretty deck.

These examples suggest that as children get older their stories become more conventional and therefore less imbued with the power to construe reality and reflect the author's inner life. They also exemplify the tendency for researchers and educators to see narrative development as a kind of neat progression towards orderliness, logic, and comprehensibility.

But when children are between the ages of $2^1/_2$ and five they energetically and enthusiastically (if unconsciously) exploit the potential for using narrative as way to construe and reconstrue their world. That is they are exploring worlds through narratives and exploring narratives themselves, at the same time. This dynamic (and often messy looking) activity has not been captured as well in our research. We haven't yet found ways to make sense of these more idiosyncratic stories children tell, though they may be ultimately the most interesting ones to try and understand.

In this chapter I want to talk about the ways in which children use stories to construe their world. I think it's essential to understand the cognitive functions such stories serve for developing children, and at the same time, to use those stories as a window into their inner life. When children tell a story they create a world. Each story not only describes a cast of characters and a series of events, it sets forth characteristics that define a particular sphere of reality. Within that world things happen in a certain way. So for instance a child might tell a story where objects can be people, or he might construct a world in which past events shape future events, or he might tell a story in which thoughts and feelings are preeminent, and action/events are invisible or unimportant. Children use the story form and the act of telling a story to draw a boundary around the events contained in the narrative, in much the same way that children often use words, objects and actions to create a boundary around their play that lets them and others know that the actions are, in Bateson's words, "real and not real at the same time".

The literary scholar Samuel Levin has said that every poem has an invisible first line, "I invite you into a world in which": the first line signals to the reader that the metaphors within the poem are to be taken literally. In the world of that particular poem, sadness is literally a cloud, or man is literally a wolf, and so on. I would like to extend that idea here and suggest that when the child begins a story whether she is telling it to someone else, or just telling it as an accompaniment to his or her play, she delineates (and announces) a world in which the actions and events she names are real. Each story offers the child a world in which for instance, objects have personalities, time moves backwards and forwards, boundaries between domains are permeable, and the relationship between symbols and referents is shifting. The actions and characters in a story are compelling, arouse emotions and have an effect on both the tellers and the listener, otherwise they would not be so powerful. On the other hand the sentences and descriptions are not actually those actions and characters. They are vivid versions of reality safely circumscribed within the narrative frame. Everything said within a narrative boundary is subject to internal rules, rather than external rules (this is what Bruner means when he says a narrative is indifferent to facts).

Heinz Werner argued that children construct a range of spheres of reality (the sphere of pretence, the sphere of aesthetics, the sphere of every day lived experience), while Schutz refers to a similar idea in his discussion of provinces of meaning.

Contrasts in children's stories

I would argue that not only do children construct stories that allow them to explore these spheres or provinces of meaning, they also explore boundaries between spheres or provinces.

Narratives offer a particular vehicle for exploring provinces of meaning and boundaries between spheres of reality because they carry with them both the meanings and distinctions important to the culture, as well as the potential to rearrange such meanings using narrative techniques. In that sense narratives are a potent tool for thinking because they are simultaneously bound by real world rules and expectations, and can also violate those rules. A story that bears no reference to our lived experience would be uninteresting and incomprehensible. But one that is no more than a dry record isn't a story. The power of stories lies in their ability to oscillate between spheres. This oscillation is exactly what we see in many narratives created by young children.

This idea, that stories represent (and function) as construals of the child's world seems to me to lead us to all kinds of possible questions and lines of inquiry. I myself am just beginning to figure out what kinds of research spring from such a perspective. What I would like to do now is tell about the first piece of this that I am tackling at a more tangible level. I want to talk about the ways in which any given story spoken, dictated or written by a child moves back and forth between different construals of the world.

There are certain contrasts or tensions that seem to be particularly salient in young children's stories. It is often apparent that children are using the narrative form to move back and forth across the boundaries that define certain spheres of reality or modes of thinking.

Let me briefly explain the five contrasts I am concentrating on in my current work. Then I'll go back and give an example of how each dimension manifests itself in an example, and finally talk about how one might actually see all these contrasts at work simultaneously.

Five narrative contrasts:
- Landscape: Inner (consciousness)   vs.   Outer (action)
- Experience: Imagined (fiction)   vs.   Real (fact)
- Actors: Self   vs.   Other
- Form: Invented   vs.   Borrowed
- Language: Opaque   vs.   Transparent

Obviously the mind does not neatly break itself up into pairs of alternatives. Yet in each case these dimensions capture the contrasts that children explore while telling stories.

One seemingly simple but important detail of this approach is that I look at each story as something that unfolds in real time. A story is a timeless text but for the child it is a process that has a beginning and an end. What a child does in the beginning of a story may be different from what he says or how he says it in the middle of the story, and the psychological functions of his story telling may shift over the time it takes to tell the tale. I am interested in seeing how children move back and forth across boundaries within the telling of a story.

Landscape (action and consciousness)

One of the most powerful distinctions made through narrative is that of internal and external landscape, described best in the work of Jerome Bruner. Every narrative paints two landscapes, a landscape of action and one of consciousness. These two landscapes can inform one another, overlap or the author can stick pretty much to one landscape or another (Joyce's *Ulysses* versus Daniel Defoe's *Moll Flanders*).

Young children tend to tell stories that describe the landscape of action.

> We really kicked butts out there. When I jumped on Jon, it was like a snake in cement. I wouldn't let him go. Then I grabbed the football. I was like a snake swallowing a frog. The football was the frog.

As they get older they are more likely to talk about the landscape of consciousness. The following was told as part of a narrative about a friend, by a ten-year-old boy.

> Sometimes he'll feel sorry because he misses his grandfather. I think he was four when his grandfather passed away. He really liked him. He misses him.

From the time a child is about three until somewhere between the ages of 8 and 12 (depending on cultural forces and the kind of schooling experience a child has) he is likely to play around with those two landscapes. Children slide back and forth between the two landscapes, finding out not only what is possible to convey in each landscape, but how far he can go manipulating the relationship between them. Let me try and give you an example of a more complex story, in which the author goes back and forth between the two landscapes. The following is a story dictated to her mother by a four-year-old girl. It involves herself (Ella) and a good friend, Tess.

> The Hot Dog
> Once upon a time there was hot dog. And that hot dog was a funny kind cause it would talk. And there were only two people who were friends with that hot dog. And their names were Tess and Ella. And they loved it cause they thought it was a HOT DOG! And they just loved it to pieces. And they were best friends. And they loved and loved each other. And one day they wanted to get married. And both the two girls were fighting over which one would want to be married to the hot dog.
>
> And so they both got married to the hot dog. And they had such a great time with the hot dog. This hot dog wasn't like something you eat. It was a real dog. Like fire. Not that hot. Like sweaty. And since they were married they loved playing with each other. But they were only about six years old or seven. But no one knows except the two little girls and the hot dog.
>
> One day someone came along walking down the street. And the two little girls and the hot dog saw the person walking down the street. And they said, "We have a hot dog." and that's how Ella and Tess made a cold dog. The end.

This story uses both landscapes, consciousness and action. But they are highly intertwined and embedded within one another. A story like this tells several stories.
It is the story of two little friends who make friends with a hot dog (action). It is the story of two little friends with a secret, and love, and jealousy, and mischief (consciousness).
It is also a story which plays with language itself (We have a hot dog, and that's how Ella and Tess made a cold dog). So much is going on in this story, formally as well as affectively. But I'll come back to that later.

Lived World versus Imagined World
A second contrast that children explore in their stories is that between fact and fiction. We are used to this tension or contrast in the work of adult writers. Philip Roth is one shining example, whose novels play with the line between fact and fiction (including his coy novel, named "The Facts" which is his way of toying with his readers who think they can figure out which parts of his novel are autobiographical and which are "pure fiction"). But with young children it is not simply that they are exploring the line be-

tween fact and fiction. They are also exploring the dynamic boundary between lived every day experience and fantasy.

Children often blend what has happened with what might have happened, or what they are afraid or wish could happen. The two most obvious forms in which this occurs are when they tell an autobiographical story but insert fantasy and when they tell made up stories and weave in actual things they have experienced. There are two kinds of experience they can draw on: direct experiences they have had, and those they have encountered through other narratives. In this way the narratives they construct give them a chance to integrate different worlds of experience (the real lived and heard about and the imagined). Werner and other developmental psychologists have argued that early on distinctions between domains of experience (real and imagined) weren't salient to children (that in some sense they didn't know the difference between reality and fantasy). I think however that narratives provide children with a form to explore boundaries between lived, overhead and imagined experience. Through these explorations children develop a sense of how and when boundaries between domains of thinking are operating.

We know that children borrow genres and styles from the stories they hear and read. But they also borrow experience, and often between the ages of 4-10 their stories reflect their interest in exploring the relationships between their own experiences and the experiences of others. This lies at the core, after all, of the power of stories, the power to give us experiences beyond the immediate. It is amplification of what Luria called the second world, the world afforded through symbols, particularly words. When children borrow the experiences of others it is one way they share consciousness, a fundamental if not intrinsic aspect of what it is to be human.

In the following somewhat extended example, a child shifts back and forth between pure fantasy and information about another person's life (Jane Goodall), and information from his own direct experience:

> The Story of Jane Goodall
> Long long ago, hundreds of scientists from all over the world were going to the jungle to study animals. But people kept on disappearing when they went to the jungle. Nobody knew why they were disappearing. Finally, the ruler of Zuubaarra, told six very brave explorers to invent something to find out what the thing was that kept making people disappear.
> John, Jack, Bob, Bishop, Ariel and Matt were the scientists' names. For five years they built a machine. It flew above the jungle. It had a sensor that took pictures of any sights of life. Finally on April 23, they sent the machine on its mission. The six brave explorers kept on tracking the machine they had sent. They used their tracking machine to track it. On the sixth month they decided to give up. They thought the machine would never come back. Eventually one whole year passed and the machine came back. The machine had taken 3000 pictures. So they got the film developed. They looked at all the pictures. All of them were of birds, tigers, and jaguars, except for one. It looked like a hairy human and it walked on two legs just like a human. So the six scientists decided to

invent a trap and go to the jungle. It took them over one year to finish the trap. The scientists went to the jungle with the trap. Time passed, and eventually they made it to the jungle. The scientists waited in the jungle for the weird man-like animal to get trapped in the trap. The scientists waited all day and all night. In the morning when the scientists woke up the animal was trapped in the trap. The scientists were so amazed. At first they didn't know what to do. The scientists decided somehow they had to get the cage with the monkey in it into their boat. So all six of them grabbed onto the bars. They lifted and lifted and they got it up into the air and boom! They got it into the boat and luckily the boat didn't break. The six scientists jumped into the boat. The scientists started rowing the boat. After three hours they made it home. They pulled the cage out of the boat. The scientists dragged the cage into the lab. The scientists ran lots of tests. They put wires all over the thing. They ran a stress test. But after a couple of weeks something bad was happening to the scientists. They were throwing up and getting bad bloody noses, and much more. They decided to go to a doctor. It turned out they had gotten a disease from the jungle.

They had to stay in the hospital. They never lived to find out what the thing was. 50 years passed. Things changed. But there was one lady who remembered those six scientists as heroes. Her name was Jane Goodall, and she wanted to go to the jungle and find out what those things were. She thought about if she should go or not. And there were reasons she shouldn't and there were reasons she should. But after all it wouldn't be too bad, so she decided to go. She packed up her bag with food and drinks and medicine. She rented a canoe and went to the jungle. When she got there she thought it was a little cool. She got her backpack and went out. She was exploring the jungle and going to all different places. Finally she got to this little cave-ish like thing that was made out of sticks and leaves. She went inside the cave. There were those things that nobody knew what they were. At first she was a little scared by them. Then the things jumped on her and they started petting her and hugging her. She noticed they weren't scary. So she started going farther into the cave. In the back of the cave there were all these old people that were trapped in there as slaves. She got the people up and helped them out of the cave. The monkeys started following her but then when she went out of the cave they stopped. She helped the people go back through the jungle. They got in her boat and they went home. She let the people out. She helped the people build new homes. She decided that she wanted to keep on going back to the jungle. She studied the things and decided that they weren't anything like humans except for their intellect. She named the things Chimpanzees. And that's the story of Jane Goodall.

In this story the author explicitly combines some factual material (Jane Goodall) with a completely imagined scenario about explorers in a jungle. But several other kinds of genres and texts are borrowed and integrated into the story. This author had heard a sibling reading the novel Congo out loud, and clearly took some strands regarding a dangerous hidden colony of apes, as well as the idea of a disease (probably Ebola, which had interested this child greatly) carried back from the jungle.

Invented Versus Borrowed Forms

Children often move back and forth within one story between a kind of free form exploration of language and language play, and the use of forms he or she has heard in other people's stories (written and spoken).

In the following example, a six-year-old boy wrote a story over a period of several days, in school. Details of how he came to write the story help the researcher understand what the form and content of the story itself can tell us about narratives. The little boy who wrote the story had a favorite book during the year, called The Paper Dragon about a Chinese artist who fights a dragon. He had been reading the book somewhere between once and four times a week over a period of several months. As his story demonstrates the book had a powerful influence on the story he created.

The Dragon People

A long time ago there lived a young painter. His favorite thing to do was painting dragons. He was the best painter in the village. It seemed to the other people in the village that he painted all day. His favorite thing to paint were dragons. But one day a little boy came up to him and said "Will you paint a portrait of me?" "Sure" the painter said.

So the painter started painting the little boy. Then the little boy heard his mother calling him for dinner.

Since the boy was gone the painter started turning the boy's painting into a dragon. Suddenly the painting started moving. Then the dragon stepped out of the painting and started walking. More and more creatures stepped out of his paintings. Then the little boy came running back. The minute the boy saw the creatures he turned into one of the creatures. The painter ran home. Finally he got home. He gasped and told his parents the story of his paintings.

Then his mom said "There is a legend that sounds like your story. A long time ago there was a young painter. He painted a half –boy, half-dragon that came to life. He tried everything to make him disappear. Finally he gave them love and they disappeared. The only way to make the creatures come back is to paint the same picture.

After listening to his mother's story, the painter ran back to his hill where he was painting. Before he knew it, sure enough, there were the creatures. So the painter tried to be nice to the creatures but he did not make them disappear. The reason he couldn't make the creatures disappear was because the creatures were not from the boy's picture but from the old legend. He had made them reappear through his painting.

It seemed to the painter that there were more creatures than the boy creature. Finally the painter ran home.

He screamed "MOM, DAD, WHERE ARE YOU?" There was no answer. So he went to his neighbors. He looked around. His neighbors weren't there either. Before he knew it he had gone to every house in the village. No one was in their house.

He went back to his hill. It seemed like there were more creatures than there were before. Then he saw one with hair just like his mom. He thought and thought. If there was a creature that looked like his mother and she wasn't home that could mean only one thing. She had turned into one of the creatures. And so had everyone else in the village.

He took the painting of the boy out of his pocket. He started writing a poem called *Dragons Play and Dance and Have Fun*. He went home. He got a rope out of his father's chest. He ran back to his hill. He tied the rope to the poem. He threw the poem over to where the creatures were. One of the creatures looked at the poem. Then some more and more came to look at the poem. Finally all the creatures came and read the poem. *The poem:*
Play and dance,
Have fun and love,
Clouds drift by,
And birds fly.

The creatures started turning back into humans because the creatures remembered that they were loved before.

Then the painter and his mom and the boy and everybody else went back to the village.

The end.

One remarkable feature of this story is that it reveals so clearly the way in which young storytellers explore the very idea of genres and text in their stories. This story is about a painter who represents reality visually. It also contains a legend, an autobiographical account of what had happened (then he told his parents the story of his paintings) and a poem. In other words it not only borrows from another text, it uses the narrative form to explore kinds of text, and the boundaries between texts. It also deals quite explicitly with the boundary between representations and the things represented what can come off of a page (how a remembered story might actually affect current reality).

The story is long and complex. Though there is a clear plight, and its resolution, there are several twists and turns to the story, and some of them are confusing. On one level of analysis the story simply reflects incomplete command over the formal aspects of a narrative. It illustrates the ways in which six-year-olds do not yet adhere to a linear form for their stories. But on another level it also reflects the function story telling is serving for this six-year-old. For instance, the painter is suddenly running home to his mother and father, which seems unusual for an adult, and one cannot help but wonder if the author has gotten confused between the boy and the painter. In a sense the young author is lost in his own text. While this leads to confusion for the reader, it also reflects the way in which story telling is still, for this child, a dynamic form of play. What he is imagining and feeling as he tells the story is more salient to him than his ongoing sense of what his audience is hearing or understanding. The line between story as finished text and story as creative process is moveable at best for young authors. While some aspects of stories like this suggest immature command over narrative form: incomprehensible jumps in time, location, perspective, or character; ellipsis, abrupt switches in plot, these same features reflect what the story is doing for the child at that time. The story as text reveals certain aspects of the child's narrative ability. The story as process shows what narrative "problems" the child is exploring, and shows him making sense of a range of influences on his inner life.

Opaque and transparent uses of language

This brings me to the next contrast that children explore in their narratives: the use of language as opaque versus transparent. Much of the time that children are telling stories, particularly autobiographical stories, they use language transparently. That is, the language is not interesting or important in and of itself, but is a vehicle for communicating about events. On the other hand, there are moments within a story where children will sometimes begin using language more opaquely. The language itself becomes part of what is important or meaningful or pleasurable about the story. For instance, in my Harmless Inside Heart it is clear that alliteration and rhythm are as important as the meaning of the words. Here is an example of a narrative in which language is opaque.

Written by an eight-year-old girl:

The Ocean

The ocean
I can see you in the ocean.
Even if you're gone.
Even if you live with the angels.
I can still see you in the ocean.
I can still see you beautiful eyes in
the ocean. I can still see the olive
green in your skin. Because I always knew
that was your color.

In this example repetition of words becomes an important part of the function and meaning of the narrative.

In the Hot dog story too, the author shifts back and forth between opaque and transparent uses of language (e.g. This dog wasn't something you eat, it was a real dog. Like fire. Not that hot. Like sweaty).

Self versus other

Finally, there is the dimension of self versus other. In the following story told by a little boy about his friend, it seems clear that he is vacillating between putting his friend at the center of the narrative and putting himself at the center of the narrative.

> Dictated by a four-year-old boy:
>
> Carter plays with me, and he talks with me. And he plays with me at home. And he plays…Carter, well, plays sandbox with me…and he said, "You can come to my party and whack my piñata." And he goes whacking hard. But yesterday there was a piñata and I whacked it hard and all the candies came out. Yesterday was Carter's birthday and I saw a sack of piñata and I whacked it. We had the birthday party at school.

As you can tell by now it is hard to show a story by a child that manifests only one of these dimensions. In each example I was tempted to show you how the other dimensions were also at work. That is because, I think in order to fully understand a child's story one needs to see that all of these dimensions can be at work simultaneously. Children make many shifts within a narrative.

It seems that we are ready to look at narratives as both multilayered and dynamic. I have begun to look at how we might actually track shifts along these five dimensions within a given story. Let me show you using some of the examples I have already presented.

We coded each story, utterance by utterance, and gave it a number of 1,2,3 on each dimension. This part is subject to rethinking- some of you might think that each dimension has only two values, or another might think a more continuous scale would work better. My goal here was simply to see if one could chart these dynamics at work within a story, and whether taken together they give a visual image of the complexity and the mental activity within a story.

I think that we might find that looking at stories this way enables us to find out which dimensions are salient at given stages of development, under various story telling conditions, or for given children. It allows us to look for patterns and general principles that reveal how children think, but it retains, I hope some of the dynamic and oscillating nature of story telling.

Implications for creating narrative opportunities for children and for what we can learn from children's narratives

The following brief discussion of implications is addressed to researchers interested in what narratives tell us about children, what more there is to learn about narrative development, and what further questions we should be pursuing about children's narratives. But it is also addressed to those readers who are interested in the applications of this work- what does it mean for teachers and people who work with young children in educational settings?

First of all, I hope I have demonstrated that there is a great deal of dynamic in children's stories. They are text, but the construction of those texts is as important as any ability or way of thinking that is conveyed in the text itself. When children tell or write a story, their experience as they make the story is one way they explore spheres of reality and modes of thinking. Not only do they "work on" whatever content is in their story, they also "work on" how to blend, contrast and integrate different spheres of experience and different modes of thinking.

For the researcher this means that we need to look at the dynamic shifts within stories, and pay close attention to the spheres of experience of modes of thought that they use for various kinds of content, or in specific circumstances.

For the educator this suggests a couple of things. First and foremost, the ideas I've described in this chapter suggest that children need opportunities to tell stories in many different situations, and for many purposes. Autobiographical as well as fictional stories are important, as is story telling that is or accompanies play (in the block corner, in the dress up corner, or wherever it occurs). These different domains may give rise to different explorations of the boundaries between spheres of experience.

Secondly, it is important that children's stories are recorded as often as possible, because of the clues they offer about development in general, and a given child in particular. While a teacher or observer might easily recall the theme or gist of a child's story, the kinds of information I have written about in this chapter are only available in a close reading of the specific text.

But it is also important to remember that the contexts in which stories are told become more differentiated. So the story one writes for an assignment at school will be very different, in form, content and function, from the story one tells while playing in a hidden spot with a friend. To the extent that children use stories to actively construe, and reconstrue their worlds, the situations in which their narratives spontaneously unfold are often more revealing than those that are more highly structured by an adult (a story a child tells during the flow of conversation, or in the midst of play, is more likely to reveal his construal of the world, than a story assigned by a teacher to serve some academic purpose).

W.H. Auden once said, "A poem is a contraption with a guy inside." I would like to suggest that a child's story is a contraption, with several worlds inside.

References

Bateson, Gregory (1956). The Message This Is Play. In Bertram Schaffner (Ed.), *Group Processes*. New York: Josiah Macy Foundation.

Bruner, J. & Lucariello, J. (1989). Monologue as Narrative Recreation of the World. In K. Nelson (Ed.), *Narratives from The Crib*. Cambridge, MA: Harvard University Press.

Engel, S. (1995). *The Stories Children Tell*. New York: WH Freeman Pubs.

Levin, S. (1976). Concerning What Kind of Speech Act a Poem is. In T. A.Van Dijk (Ed.), *Pragmatics of Language and Literature*. Amsterdam: North Holland Publishers.

Roth, Ph. (1988). *The Facts*. New York: Random House

Schutz, A. (1971). *Collected Papers*. The Problem of Social Reality, Volume 1, The Hague.

Werner,H. (1948). *Comparative Psychology of Mental Development*, New York, International Universities Press.

[4]
Children's mathematical narratives as learning stories

Leone Burton

Introduction: Why does a narrative approach help children to learn mathematics?

Narrative is what we use to impose coherent meaning on experience. But narratives must not only be coherent to the narrator and the listener, or reader, they must also be connected, that is have a story to tell, as well as communicating that story in an accessible form. A narrative, I am claiming, engages narrator and listeners in an attempt to understand and explain the experience provoking it.

Narratives are personal to the narrator so that each account of an apparently shared experience will be different for each narrator. In mathematical terms, they will be similar but not congruent. We use narrative in order to pose, explore and respond to questions, to examine implications and to pursue and test conjectures against the substance of the experience. However, recounting a narrative requires a participatory audience, present or not. It is something we do in a community, rarely on our own.

A classroom constitutes a community of learners where narrative is often expected and recognised, although rarely when mathematics is being taught or learned. So it falls to me to convince you that narrative is as appropriate to the learning of mathematics as it is to other kinds of learning. To do this, we have to share a number of stories.

The first story is about mathematics itself, the nature of the discipline. As I pointed out elsewhere (Burton, 1996):

> Despite a century of reinforcement for the notion of the Queen of Sciences as objective, universal, certain and infallible, ... recent work by sociologists, philosophers and historians makes the relationship of mathematics to its social and cultural (including political) roots more and more evident. Much of what is taught as immutable mathematics, especially at school level, is a social distillation of the results of refining strategies which have been particular to space and time. (p.31)

Mathematics, for me, then, is a socio-cultural artefact, like language or the arts. As such, it is available to the members of any community for them to revise, revisit, and play in order to improve its efficacy. Understood in this way, mathematics becomes a socio-cultural story told in a socially negotiable context. The fact that mathematics is shareable across many communities and cultures relates more to its utility and the development of its shared discourse than it does to how it is derived and the consequent meaning it carries.

So, next, we must turn to the classroom as a place where mathematical meaning is negotiated with learners. As with all negotiation, this depends upon a number of factors, which are not present in the majority of current mathematics classrooms. These are, first of all, using Etienne Wenger's (1998) terminology, participation together with reification. But, additionally, there are the components of a necessarily supportive classroom environment and expectations on learners to be agentic authors of their own mathematics. Finally, there is the role of discourse through which meaning is negotiated.

Participation and reification

Etienne Wenger points out that "through the negotiation of meaning, it is the interplay of participation and reification that makes people and things what they are." (1998: p. 70). So participation, for Wenger is "a complex process that combines doing, talking, thinking, feeling, and belonging" (Ibid: 56). The classroom implications of this point to activity, discourse, and social interaction but also to a recognition that participation, by giving meaning to our experiences, becomes "a constituent of our identities" (Ibid: 57). Reification, on the other hand, is "the process of giving form to our experience by producing objects that congeal this experience into 'thingness'" (Ibid: p.58) and "any community of practice produces abstractions, tools, symbols, stories, terms, and concepts that reify something of that practice in a congealed form" (Ibid: p.59). He sums up that "one advantage of viewing the negotiation of meaning as constituted by a dual process is that we can consider the various trade-offs involved in the complementarity of participation and reification" (Ibid: p.64). For me, one of these trade-offs is the recognition that the learning of mathematics is not simply a cognitive matter but involves people in their entirety.

The classroom environment

To ensure that participation and reification operate in a balanced way requires that the classroom environment is supportive of both, separately, but also of how they interact together to produce negotiated meaning. Pupils have to be trusted to assume responsibility for themselves and their learning and to exercise that responsibility judiciously with respect to one another and to their teacher. The classroom has to be a place where there are stories to tell, so the work cannot be replicative; the pupils must be ready and willing to levy and respond to questions, have enquiry strategies to drive their activity and be reflective and convincing in presenting and arguing their summative stories.

Agency and authorship

The kind of story-telling which underpins the learning of mathematics is not arbitrary. A teacher has to create the conditions to make the connections, using Bruner's (1986) terms, between the "imaginary" and the "paradigmatic" (and see Burton,

1999b). Instead of teaching mathematics as cognitively driven and unproblematically paradigmatic, using a narrative approach helps to locate the agency and the authorship of the learner in creating, arguing for and, ultimately, justifying the transformation of personal, or community, knowing into accepted public knowledge. As I wrote elsewhere (Burton, 1999b: 23): "Preferred versions of knowledge are often consistent with Jerome Bruner's description of paradigmatic presentations. Nonetheless, they are narratives scribed by members of the community and offered as conforming to well-authenticated, acceptable conventions within a shared 'discourse community' (Resnick, 1991) with its own 'social language' (Bakhtin, 1986)."

Such an approach must expect some stories to conflict, and some pupils to pursue pathways not predicted by the teacher. Unlike a conventional classroom where "knowledge conflicts cannot emerge. A disagreement will always indicate that somebody has misunderstood something" (Skovsmose, 1993: p.175), a classroom in which meaning is expected to be negotiated values disagreement as an opportunity to explore different understandings and search for communality.

Discourse

Bruner (1986:25/6) lists three features of discourse that I see as being necessary to mathematical narrative. They are *presupposition, subjectification* and *multiple perspectives*. Presupposition allows the creation of implicit meanings. Subjectification places those who are undertaking the enquiry and, consequently, their questions, their strategies, their reflections, at its centre. Multiple perspectives recognise, indeed celebrate, many views on the same activity or work.

To summarise, then, to accept a narrative approach to the learning of mathematics requires an acknowledgement of the agency and authorship of the learner in a supportive, discursive classroom climate where learners participate and are engaged in, and responsible for, the formulation of the reifications which ultimately are recognized as their learning.

What are the features that such an acceptance imposes on an effective mathematics classroom? They are:

- Activity
- Social interaction
- Discourse
    - presupposition
    - subjectification
    - multiple perspectives

supported by a classroom environment which values the telling of stories. As part of mathematical story telling pupils are expected to:

- Question
- Challenge
- Enquire

- Reflect
- Communicate

Under these conditions, what are the narratives that children can and do tell? I am using these narratives to draw attention to four aspects of what children can do as agents of their own learning of mathematics. The four aspects are:

- Authoring
- Sense-making
- Collaborating
- Using non-verbal narratives

The data

The transcriptions that I am presenting here are mainly taken from the thesis of one of my students, Gay Vaughan, who worked with pairs of five-year-old children in order to map their zones of proximal development as, in different contexts, they attempted to come to know number. She was concerned that there appeared to be "a widespread belief in schools that the National Curriculum levels provided an effective linear hierarchical framework for planning children's numerical development" (Vaughan, 1999: 26) whereas she felt that an assessment model which sought to map zones of proximal development would be more likely to uncover richer learning.

In terms of the features already listed which I claim to be necessary to narrative functioning as an effective way of learning mathematics, Gay was careful to set up activities, which provided a context, in which the children wanted to use number, and where they took agentic control of their use of number. These included a dartboard where one child moved the dart in the outer circle, while the other had to say what the dart would score if it landed in a particular position; Roamer, an electronic toy which can be programmed to move; a measuring tape to take wrist, head and waist measurements; baby's feeding bottles labelled differently; shopping coupons, and other similar contexts. The assumption was that contexts would be meaningful for different children but that the variety would be sufficient for the data provided by each child to be meaningful. Gay worked with pairs of children, each of which pair was matched with a similar pair who did not have the experience of working with her so that assessment information could be compared. The exchanges were dialogic with Gay introducing into a conversation a question or an activity and inviting the children to respond and comment. For example, in her first interview she chatted with the children about things they particularly liked to do in and out of school. Once they seemed relaxed, she said:

> "I've spoken to a lot of people and they've said to me that little boys/girls about as old as you don't know much about numbers and worse than that, some of them have said that you don't know anything about numbers. Is that true?" (Ibid: p.86)

In this way, social interaction and discourse were a central feature of the exchanges between Gay and the children. Additionally, she encouraged the children to reflect on cognitive conflict and to listen and respond to each other, frequently requesting their opinion of something that their partner had said. In my terms, she was inviting them to author their responses. If she deemed information was necessary for a child to be able to make sense, she provided it without comment as is the case for adult authors.

Children's narratives

From the extensive transcriptions in Gay's thesis, I have chosen to focus on evidence of the children behaving in four ways that contribute to their learning; these are authoring, sense-making, collaborating, and using non-verbal narratives. The first of these is authoring.

Authoring

"As an author, the learner uses his or her mathematical voice to enquire, interrogate and reflect upon what is being learned and how. What does it mean to say that a learner of mathematics is an author? For the majority of classrooms, authorship appears to be vested in the mathematicians who determine what is to be learned, and the texts through which that mathematics is conveyed. We believe that such a view ignores what is known about the process of coming to know which, far from being one of cultural transmission, is necessarily one of interpretation and meaning negotiation in the context of current personal 'knowing' as well as knowledge situated in the community. This we believe to be a lifelong struggle to accord meanings to the narratives that describe the personal, the socio-cultural and, inevitably, the political" (Povey & Burton, 1999: 232).

Nathan was counting from 1. He reached 12, and then jumped to 31. Gay pointed out:

"At this time Nathan was struggling to make sense of teen symbolizations, their linguistically similar decade forms (17 and 70) and reversals (35 and 53). Thus, saying 31 after 12 is significant in the sense that it is the translation for the reversal of the next symbolization" (Vaughan, 1999: 115).

With this explanation, Nathan's attempts to create a story that made sense to him made it obvious how misguided can be the reading of such counting habits as 'errors'. Nathan continued to count until he reached "thirty ten and thirty twelve", composite terms often employed by children at this stage in their learning as they attempt to make meaning of some of the absurdities of counting in the English system. Having learnt to count from 1 to 10, it seems eminently sensible to extend and use this pattern with numbers higher than this, an example of the use of presupposition.

At the start of Gay's study, Elizabeth knew four of the numbers 1 to 10, did not know any of the numbers higher than 10, and would not make suggestions even with encouragement. Part-way through the study, Elizabeth was struggling to make sense of the relationship between digit position and name particularly with respect to decade names. When looking at the dartboard, she gave 41 as the translation for 14, and called 12, the next symbolization on the dartboard, 42. Later, 17, followed by 19, provoked 71 then 79. Later, Elizabeth was translating teen numbers quite successfully and any mis-takes were to do with decade names (13 called 33), linguistic similarity (14 called 40) or reversed symbolizations (17 called 71). Elizabeth, challenged to read three digit numbers and despite not having been exposed to their additive components, accepted the challenge and referred to 134 as "34 and a 100", a fair and accurate reading which, historically, is possibly nearer correct. Gay commented:

> "I believe that my research indicates that if traditional assumptions with regard to appropriate learning experiences were ignored and young children were allowed to define the limits of their own learning and participate in the framing of learning experiences, then they might be empowered to come to understand a great deal more about the structure of the number system than they do at present." (p.138)

Later, I will take up the implications for teachers. Now I move to the second aspect.

Sense-making
Elizabeth and Mel were ordering double digit numbers, 33, 44 and 55. Gay repeated their findings:

Gay:	The biggest was 55 because if we put them in order it would be 33, then 44, then 55.
Elizabeth:	Because a 3 goes by a 4 and a 5 goes there.And then it's supposed to be a 6 and a 7 and an 8, then a 9, then a 10.
Mel:	They are both countings.
Elizabeth:	It goes 8, then 9. 8 goes there.
Mel:	6, 7, 8, 9.

Here, we see the effectiveness of children working together to construct joint stories but also how far children can exceed adult expectations when challenged. In contrast, Mel was perceived by her teacher as the least 'able' child in the class with respect to number and the teacher had commented that Mel seemed "to be going backwards in class...She has already been through the work twice, numbers 2 and 3 and is going through it for the third time and she is still not grasping it. I asked her to draw 3 things this morning and she drew one and that was within 2 minutes of explaining it to her." Frequently, children are labelled by their teachers and, subsequently, live up to their labels rather than the exploitation of their potential.

For some different examples, I turn to *Mathematics for Young Children* (1991) a book by Marion Bird. She wrote about Sam aged 5.03, who made configurations of 5 black dots in a 3 x 3 square. Of the first two in his middle row, he made an unprovoked observation of their symmetry, saying: 'That one's facing that way and that one's facing that way' (p110):

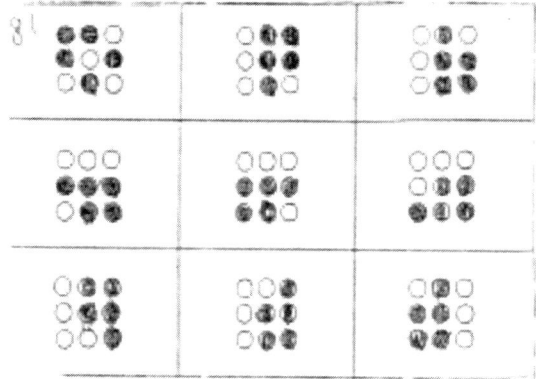

Figure 4.1: Sam's sheet

Sam, building upon his interest in visual stories, went on, in a highly systematic way, to make all the available different patterns of 8 dots simply by identifying the positioning of the ninth:

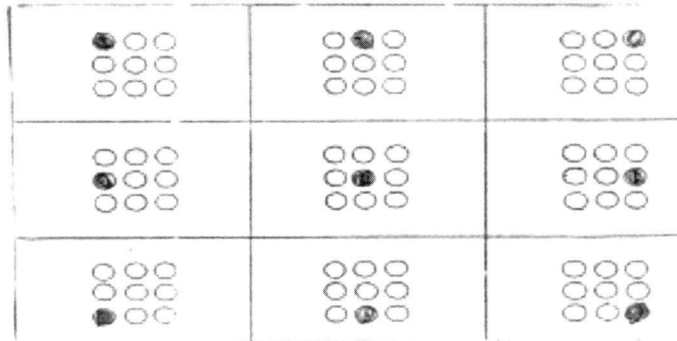

Figure 4.2:
Sam's second
sheet, showing
his pattern
of single spots

Sam had clearly exhausted all possible positions in a mathematically highly convincing and meaningful way. He authored this himself using a diagrammatic form of story-telling.

The third aspect to which I want to turn as an influence on the learning of mathematics is collaborating, of which we have already seen some benefits. There follow further examples.

The benefits of collaboration

Nathan and Stephen were asked what was the biggest number they knew. Nathan suggested 252 thousand million 2000 whereupon Gay asked him to think about what he had just said. He looked thoughtful and then changed his response to 252 thousand million. Stephen then formulated his offering of 252 and 20 million trillion and Nathan responded by saying 252 thousand million trillion. Gay referred to this as 'mirroring' where one child uses some of the other child's response in an imitative way but makes it her/his own by extending it. I think it is noticeable how enjoyable it is to children to play imaginatively with number constructions in this way. It can also be very useful to a teacher in mapping zones because it is indicative of inter-subjectivity.

Oliver and Greg were asked, by Gay, if they could do some adding up sums.

Oliver: Umm, well, not very hard ones like 100 add a 100.
Gay: You couldn't do a 100 add a 100? [Pause 2 seconds.] Umm, well, what if I asked you to do 20 add 1?
Greg: That's too hard for me.
Gay: What about you Oliver? If you pretend that in your head that you have got 20 and then in your head you put 1 more?
Oliver: 21!
Gay: Yes, you see you can do it. Pretend in your head you have got a 100.
Oliver: Arh!
Gay: And one more.
Oliver: 100 and 1!
Gay: Pretend in your head you have got a 1000 and 1 more.
Oliver: A 1000 and 1.
Greg: [very quietly] A 1000 and 1.
Gay: OK, pretend in your head you have got a 100 and 10 more.
Oliver: A 100 and 10. I just guessed that!
Gay: OK, Greg pretend in your head 200 and 1 more comes along.
Greg: 200 and 1.
Gay: Oliver, in your head you have got 200 and 20 comes along.
            [2 seconds pause]
Greg: I will help you. 200 and tw..., tw..., tw...
Gay: Well done, Greg.
Oliver: 200 and 20.

Gay used this transcript to exemplify scaffolding at work between Oliver and Greg. She pointed out that their awareness of relationships between numbers was facilitated by the presentation of measure embodiment experiences and these allowed them to begin to make sense of the additive place value component of numbers. Furthermore, she believed that they were coming to understand how to use this knowledge to calculate as, when Oliver paused, it provided some evidence that he was not just repeating the number names he heard but had made a connection which enabled him to work out the answer. However, for me, what is central to this piece of transcript is that the two boys are together building a story about the construction of big numbers, a story which is essential to their ultimate understanding of how place value functions.

Non-verbal narrative
Finally, we move to non-verbal narrative. Katy's partner asked her to make the calculator display 230. The constant had been set to +10. She approached this problem by stopping on 30 and staring at it, then stopping on 130 and commenting that there needed to be a 2 at the front before finally stopping on the correct symbolization. Gay interpreted Katy's actions as reflecting a sub-division approach, which Gay had modelled on numerous occasions, thus enabling Katy to acquire it's use herself. Gay suggested that it can be inferred from this example that it is possible, through her reflection, for a child to learn to be simultaneously the 'more knowledgeable' other, and the learner, thus breaking down the supposed distinction between scaffolding and apprenticeship (see op.cit: p.117).
As teachers, what guidance do children's mathematical narratives give us?

Children's narratives as guidance for teachers
The children's narratives and the sense that the teacher makes of them rely on the assumption that children are always trying to make meaning. This underlines both their agency and their authoring. As teachers and researchers, instead of identifying errors, or looking for differences from the mathematics as taught or offered in the text, I believe we have to create the opportunities for the making of narratives and then look inside the children's stories to try and make sense of their meanings. Such a process is highly informative as well as being supportive of the children. In the case of a child imposing, on some mathematics, a sense that is inconsistent with convention, I prefer to describe this using the English word 'mis-take' rather than 'error'. There is then nothing to stop new 'takes', which explore the space between imaginative and paradigmatic narrative.

What then are particular features of utilising children's narratives, that are informative to teachers? I would like to draw attention to four, which I believe to be of great importance. The first is the message provided by instability. The second is teachers deliberately using mis-takes, in this case about counting, as information about children's mathematical development. The third is avoiding the domination of the written and the fourth is inconsistency between knowledge and understanding of structure.

The message of instability
Gay worked with Matthew in his first term in school. In the first interview Gay had with Matthew and his partner, Matthew's string from 18 to 28 was correct, except for the omission of 20. His stable correct sequence increased during this first term at school while working with Gay. By the end of that term, however, Matthew omitted 15, 21 to 25 and the whole of the twenties decade appeared to have become unstable. Gay suggested that a reason for this might have been that Matthew's classroom experiences had focused on the numbers 1 to 10 so he had not had opportunities to reflect on the number name sequence beyond this and, as a result, the connections he was beginning to make had not been maintained. If this conjecture is correct, two issues

become critical for teachers. One is that children require appropriate presentations to maintain the width of their zone of proximal development. The second is the teacher's need to recognise and nurture reflection as a necessary condition for learning mathematics. When a child appears to regress, the focus of questions must be on the classroom experience and not on the child.

Counting mistakes as information

When children learn to count, they do so by demonstrating an observation of pattern, which, in the case of the English number system, is not always reliable. The counting story that they tell, consequently, is not redolent of error but is informative about their pattern observation. A child who counts to nine and then names ten as onety, for example, following this with onety-one and so on up to twoty, then threety is being entirely consistent with what, conventionally, follows with forty, fifty, and so on. The fact that we do not count in this way in English is an historical accident and a response to other cultural conditions, not an 'objective' reality. There has been extensive research within mathematics education on the many different cultural variations of number naming constructions and the advantages to the learner, over English, of being born into a culture that has a counting style which is consistent and logical.

Nathan, whom we met earlier, was asked to name the numbers in order. He correctly recited 1 to 14 followed by 52, 53, 54 and 55. At the end of that same term, Nathan could only recite correctly to 12 but followed this by a string from 31 to 38, with two omissions, 34 and 35 and then with thirty ten and thirty twelve. This, at first sight, suggested that Nathan's correct sequence had decreased. However, as pointed out earlier, the incorrect sequence may have lain in Nathan's struggle to make sense. Gay claimed that the apparent regression in Nathan's correct sequence might best be interpreted as indicative of cognitive advancement in symbolisations, which would be a help to the teacher in mapping Nathan's zone of proximal development.

Avoiding the domination of the written

The overwhelming message, which reaches children when they start school, is of the importance of the written form. English children frequently complain that the trouble with going on an outing from school is that, afterwards, they will have to write about it!

As Götz Krummheuer (2001) has pointed out, a strength of narrative is that it is oral in form. We tell stories, in the first instance. Subsequently, writing provides an opportunity to reflect again, confirm and substantiate the argument, make 'visible' the ephemeral of the spoken. "The children are supposed to find means of presenting their thoughts which last over a longer span of time" (Ibid: 132) as well as providing the teacher with a more stable format on which to work with the children.

Marion Bird, an acknowledged superb teacher and recorder of working with young children, in the book already referenced, described giving Vanessa (5.07), Ben (5.05), Anne-Marie (5.08) and Helen (5.03) each "a small plastic bag containing a set of nine squares of card with dots on them. The squares were jumbled but the children's first reaction was to sort them into groups with the same number of dots on each square, commenting on the numbers of dots as they were doing this" (1991, p.45). She then gave them some blank 3 x 3 square grids which the children used to record their arrangements and asked them to record how many dots were in each row. Finally, she asked the children to arrange their squares in different ways on fresh grids

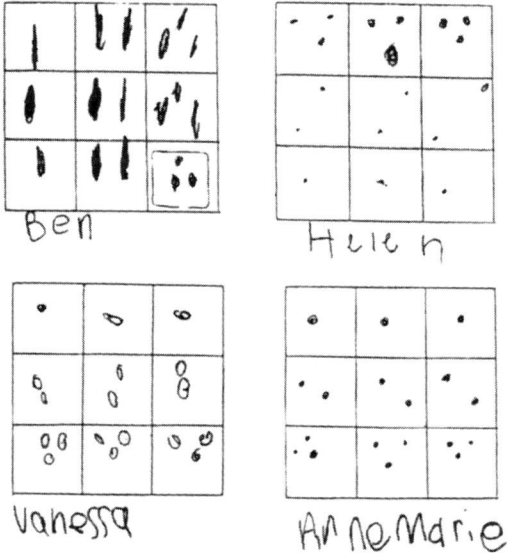

Figure 4.3: Examples of the children's work on the grids

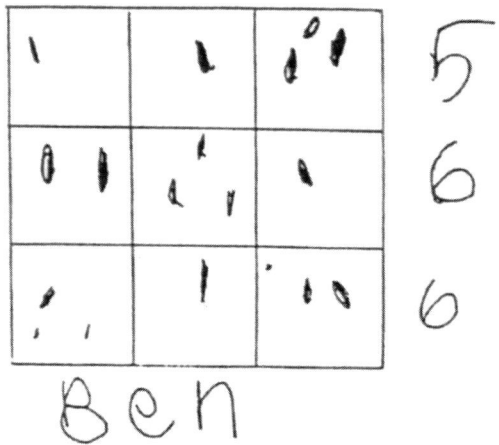

Figure 4.4: Ben's work on the grid

Marion Bird recorded the children's comments about the activity:

(1) "Ben was delighted that each of the rows of numbers in his first square came to six. He said that they were 'All the same number' and added 'I didn't know I could make a six with a two, a three and a one!' He also commented that he had 'Got two sixes' in his second example...A quick glance at what Ben had done revealed that he had four lots of one dot instead of three. I decided to ask him how many one dots, two dots and three dots he had on his grid. He counted and showed some surprise at there being just two twos but four ones. To my surprise he realized immediately that he needed to switch a one dot to a two dot, which he then did in the third row. Furthermore, apparently without any further counting, he changed the '6' to a '7'". (Ibid: p.47/48)

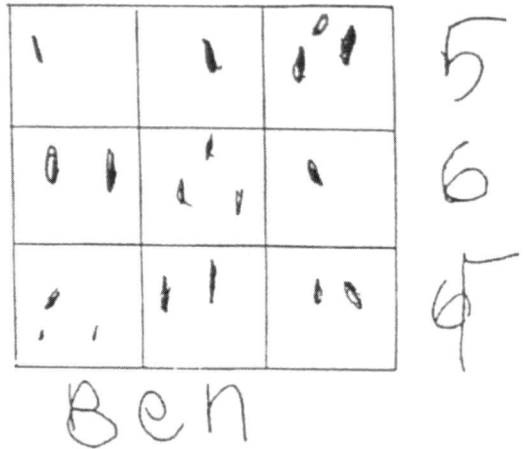

Figure 4.5: Ben's corrected grid

(2) "Helen had completed her first example as shown (Figure 4.3). For her second example, (Figure 4.6) she put three, two and one along the top row as shown. When she looked at this afterwards, she was intrigued to find that what she had going across the paper in her first grid, now went down the paper in her second grid! She decided to write her original totals of nine, six, three along the bottom of the second grid. She also totalled the dots going across the bottom row and, having found that this gave six, said that the other rows would be six too. Furthermore, she counted to see how many dots she had on her grid altogether. She reached 18 correctly and wrote the numerals for this, also correctly at the side of her grid." (Ibid: p.49).

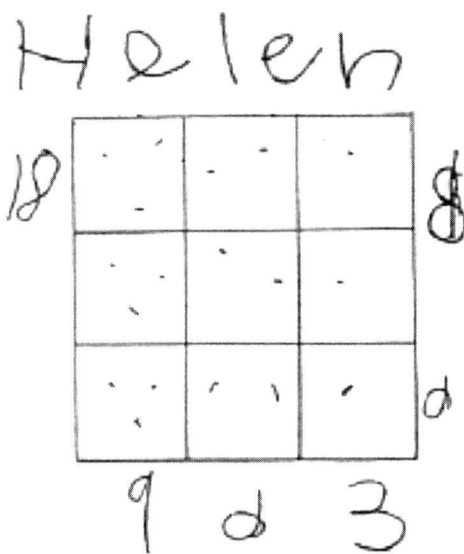

Figure 4.6: Helen's grid

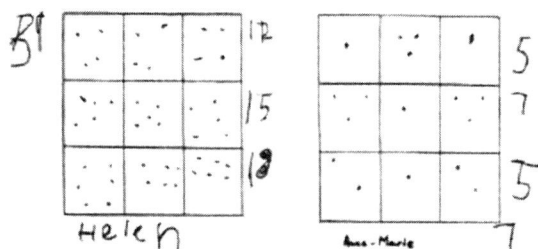

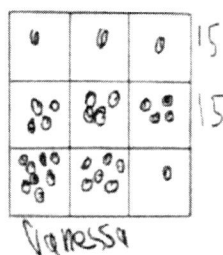

Figure 4.7: A selection of the children's own cards

(3) "Vanessa drew the dots on her grids without putting any on the squares of card. When I first saw her grid she had written just one '15' on it, the one by the side of the middle row. I thought that perhaps she had counted the three fours incorrectly but when I asked her to tell me about what she had done her comments revealed that she had counted the number of dots in both the top and middle rows. I expressed some surprise and said that I had thought, wrongly, that the '15' referred to just the middle row.

Immediately she wrote on the other '15' and said that this was to help me see what she meant! It is also interesting to see that her dots in the third row total fifteen as well and to ponder whether she made this so on purpose." (Ibid: p.52)

These children were making use of two things that are essential to this kind of classroom. First, they were exploring stories in pictures as well as words, a facility which is profoundly useful in mathematics and often ignored. Second, they were involved in a community of learners challenged in a similar way. The productions of these children, therefore, should not be seen as personal but as the results of interactivity.

Another example, provided by Marion Bird, of the productive interactivity of children and their creative response to a puzzling situation follows:

"A group of 4 and 5 year olds had spent a session colouring-in strips of squares of different lengths using red and green pencils alternately. They had become interested in which numbers of squares gave two red ends, two green ends, or one red and one green end. When I brought in the strips the following session for the group to continue working with them, I commented on them being in a muddle in the envelope and invited Xanthe (4.09) and Leanne (5.00) to sort them out in some way. Leanne started to collect the strips with two red ends saying, 'All the reds on this pile'. Xanthe added 'And all the greens on this are coming over here', and started to collect the strips with two green ends. After a while, I noted that Leanne had included in her pile strips with one red and one green end. I asked Xanthe what she thought about that and she claimed that it should be on her pile. Then suddenly she had another idea. She turned the strip round and placed it so that the red end went on Leanne's pile and the green end went on her own pile. With an air of satisfaction she announced 'Half goes on each end'." (Ibid: p.108/109)

The teacher, on this occasion, encouraged this resolution by creating conditions for learning that depended upon the pupils working together, assuming responsibility for their learning, having their offerings valued and being expected to arrive at, and communicate, a sensible outcome.

Inconsistency between knowledge and understandings of structure

The example of Infinity
Nathan, our young friend already encountered working with Gay, counted from 100 to 103 and then said:

past a thousand, 1000, 1001, 1002, 1003, 1004, 1005, 1006, 1007, 1008, 1009, 1010, 1011, 1012, it keeps going for all of the numbers of a hundred then trillions.

This was at the same time that Nathan was demonstrating difficulties in the teen sequence and the linguistic and the symbolic similarities were constituting an obstacle to his recitation. Yet despite this, he had knowledge of the relationship between terms much further on in the sequence. He knew that 64 came after 50, 510 came before 990 and 940 came after 870. Gay conjectured that his knowledge of the decade sequence had begun to mature along with his knowledge of the order of name changes and when to make them. Consequently, she claimed that the relative shortness of his number name recitation was misleading with regard to the state of his coming to know. His statement inferring infinity indicates that his understanding of the structure of the numbers was greater than his knowledge of how to name a particular sequence, which could be very misleading for his teacher. This is a pointer to the damage that can be done by an over-zealous reliance on the limitations of a text or of textual material, in the absence of the space and time to explore the meanings of the text for the children as well as their linking stories i.e. the stories that one activity provokes them to tell about another.

Conclusion: Trusting children to identify their own understandings

The teacher's comments about Mel, already noted, surprised Gay as Mel was able to make sense of 3 digit symbolisations and displayed great tenacity when she and Elizabeth were faced with a challenge. In her final interview with Mel's teacher, Gay found out that Mel had been referred to the Educational Psychologist for assessment. Gay forwarded her summary statements to him with a covering letter, but received no reply. It would appear that, for this teacher and this Educational Psychologist, an alternative perspective on Mel's performance would have provoked too many questions about what was being offered to Mel in class and how expectations were being laid on Mel which might, ultimately, constrain and distort her approach to learning mathematics.

The kinds of narratives that have been reported here are rich with information for the practising teacher, if she is open to such observations and encounters with children. In a classroom where such information is valued and encouraged, and where learners are expected to reflect, and make and justify their inferences and deductions, the children themselves freely identify their own understandings.

For example, Alice, Katy and Gay had each thrown three dice and scored 443, 655 and 556 respectively. The biggest number was the winner but Alice had no idea whose number that was. Katy explained:

> "I had a 6, you had a 4, Alice, and Gay had a 5."

While Katy was speaking, Alice was looking around the room and Gay was unsure if she had heard what Katy had said so she asked Alice to repeat it. Alice retorted:

> "I know what she said, 6, 4 and 5, but I don't know what she means actually".

Alice was able to identify what she did not understand because she had been engaged in a programme which encouraged her to reflect and vocalise.

In summary, then, left to their own devices, children are natural story-tellers and they practice this in all aspects of their learning, including mathematics. The ways in which we constrain the learning of mathematics, however, distort the potential for the kinds of experiences which can feed their narratives and which can help them to make sense of these narratives as well as shift them towards the narratives that are conventionally recognised. The experience, across many countries, of the dysfunctionality of teaching paradigmatic mathematics in the absence either of the children's need to know, or of connections to their knowing style, should be evidence enough of a pressing requirement for change in classrooms. There is, additionally, evidence of how practising research mathematicians utilise the very narrative strategies that, here, I am identifying as productive for young children's learning (see, for example, Burton, 1999a, Burton, 2001). What a pity that a search for mathematical meaning by young children cannot be as recognised and valued by them, their teachers and their communities, as the published research outcomes of pursuing similar strategies by mathematicians. I believe that the learning of mathematics is locked into a 'normal science' (Kuhn, 1970) paradigm that fails to distinguish between knowing and knowledge, between the construction of narrative and its formalisation. Within such an approach, I believe it is not difficult to comprehend why children find mathematics both unpalatable and unacceptable – in their words, "boring". I have offered an alternative perspective on mathematics, one that is consistent with approaches to the learning of other disciplines but also one that enables the learner to inhabit and make sense of the mathematical world that they are entering. Since such an approach is the one naturally used by mathematicians engaged in attempting to make sense of a research problem when they, themselves, are trying to learn, how appropriate it would be to take these practices as normal and natural to *all* learners of mathematics and treat early, indeed all, learning as a research practice in which story telling, the construction of convincing narratives, is the name of the game.

References

Bakhtin, M.M. (1986). *Speech Genres and Other Late Essays*. Austin: University of Texas Press.

Bird, M. H. (1991). *Mathematics for Young Children*. London: Routledge.

Bruner, J. (1986). *Actual Minds, Possible Worlds*. London: Harvard University Press.

Burton, L. (2001). Research mathematicians as learners – and what mathematics education can learn from them. *British Educational Research Journal*, 27(5), 589-599.

Burton, L. (1999a). The practices of mathematics: What do they tell us about coming to know mathematics? *Educational Studies in Mathematics* 37, 121-143.

Burton, L. (1999b). The Implications of a Narrative Approach to the Learning of Mathematics. In: Burton, L. (Ed.), *Learning Mathematics: from Hierarchies to Networks* (pp. 21-35). London: Falmer Press.

Burton, L. (1996). Mathematics, and its Learning, as Narrative – A Literacy for the Twenty-first Century. In: D. Baker, J. Clay, & C. Fox, (Eds.), *Challenging Ways of Knowing: In English, Mathematics and Science* (pp. 29-40). London: Falmer Press.

Krummheuer, G. (2001). Narrative Elements of Children's Argumentations in Primary Mathematics Classrooms. In: H.G. Weigand, et al. (Eds.), *Developments in Mathematics Education in Germany* (pp. 125-133). Berlin: Franzbecker,

Kuhn, T.S. (1970). *The Structure of Scientific Revolutions* (2nd edition). Chicago: University of Chicago Press.

Povey, H. & Burton, L, with Angier, C. & Boylan, M. (1999). Learners as Authors in the Mathematics Classroom. In: L. Burton, (Ed.), *Learning Mathematics: From Hierarchies to Networks* (pp. 232-245). London: Falmer Press.

Resnick, L. B. (1991). Shared Cognition: Thinking as Social Practice. In: L.B. Resnick, J.M. Levine, & S.D. Teasley, (Eds.), *Perspectives on Socially Shared Cognition* (1-20). Washington, DC: American Psychological Association.

Skovsmose, O. (1993). The Dialogical Nature of Reflective Knowledge. In: S Restivo, J.P. van Bendegem, & R. Fischer (Eds.), *Math Worlds*. Albany, NY: State University of New York Press).

Vaughan, G.F. (1999). *An Investigation into Using Vygotsky's Zone of Proximal Development for Assessment*. M.Phil. thesis. The University of Birmingham.

Wenger, E. (1998). *Communities of Practice: Learning, Meaning and Identity*. Cambridge: Cambridge University Press.

[5]
The logic of young children's (nonverbal) behaviour

Elly Singer

Introduction

S tudying videos of free play among toddlers in Finnish and Dutch day care centres, Maritta Hännikäinen and I became fascinated by the different educational approaches adopted by teachers to guide peer relationships among these children. The Finnish teachers we observed monitored the children's interactions closely and were actively involved in their play. In the Dutch day care centres, we saw several teachers taking a break during free (i.e. unstructured) play and taking care of the children only on demand. At first we were quite convinced that these Dutch teachers were failing to meet the current standards of high quality care. But studying peer conflicts, we became aware of certain important benefits of their approach. Those teachers who closely monitored the children in their care noticed every conflict arising between the children and were quick to intervene; whereas many Dutch children solved their conflicts on their own, often in a highly creative and pro-social way. We even had to acknowledge that sometimes a disagreement only turned into a full blown quarrel after the teacher had intervened.

These observations reminded me of the traditional wisdom of Dutch mothers: refrain from intervening in children's quarrels. I also remembered the intriguing comment made by a Japanese educator on an American preschool in Tobin et al.'s famous book *Preschool in Three Cultures* (1989). Small classes, he thought, were fine if the teacher was sensitive, but many are not. And 'if the teacher is mediocre (...), in a large class, children can more easily find a kind of safety or haven in the group.' (p. 63) 'Sensitivity' is a key concept both for this Japanese educator and currently for western experts; but what does this concept mean in the context of peer conflicts among young children? This is the question I want to discuss. I will argue that teachers have to understand the logic of young children's behaviour, that is, in their joint play and in their conflicts. Children construct logic-in-action (procedural knowledge) long before they are able to verbalise their logic in narratives.

The basic assumption of this paper is that there is a functional continuity between the logic-in-action of young children and the verbalised logic of children's narratives. Firstly, I want to look at the concept of 'logic' and the basic human motive to construct a 'logic' world at the subjective level. I will then discuss young children's logic-in-action of the sensorimotor period (Verba, 1994). Secondly, I shall relate this to some studies of children's co-construction of meaning in peer relations, and their pro-social behaviour during or after peer conflicts. In peer conflicts, with or without their teachers' help, young children socialise. This is a natural heritage, also shared with non-human primates in situations of conflict resolution. Finally, the teacher's role in peer conflicts will be discussed.

The meaning of logic in young children's life

Piaget, Vygotsky and current constructivist psychologists assume that the urge actively to adapt to the environment is basic to human development (Emde et al., 1991; Piaget & Inhelder, 1969; Vygotsky, 1978). From the start, the infant explores the environment, seeking what is new in order to make it familiar. Confronted with the environment, there is a basic motive to "get it right". This process of achieving balance, or equilibrium, leads children to develop new, adaptive psychological structures (Piaget, 1967). At a subjective level, this means that children as well as adults need to experience their own actions as logical and sound.

For young children, the environment is first and foremost a social environment. They are focused on understanding their social world. This is probably related to another basic motive, to maintain social relationships, and their need to bond (Bowlby, 1969; Emde et al., 1991; De Waal, 2000). Infants come into the world pre-adapted for initiating, maintaining and terminating human interactions (Schaffer, 1977). By 3 months of age, infants and their caregivers are jointly experiencing pleasure in simple face-to-face interactions. Within this familiar frame of joint play infants learn to "read" their mother's faces and they develop particular emotional procedures for monitoring their caregiver's emotional availability. From 10 to 12 months, most infants engage in social referencing. They use their caregiver's emotional expressions as a guide to how they are expected to feel and act in a particular situation. They know that a smiling mother means OK; and a stern looking mother means: Stop it, don't be naughty! It often frightens young children when a trusted parent turns into a 'stranger', for instance by putting on a facial mask.

A child's motive to understand and fit into social relations is most clearly seen in its "why" questions (Miller & Aloise, 1989). Piaget (1930) found that children's earliest "why" questions usually concern human actions. He observed that preschoolers are always looking for causes and more especially for intentions. They seem to believe that all behaviours are deliberate, voluntary, and not accidental. Sometimes young children think that physical events are also magically caused by human intentions: for instance, that the tree has fallen on daddy's car because I was mad at him; or that the sun rises because he wants to give us light. Young children's urge to understand their social world leads them to over-attribute to human intentionality. Even in western countries, with their denigrating attitude towards magical thinking, most children do not understand the concept of 'coincidence' or 'sheer accident' before they are eight or nine years old (Kuzmak & Gelman, 1986).

Young children's reasoning is often a source of pleasure and amusement for adults. In Holland we have a popular TV-program, called *Praatjesmakers* (Little Boasters) especially designed for us to laugh at young children's logic. The host acts as if he is really interested in the child, because the audience derives most amusement from a child seriously linking things up in an irrational way and drawing illogical conclusions. Adults, after all, we assume are logical and superior, and children illogical. This is great fun. Even though Piaget was one of the first psychologists to open our eyes to the specific cognitive structures of young children, his theory also reinforced this denigrating attitude towards young children's reasoning. Piaget's model of cognitive development is serial and hierarchical; it describes a sequence of stages through which the infant and child must pass before he or she can perform truly logical operations at the age of 11 or 12 years old. To perform logical operations means in his view: to reason logically about propositional verbal statements, manipulating propositions and drawing inferences in a deductive manner and to understand probability (Piaget, 1967, 1969). Despite preschoolers great interest in "why" questions, Piaget described their thinking as pre-causal, because they do not follow the procedures of either deductive or inductive reasoning (Piaget, 1930). But thinking propositionally and being consciously aware that one is thinking propositionally are not the same. Even infants are trying out their expectations by active manipulation of their world. Young children construct their logic at a sensorimotor level, long before they can verbalise their logic. The fact that this reasoning does not arrive at a conclusion judged by adults to be true or reasonable does not negate the fact that the process was one of generating hypotheses and arriving at logical, if frequently mistaken, conclusions.

The term 'logic' refers to two different meanings (Collins' Dictionary, 1998; Van Dale, 2000). Firstly, the term 'logic' refers to a method of reasoning, to the principles of abstract thought or to the 'laws of logic'. That is, it describes and prescribes the basic patterns of *consistent thinking*, based on a scientific philosophical system. However, the term 'logic' also refers the way in which individuals or social groups *consistently think;* to a particular logic of an individual or social group. Piaget's theory is based on the first notion of logic, and much of the research of his followers was focused on the logical failings in young children's thinking. This line of research has significantly impeded our understanding of the way young children do think. If we take the secondary notion of logic, the way that young children consistently think to construct a sensible and logical world, they are far from being pre-logical thinkers. According to Donovan and McIntyre (1990), they are, in fact, *obligatory slaves of logic* (p. 22). They need to understand their world; they spend much of their energy with playing, experimenting, learning by doing, looking and imitating, and communicating with their caregivers and peers. And young children are slaves of their own 'logic', because they miss the metacognitive skills of older children and adults – their objective logic in the sense of Piaget. Young children are unable to see the results of their reasoning as a subjective interpretation of the world; they are unaware of the premises of this thinking or of the na-ture of the inferences they make. For them, their particular logic is 'the truth' and one of the pillars of their existence and of their feeling of security.

What, then, is the lesson of this discussion of the logic of children's thinking and its significance in their lives? The main question in my lecture was: what does the 'sensitivity' of teachers mean in the context of peer conflicts in day care centres? With regard to that question, we have learned that teachers have to be sensitive to children's ways of thinking. If they do not respect children's logic, they will be a threat to these children's feeling of security. Later I will discuss what happens when teachers intervene in conflicts between children without understanding their logic. But first I want to look more closely at the caregiver's role in creating a shared, logical world.

The caregiver's role in the construction of a shared logical world

The child's development takes place in the context of an intense dialectical relationship with the world, a relationship of mutuality. I have already mentioned the caregiver-infant interaction. That the infant learns to "read" his or her mother's different faces is the result of a joint activity to construct a shared world (Schaffer, 1977). The mother, as the more experienced party, attributes certain meanings to the infant's diffuse movements. She mirrors and imitates her child. She interprets her child's movements as communicative cues that suggest some joint course of action. If the child constructs some kind of logic in their joint play, this is not the result of a purely cognitive activity, even less the achievement of a lonely thinker. It is also an affective achievement. I want to discuss this insight in more detail for two reasons.

1. Respecting the child's logic is not enough. Caregivers also have an active role in co-constructing a shared logic.
2. The basic motive to "get it right", to construct a consistent and logical world, is not purely cognitive. This motive is deeply related to the co-construction of rituals and routines; moral and social rules; the development of a self; emotional security; and a sense of belonging to a cultural group.

Constructivist psychologists assume that thoughts, affects and (social) behaviour form an indivisible whole in human behaviour. In line with Vygotsky and Piaget they emphasise that all our activities, including our thinking, are motivated (Piaget, 1967; Vygotsky, 1934/1987); and that all our emotions and moral affects suppose cognitive processes to signal that important interests are at stake (Frijda, 1986). They try to overcome the dichotomy within traditional developmental psychology of studying cognitive development and social-emotional development as separate domains. This requires new theoretical concepts. Fischer at al. (1990), for instance, use the concept of *'script'* to refer to the socially embedded knowledge of children as to how to act, to feel and express their emotions in specific situations. Another example is the concept of *'cognitive-affective structures'*, by which is meant complex synthesising structures integrating *cognition* (in the form of appraisals, expectations, and beliefs) with *motivation* (in the form of needs, interests, goals, emotional action tendencies), *affect* (in the shape of physiological arousal and sensory and bodily feeling) and *actions* (in the form of motor responses and social procedures and methods for acting (Miltenburg & Singer, 2000). Personally I prefer the concept of 'cognitive-affective structures', because 'structure' directly refers to the self-evident frames in which a person observes, feels and acts, i.e. to their 'inner logic'.

These new conceptualisations of the relationships between cognition, motivation and (social) activities lead to new insights into the development of a self. The cognitive-affective structures of infants are sensorimotor structures. According to Emde et al. (1991) these structures are stored as procedural knowledge of the infant's most emotionally engaging experience with their caregivers. They argue that the co-construction of procedural knowledge is crucial for the development of a 'moral self' in infants and a sense of belonging to a parent, family and cultural group. As a result of face-to-face turn-taking behaviour with caregivers, infants learn rules for reciprocity, for give and take, together with the powerful motive for using these rules: 'together' is so pleasurable. They argue that this procedural knowledge is a basic form of morality, long before the child is able to verbalise moral rules. 'All systems of morality have a sense of reciprocity at their centre with a version of the Golden Rule: "Do unto others as you would have them do unto you"' (Emde at al., 1991, p. 261). Procedural knowledge and the experience of togetherness are also constitutive of other aspects of the developing self. Because of shared regularities, infants know how they can influence their caregivers; this gives them their first sense of control and agency. Later on, shared procedures, for consolation for instance, are put to use by the toddler as tools for self-regulation of his or her emotions. One might think here of children who imitate with their teddy-bear the rituals of consolation they have constructed with their caregiver, or of those little rituals that children have with their special piece of cloth before they fall asleep.

Emde et al. (1991) conclude that early morality is surprisingly positive. It is based on a strong motivation to share and to connect, and to construct shared rules. Even conflicts between parents and their toddlers often happen in a positive relational context. We all know of the 'terrible twos'. But these obstinate toddlers repeatedly look at their caregiver, either after or before a prohibited act. When they transgress parental rules, they often produce that special smile of naughty children (Juen & Banninger-Huber, 1999), partly as an attempt to induce their parents to relent, partly as a strategy to repair the relationship in advance. After a conflict young children often show an enormous need to be kissed and cuddled, to "make it right again" and to restore the feeling of togetherness.

The teacher's role in the construction of a shared logical world in day care centres

What do the foregoing insights have to do with the role of teachers in day care enters? Firstly, teachers have to offer procedures at group level in which young children can join in and actively participate to construct a shared logical world. The tools available to teachers are well-known: the daily routines, the structuring of time, space and play material and some explicit 'dos' and 'don'ts' (Jones & Reynolds, 1992). Secondly, it means that teachers have to create procedures that create a strong sense of belonging and togetherness. This is not merely a matter of shared togetherness between the teacher and an individual child, as is assumed in many studies of the teacher's sensitivity and attachment behaviour (Singer, 1998). What is equally important are the feelings of solidarity between the children and in the whole group. Rituals are powerful tools to give shape to communal life and shared values (Butovskaya et al., 2000; Corsaro, 1988, 1997). For instance, rituals to welcome a new child in the group; rituals to celebrate birthdays and (religious) feasts; often with the active involvement of the parents; and also rituals for the regulation and sharing of emotional events; for consoling a hurt child or for keeping in touch with a sick playmate who has to stay at home for a long period.

This emphasis on the importance of structure, rules and rituals also serves to highlight certain pitfalls for teachers in daycare centres. I want to mention here three that are related to the above theoretical discussion. Because the child's construction of cognitive-affective structures is a co-construction, involving the active involvement of the child and indivisible relations between cognition, motivation and social activities, teachers' structures should not be based solely on their need to control, and their rules should not merely relate to the day care centre as an institution. Routines that are mainly based on institutional rules can make children feel powerless or obstinate (Jones & Reynolds, 1992; Hakkarainen, 1991). They are not helpful to the child's development of a sense of agency. A simple strategy to make children co-constructors of a consistent, logical, shared life in which they actively participate, is to ask their opinion and to give them responsibility in solving problems. For instance when John is ill: shall we make a present for him? What shall we make?

A second pitfall is that the routines easily become boring, everything becomes too predictable and too safe. Children strive to make new things familiar, and therefore they need risks and new challenges. They want to understand the whole world!

A third pitfall has to do with the processes of co-construction between the children themselves. Peer relationships differ from the teacher-child relationship. Teachers should give young children room for their own jokes, their own style of constructing a shared life and strategies for solving problems. In the following I will discuss in more detail the teacher's role in the development of children's peer-relationships.

Studies of peer interactions

Until the 1980's, in mainstream developmental psychology the peer relations of children under three years of age were considered to be rare, short-lived and often aggressive (Schaffer, 1984; Verba, 1994). That opinion was hardly based on research. But since the increase in use of day care facilities for very young children, peer interaction research has been receiving more attention. In Europe, important and innovative research for studies of peer interactions of young children, has been conducted by the CRESAS in Paris (Centre de Recherches de l'Education et de l'Adaptation Scolaire); often in cooperation with Italian researchers like Bonica and Mussati (Stambak et al., 1983; Stambak & Sinclair, 1993; Stambak & Verba, 1986; Verba, 1994). In former East Germany and other east and west-European countries there also were (small) groups of researchers who have done innovative work in this field; because of languages barriers, these studies only recently have become available for an international public

(Lamb et al., 1992). These psychologists try to understand how babies and toddlers are able to construct shared meanings during their social play, mainly through nonverbal means. Reading their studies, one cannot but be impressed by the way very young children manage their interpersonal relationships, being attentive to their playmates, either waiting patiently or taking the initiative, by accepting proposals or modifying them. Far from being aggressive, they found that young children invest a lot in sharing and social participation.

One of the most radical defenders in the USA of the value of peer relations is the sociologist Corsaro (1997), who studied children's peer cultures in day care centres. His studies show that toddlers spontaneously construct specific routines (run and chase; rough and tumble; building things) that give them a 'we-feeling' and an escape from their teacher's control. His analyses reveal how children creatively appropriate adult's roles and routines, and how they use information of the adult world to deal with practical problems in their peer culture.

Personally, I owe a great deal to Brazilian researcher Zilma de Oliveira. During her stay in Holland, we discussed a video of two girls (Vania, 21 months; Telma, 23 months) in a Brazilian day care centre. She taught me how to observe a collage of different story lines in their cooperative play (see for an extensive analysis of joint play episodes Oliveira & Rossetti-Fereira, 1996). The two girls in this video are too young to discuss in advance a script for a joint play. Nevertheless they succeed in co-constructing a joint play by enacting fragments of well-known routines and roles daily experienced in their homes or in the day care. In their play you can see, among other things, fragments of a birthday singing ritual, a combing-and-washing-the-baby-routine and the game of building up a pile of blocks and knocking it over. These young children's use of rituals and routines seems to confirm the importance of procedural knowledge I have discussed before (Emde et al., 1991) and Corsaro's emphasis on routines.

In the most dramatic part of this joint play episode, Vania uses various strategies, trying to involve Telma in the role of baby-to-be-taken-care-of. Vania acts as a mother in a very expressive way. She looks at Telma, smiles to persuade her and touches her in a gentle way. But she also assumes an authoritarian postural attitude, trying to force Telma into submission, and is quick to reconcile the ensuing disagreement to prevent any escalation. Telma initially remains more passive, but later on she tries to escape from the script proposed by Vania by introducing a new script of her own. At the moment of crisis, both girls look at the researcher. Telma is almost crying and seems to ask for help, while Vania produces a kind of vague smile that is characteristic of naughty children (see Bonica (1997) for an analysis of social referencing by young children during quarrels). Though the researcher refrains from intervening, Vania probably knows that she has gone too far. In any case, she gives way and for a while complies with Telma's proposal to play with the blocks.

Prosocial behaviour in peer conflicts

Recently researchers have become aware of the pro-social behaviour of young children during conflicts. Surprisingly, perhaps, we owe this new interest to researchers of non-human primates, specifically to the work of De Waal on chimpanzees (De Waal, 2000; Aureli & De Waal, 2000). De Waal and his colleagues argue that, whereas aggression in chimpanzees was traditionally considered to be an antisocial instinct, we have to replace this notion of aggression with a conceptual framework in which it is a tool of competition and negotiation. When survival depends on mutual assistance, the expression of aggression is constrained by a need to maintain beneficial relationships. De Waal and his colleagues found that chimpanzees kiss and embrace after fights, and that other non-human primates engage in similar acts of "reconciliation". According to them, in human groups (families, day care centres and schools) aggressive conflict is subject to the same constraints as those now known in cooperative animal societies. Wherever social relationships are valued one can expect the full complement of checks and balances. This new theoretical approach to aggression has led to cooperation between non-human primates ethologists and researchers of preschoolers in day care centres. These studies confirm the insights mentioned above of the French and Italian researchers: that young children are focused on a project of sharing and a concern for continuation of their interactions with peers (Verba, 1994). Among preschoolers, peaceful associative outcomes, in which both opponents remain together and work things out on the spot are very common. Forms of child reconciliation, expressed in invitations to play, body contacts, offers of objects, self-ridicule and verbal apologies, all serve to enhance tolerance (Killen & De Waal, 2000; Verbeek et al., 2000). In addition to these resources, young children also use verbal strategies to construct a sense of togetherness, for instance by using nicknames for each other (De Haan & Singer, 2001).

In our study of peer conflicts, Maritta Hännikäinen and I arrived at comparable conclusions. In our study we distinguished three types of conflicts:

- *bad luck* when the 'victim' hardly reacts to being hit, pushed or rejected;
- *disagreement* when children persist in their resistance or communication of their ideas and feelings, either non-verbally (hitting, smiling, giving an object) or verbally (directing, clarifying and justifying), until a compromise is found or one of the children gives way;
- *crisis* when children show strong emotional reactions, such as crying, getting angry or showing remorse.

We studied almost 40 hours of video-taped data of two- and three years olds during free play, in nine Dutch day care centres and in one Finnish day care centre. We found that crises were rare. Of a total of 222 conflict episodes, the children developed a crisis in only 47 (21%) of these episodes. Most of these crises (75%) lasted less than one minute. The young children in our study seemed to be aware of the relational dangers of crises. Their use of nonverbal strategies for de-escalating a disagreement were characteristic. Three year-old Jan, for instance, wants to participate in Bert's play with a xylophone. Jan keeps on trying for more than 20 minutes before he manages to be accepted by Bert as a playmate. The whole time he follows Bert around while Bert wanders round the room with his xylophone, playing a bit, then walking on again. Sometimes Jan is allowed to touch the xylophone, but Bert is keen to keep his control over the xylophone. Every time Bert resists Jan's advances by pushing him away or hitting him, Jan withdraws and gives in. But he does not give up. After a few seconds he tries again. In our data, this pattern of withdrawal, giving up and trying again, belonged to the most common strategies of the children: to stick to their own activity and ideas and to prevent a disagreement escalating into a crisis.

Almost all conflicts started with simple forms of resistance, that is pushing, hitting, saying or shouting 'no' or 'don't'. But during the negotiations there were also a lot of positive gestures and smiling, and the children often proposed and accepted alternative objects or activity ideas. Though the children did use verbal directives and arguments, the solution was mainly found at a nonverbal level. It is very difficult for young children to verbalise their plans in advance or to discuss proposals for resolving their conflict; at least without help of their caregiver or teacher. But they are masters in nonverbal communication and in using procedural knowledge of give and take. Most conflicts between the children arise during joint play or parallel play (60%), and of these conflicts only 10% end by splitting up. One of the best predictors of peacemaking seems to be the degree of positive contact between the children before the conflict erupts (De Waal, 2000).

The teacher's role in peer conflicts

If young children are so skilful at solving peer conflicts on their own, what then is the teacher's role? In our study, teachers intervened in a third of all conflict episodes; 79 episodes compared to 143 episodes without teacher intervention. Our data clearly show that, in general, teachers are no better at resolving conflicts than young children. When children are playing together and the teacher intervenes in their conflict, they end by separating in 20% of the cases; in similar conflict episodes without teacher intervention that happens in only 8% of the cases. Nor is this because teachers tend to intervene in more serious conflicts. Many crises are resolved without the assistance of the teacher, and teachers often intervene without any appeal from the children. Moreover, it happens quite frequently that a crisis develops only after the teacher has begun to intervene (in a third of the episodes in which a teacher is involved in a crisis between the children). These crises tend to last longer (there was a teacher involved in all but one of the crises that lasted longer than a minute). Should we conclude from these data that teachers ought to refrain from intervening in conflicts? Yes, I think it is often better to refrain than to intervene. But I also think that teachers need to develop a special sensitivity and skills for solving children's peer problems.

First of all, teachers have to ensure that they do not become part of the conflict. In this respect, teachers often failed, mainly because they resorted to high power strategies

(Singer & Hännikäinen, submitted). Half of the teacher's interventions could be classified as a form of high power strategy, in which the teacher is following her own agenda solely to restore order. In the other half of the interventions the teacher tried to mediate between the children. When the teacher takes side by helping the 'victim', blaming the 'wrongdoer', or by imposing a solution, she runs the risk of destroying the balance of power between the children. Often she (unintentionally) reinforces the power of one of the children. The child who has the support of an omnipotent adult tends to stick to his or her position. Some of the children, we noted, took advantage of the teacher by crying loudly to enlist her support. Any unfair treatment by the teacher appeared to evoke more violent emotions by the 'victim' than unfair treatment by a peer. This was probably because a 'victimised' child feels more powerless against the teacher; and because the violation of the child's moral logic by a teacher who is supposed to take care and to protect, induces fear. We saw several examples of children who take their revenge on a peer after an unfair intervention by the teacher. Unfair treatment of the teachers merely fuels further conflict between children.

For teachers, it is hard to know what solution will be acceptable for all children involved. In most cases she will not know the full history of what happened before the conflict erupted. Even the children often do not know the lines of their script before they are acted out; so how could the teacher know what's best? And most conflicts cannot be resolved by applying social or moral rules, because contradictory rules could equally be applied. When a child wants to participate in the play of another child, what rule should be applied? 'Children should learn to share and play together'; or 'children should not disturb each other'? (for analysis of this apparent contradiction, see Corsaro, 1997).

Of course, in cases where children are bullying each other teachers have to intervene immediately. In such a situation she has to forbid the means (biting, spitting, hitting that causes pain) that children sometimes use to enforce their will. In her role as protector and guardian of the rule 'you should not harm each other', the teacher is accepted by all children. In fact, most children look to the teacher or the researcher before or after that rule is violated. But the teacher can do more to participate in the resolution rather than become involved in the conflict. On the basis on my previous thoughts on the logic of young children's nonverbal behaviour, five obvious suggestions can be made.

1. The natural tendency of young children to use nonverbal strategies to de-escalate a conflict should be strengthened by fostering a sense of belonging. Teachers can foster this sense of belonging by introducing rituals and routines in which the children actively participate.
2. The teacher can offer 'tools' for the cultivation of this natural tendency for pro-social behaviour during conflicts. For instance by using maxims like "don't hurt", "use your words" and "take turns", that can be adopted by the children; and by teaching songs or ritualised gestures for reconciliation (Butovskaya et al., 2000).

3. The teacher has to understand that conflicts are a natural part of social life and playing together. By structuring the room, time and play objects, she can prevent an excess of conflict, but conflicts over the content of joint play, or the use of objects and over the rejection of children who want to join in, are normal phenomena in day care centres. In general, young children are well equipped to resolve these conflicts on their own.
4. In the case where the teacher has to intervene, she has to respect the logic-in-action of all children involved. She has to mediate between the children and aim to ensure that the children's play continues (for a further discussion of mediation, see Singer & Hännikäinen, submitted).
5. In cases where the teacher wants to discuss the conflict with the children, she has to function as a more experienced other who actively helps the children to verbalise their feelings and activity ideas: she has to ask questions. And she has to be careful not to obstruct their nonverbal skills of communication.

In conclusion

Children younger than four years old construct and co-construct a shared logic during their play and they rarely discuss the ideas that underlie their play in advantage. This can result in conflicts and in a collage of different story lines that seem illogical or even without sense to an adult. But adults usually cannot get things 'straight' for young children. In my introduction I quoted a Japanese educator who held the view that small classes are only fine if the teachers are sensitive. He warned against too much interference of the wrong kind. I think this educator makes a valid point: it is not at all unusual for teachers to fuel peer conflicts. But I do not agree with his plea for large groups. As Stambak and Verba (1986) have argued: young children need teachers who are nondirective, but nevertheless highly interested. When they are playing together, young children often look to the teacher for reassurance, especially during conflicts. Working with very young children in groups is a relatively new profession, a profession that demands the development of skills that are different from the skills of caregivers at home. Therefore teachers need training to understand the logic inherent in young children's behaviour. They need someone who teaches them to look at young children differently, just as Zilma de Oliveira did to me. Teachers have to develop a day care culture, in cooperation with the children, that fosters the construction of a shared logical world.

References

Bonica, L. (1997). *Regulating Processes Between Children in Group Situation: Children's Observation of an Adult Consoling Another Child*. Paper presented at the 7th European Conference on the Quality of Early Childhood Education, Munich 3-6 September 1997.
Bowlby, J. (1969). *Attachment and Loss: Vol 1.. Attachment*. New York: Basic Books.
Butovskaya, M., Verbeek, P., Ljungberg, T., & Lunardini, A. (2000). A multicultural view of peacemaking among young children. In: F. Aureli, & F. M.B.De Waal, *Natural Conflict*

Resolution (243-258). Berkely: University of Calofornia Press.

Corsaro, W. (1988). Routines in the peer culture of American and Italian nursery school children. *Sociology of Education*, 67, 1-26.

Corsaro, W. (1997). *The Sociology of Childhood*. Thousand Oaks, Cal.: Pine Froge Press.

Donovan, D.M., & Mcintyre, D. (1990). *Healing the Hurt Child. A Development-contextual Approach*. New York: Norton.

Dittrich, G., Dörfler, M., & Schneider, K. (Eds.). (1998). *Konflikte unter Kindern Beobachten und Verstehen*. Munich: Deutsches Jugendinstitut.

Dittrich, G., Dörfler, M., & Schneider, K. (1999). *Konflictverhalten von Kindern in Kindertagesstatten. 5 Materialbeispiele fur die Fortbildung* (50 Min., VHS/PAL). Munchen: Deutsches Jugendinstitut.

Emde, R.N. van, Biringer, Z., Clyman, R.B., & Oppenheim, D. (1991). The moral self of infancy: affective core and procedural knowledge, *Developmental Review*, 11, 251-270.

Fischer, K.W., Shaver, P.R., & Carnochan, P. (1990). How emotions develop and how they organise development. *Cognition and Emotion*, 4, 81-127.

Frijda, N.H. (1986). *The Emotions*. Cambridge: Cambridge University Press.

Haan, D. de, & Singer, E. (2001). Young children's language of togetherness, *International Journal of Early Years Education*, 9, 117-124.

Hakkarainen, P. (1991). Joint construction of the object of educational work in kindergarten. *The Quarterly Newsletter of the Laboratory of Comparative Human Cognition*, 13, 80-97.

Jones, E., & Reynolds, G. (1992). *The Play's the Thing. Teachers' Roles in Children's Play* .New York: Teachers College Press.

Juen, B., & Banninger-Huber, E. (1999). *Conflict Regulation in Early Mother-child Dyads*. Paper presented at the 8th European Conference on 'Facial Expression, Measurement and Meaning', University of the Saarland, Saarbrucken (Germany), September, 27-30, 1999.

Killen, N., & Nucci, L. P. (1995). Morality, autonomy, and social conflict. In: M. Killen & D. Hart, (Eds.), *Morality in Everyday Life. Developmental Perspectives* (pp. 52-85). Cambridge: Cambridge University Press.

Killen, M., & de Waal, F.B.M. (2000). The evolution and development of morality. In: F. Aureli & F.B.M. de Waal, (Eds.), *Natural Conflict Resolution* (352-372). Berkely: University of California Press.

Kuzmak, S.D., & Gelman, R. (1986). Young children's understanding of random phenomena, *Child Development*, 57, 559-566.

Lamb, M.E., Sternberg, K.J., Hwang, C.P., & Broberg, A.G. (1992). *Child Care in Context. Cross-cultural Perspectives*. Hillsdale NJ: Lawrence Erlbaum Ass.

Miller, P.H., & Aloise, P.A. (1989). Young children's understanding of the psychological causes of behavior: a review. *Child Development*, 60, 257-285.

Miltenburg, R., & Singer, E. (2000). A concept becomes a passion. Moral commitment and the affective development of the survivors of child abuse. *Theory & Psychology, 10*, 503-526.

Oliveira, Z. Moraes Ramos de, & Rossetti-Ferreira, M. C. (1996). Understanding the co-constructive nature of human development: role coordination in early peer interanction. In: Valsiner, J. & Voss, H.H. (Eds.), *The Structure of Learning Processes* (pp. 177-204). Norwood NJ: Ablex.

Piaget, J. (1930). *The Child's Conception of Physical Causality*. London: Routledge & Kegan Paul.

Piaget, J. (1967). *Six Psychological Studies*. New York: Vintage.

Piaget, J., & Inhelder, B. (1969). *The Psychology of the Child*. London: Routledge & Kegan Paul.

Schaffer, H.R. (1977). *Studies of Mother-infant Interaction*. London: Academic Press.

Schaffer, H.R. (1984). *The Child's Entry into a Social World*. London: Academic Press.

Singer, E. (1993). Shared care for children. In: M Woodhead, D. Faulkner, & K. Littleton, (Eds.), *Cultural Worlds of Early Childhood* (pp 64-83). London: Routledge/The Open University.

Singer, E. & Hännikäinen, M. (submitted). *The Teacher's Role in Territorial Conflicts of 2 to 3 Year-old Children*.

Stambak, M., Bonica, L., Maisonett, R., Musatti, T., Rayna R., & Verba, M. (Eds.). (1983). *Les Bébés entre eux: Découvrir, Jouer, Inventer Ensemble*. Paris: Presses Universitaires de France.

Stambak, M., & Sinclair, H. (1993). *Pretend Play Among 3 year Olds*. Hillsdale NJ: Erlbaum.

Stambak, M., & Verba, M. (1986). Organization of social play among toddlers: An ecological approach. In: E.C. Mueller, & C.R. Cooper, (Eds.), *Process and Outcomes in Peer Relationships* (pp. 229-247). Orlando: Academic Press.

Tobin, J.J., Wu, D.Y.H., & Davidson, D.H. (1989). *Preschools in Three Cultures*. New Haven: Yale University Press.

Verba, M. (1994). The beginnings of peer collaboration in peer interaction. *Human Development, 37,* 125-139.

Verbeek, P., Hartup, W.W., & Collins, W.A. (2000). Conflict management in children and adolescents. In: F. Aureli, & F.M.B. De Waal, (Eds.), *Natural Conflict Resolution* (34-53). Berkely: University of California Press.

Vygotsky, L.S. (1978). *Mind in Society. The Development of Higher Psychological Processes*. Cambridge, Mass: Harvard University Press.

Vygotsky, L.S. (1987). Thinking and speech. In: R.W. Rieber,, A.S. Carton, & J.S. Bruner, (Eds.), *The Collected Works of L.S. Vygotsky, Vol. 1 Problems of General Psychology* (pp. 39-285). New York: Plenum Press. Original work published 1934.

Waal, F. De (2000). Primates. A natural heritage of conflict resolution, *Science, 289,* 586-590.

[6]

A rainbow of narratives:
Childhood after developmentalism

John R. Morss

Introduction: The Developmentalism Problem

It is probably true to say that communities and professions need to share certain assumptions and values in order to function. These assumptions and values may well be very firmly embedded. But they do change from time to time, and the role they play will vary from place to place. It can surely do no harm to question them once in a while. If the assumptions and values are sound or useful then they will be re-affirmed as a consequence of this process of scrutiny. If not then we will have the opportunity to re-think them.

Research and evaluation of all kinds, including the personal reflection of members of a profession, must likewise, of necessity, involve the questioning of something that has been accepted in the past. Usually this will be something rather narrow or specific – something like a teaching strategy or a way of designing some educational facility. Someone asks her- or himself, or asks someone else, "Why do we do it this way? Why don't we try doing it another way?" This kind of everyday critical thinking is essential for any profession if it is not to stagnate, for even if some accepted method or process has been adequate in the past, a changing environment may mean that it has become obsolete.

In some ways however the sort of assumptions and values that most need to be subject to scrutiny are those we take most for granted – those that seem like mere common sense, that which is "obvious." These are the conceptual foundations of how the profession carries out its business. Above all perhaps we should ask questions about anything to which there seems no alternative, for it is by seeing alternatives where there were apparently none, that new ways of thinking, feeling and acting are opened up.

It is in this spirit that we should ask some difficult questions about "development." Do children "develop"? Should educators organise the activities of children in terms of their developmental "needs" or capabilities? It might seem that asking questions about the validity of this idea is to challenge the very basis of teaching, in early education or elsewhere. Is it possible that the idea of "development" conceals what is actually happening rather than illuminating it? My argument is that all of us – teachers, parents, policy-makers, researchers – know from our own experience that talking about children's development is somehow missing the point. Although it may take someone with a researcher's detachment and resources to work through the academic aspects of this claim, and to put in the effort to get people seriously thinking about it, it is at heart an everyday matter not an academic one. "Developmentalism" is a serious concern for the educationist (Baker, 1999).

In this chapter I shall first attempt to illustrate some key aspects of the current debate on the nature of childhood. Next I discuss the decline of naturalistic accounts of childhood. I then outline seven possible versions of a more adequate, social-constructionist approach – a "rainbow of narratives." Finally I sketch some of the ways in which a narrative framework might help us to make sense of these issues.

Developmental statements

We are all familiar with developmental statements. These are statements that make a claim about a person or group of people on the basis of age or "stage." For example, any statement about "what young children are like" or "what an adolescent needs" would be a developmental statement. Some developmental statements are very precise – for example, statements based on experimental research in psychology. Some are extremely informal and vague. A lot of the time people (including researchers, teachers, parents) move back and forth between precise and imprecise kinds. A scientific paper presented at a psychology or education conference may well contain extremely precise claims about what children of certain ages can and cannot do, but listen to the introduction and conclusion of such a paper. More often than not, the research work that is being reported is justified by reference to very general developmental assumptions.

Parents and teachers, especially teachers in early childhood settings, are often in a particularly good position to notice the inadequacies of developmental statements. They are frequently reminded of the differences between children of similar age and, just as significant, of the different ways that the same child acts in different circumstances. Yet parents and teachers (that is to say, most of us) are frequently trapped by developmental language. Perhaps it is the convenience and familiarity of developmental statements that lead us to talk this way so often, almost as if we were on "autopilot." Perhaps it is the difficulty and social awkwardness of the alternatives. For whatever reason, most of us find it familiar and comfortable to talk about other people, especially children and young people (but also at times ourselves) in ways that are stereotyped, clichéd or at least simplistic. We still hear about the "terrible two's." We raise mutual eyebrows when someone mentions a "teenager." We slip so easily into a code that classifies and characterizes people in terms of age. We recognise and concur with developmental statements made by other people because we share expectations and beliefs, culture, or experience with the maker of the statement.

There are parallels to be drawn with other kinds of stereotyping. We have (finally) noticed how damaging it is to use simplistic, lazy classifications for gender or for race – to stereotype people in terms of broad and largely accidental features. The fact that the employment of such stereotypical labels is shared within a group or community (ie sexism and racism are collective attitudes) makes things worse, not better. It becomes a matter of affiliation or conformity, or sheer laziness, to make use of shared prejudices. It may seem that I am moving too fast here. From criticising racist or sexist comments to criticising a comment about "teenagers" or "terrible two's" seems a large step. And the invention of another "ism" does not in itself demonstrate that any serious discrimination is actually taking place. After all, although we are already aware of the idea of "ageism," the term is usually applied to discrimination against the more aged rather than the less aged. But if stereotyping is wrong in general, then stereotyping according to chronological age will be wrong. An age-related term that seems no more than descriptive – a term such as "toddler" – seems inoffensive enough. What's in a name? But if the use of the word brings with it restrictive connotations (for example, brings with it the idea that such people are generally incompetent) then serious discrimination is certainly possible. People of all ages live up or down to others' expectations, so that developmental statements can become self-fulfilling prophecies. If certain actions and characteristics are expected of a person (for example on the basis of their age), then it often happens that those actions are indeed observed and those characteristics indeed perceived. Let us at least think about possible alternatives.

The decline of naturalistic accounts of childhood

As Allison James and her colleagues, among others, have shown (James, Jenks and Prout, 1998; Prout, 2000) the understandings of childhood that we are offered by psychology are almost entirely naturalistic. That is to say, the accounts are based directly or indirectly on biology (see Morss, 1990; 1996). They set out universal patterns, trends or stages for "developmental" change. There is often a reliance on biology. The explanatory role played by evolutionary theory as such varies from one account to the next, but biological or "natural" processes are treated as foundational.

Almost without exception, theories of human development put forward by psychology have been based on the idea that early development (infancy and early childhood at least) are above all expressions of biology. Human cultures, it is claimed, get overlaid on the natural baseline, and the cultural material accumulates to an increasing extent with chronological age. Cultural difference is for adults (except that very old age brings us all back closer to our biological nature). Differences due to environmental or other social factors are minor variations in a largely uniform picture. Such at least is the account offered by psychology in its main features.

It is widely accepted among social scientists writing on childhood that naturalistic accounts of childhood are now in decline in terms of influence (Jenks 2001; Lee 2001). They are being challenged, if not yet displaced, by alternative approaches. The first alternatives were presented by sociologists and were focused on socialisation (James and Prout, 1997). They represented an improvement on the biologically naturalistic, yet they were still committed to the idea of uniform and rather simplistic patterns of change with age. The alternatives which present significantly different conceptualisations of childhood both to the naturalistic account and to the socialization account can all be called "social construction" approaches. This somewhat clumsy term simply denotes the idea that we try to recognize the pervasive effects of the social context to all our activities.

Naturalistic accounts are of many kinds, as are socialisation accounts. It should therefore not be a surprise that social construction approaches are also of many kinds. For while the term social construction can properly be used in a fairly generic sense, indicating the broad domain excluded by naturalistic and socialisation approaches (Morss, 2002), it is probably more useful to think of it as a collection of more specific variants. Indeed social construction approaches are probably more varied than either of the other two orientations. James and her colleagues (1998) have identified a number of these alternative forms of social constructionism in relation to childhood. Further alternatives can be discerned. I will attempt to sketch and to discuss seven of these alternative formulations of a social-constructionist approach.

Indeed each of the seven variants discussed here can be further subdivided, at least into weaker and stronger versions. Nor, except for its happy associations with the colours of the rainbow – internationally an icon of plurality and tolerance – is there anything "magical" about the number seven. Indeed as suggested above, it is probably important that not one single view of a social construction perspective comes to predominate – "let one hundred flowers blossom."

Seven versions of a social constructionist account of childhood

In all probability something useful can be learned from each of the seven approaches discussed here, and from others yet to be described. Yet the tensions between them are as important as the communalities. Let us consider them in turn, remaining vigilant for both kinds of relationship, both difference and repetition. It may be that one of these approaches is "right" and the others "wrong," or that they can all be harmoniously synthesised into one comprehensive perspective ("*the* social construction account of childhood" – the spectrum resolved into pure white light). But it is much more likely that neither of these neat solutions is the case and that we have to live with the multiplicity.

Red: Childhood is tribal

Children share cultural or sub-cultural identities with each other, in ways that to some extent cross-cut the cultural sub-divisions of adult society. To some extent childhood is handed down from one generation of children to the next, as each generation dies (ie "grows up"). Therefore childhood is to be understood anthropologically – in terms of its coherence and internal intelligibility. Otherwise, an act of colonisation is taking place. Nothing is gained by trying to wish away the boundaries between adults and children in this sense. Childhood is foreign to those who study it: like the rainbow, it can only be seen at a distance. Involving children more actively as researchers may achieve little more than causing them to become foreign from their own experience. Childhood thus deserves scientific respect as a noble tribe, or at least a quaint tribe (think of Tolkien's hobbits).

This line of thinking can be traced back at least to the classic English work of the Opies (1959) on children's games and other activities, but more contemporary examples can also be found (James, 1993) which reflect conceptual advances within anthropology.

Orange: *Childhood is experiential*
And yet, we might want to say, the basic facts about childhood are surely located in the experience of it, not in some objective scientific reality. Do we really "understand" a rainbow when we are instructed in optics, refraction and meteorology? How could science pretend to capture this elusive phantom? Isaac Newton holds up a prism and a weak Cambridge sun delivers a miraculous splash of colour to his dark Cambridge wall. Should we not say with Tolkien's Gandalf – faced with Saruman of Many Colours – "He that breaks a thing to find out what it is has left the path of wisdom" (Tolkien, 1993: 339).
From this perspective then, childhood resides in the experience of children and of adults. In terms of explanation, phenomenology takes precedence over any supposedly objective account. Childhood deserves sensitivity as an experience (see Bradley, 1989).

Yellow: *Childhood is an oppressed minority status within society*
Portraying children as mystical or magical goes back in European culture particularly to the romantic tradition of the very late eighteenth century. Many decades later its attitude was captured, with heightened nostalgia, in the writings and the photographs of Charles Dodgson also known as Lewis Carroll (Stainton Rogers and Stainton Rogers, 1992). Yet the period of most extreme child-worship corresponded exactly with the period of most extreme and large-scale exploitation and abuse of children, as workers in the new industries of western Europe. Surely we would have to say that the myth concealed the reality? Children it seems are vulnerable, and therefore are oppressed.
We can say that, to the extent that children are separated from adults, they are discriminated against. The separation or sequestration is achieved by a variety of means, some physical, some regulatory. In many ways modern industrialised societies conceal the sequestration by relaxing the physical means of separation while increasing the regulation. For example, children of the twenty-first century "west" mix much more with the world of adults in leisure domains: children and adults watch the same movies, listen to the same music, wear the same styles of clothes, use the same vocabulary. And yet children may not vote, sign contracts, consent to or have a veto over medical treatment, and so on. This is not separate development, this is *apartheid*. Even the supposed "protection" of children (eg labour laws) function in reality to protect adults from the necessity of recognising children. Like some group stigmatised in terms of a disability, or an ethnic or religious identity, children are disposed of, "looked after."
Therefore, from this perspective, childhood is to be responded to through activism, through the assertion of the rights of minorities. As with other groupings who are the subject of discrimination, it is presupposed by this approach that the oppression of children is contingent – it can be stopped or at least reduced by political action. Therefore it *should* be stopped. Children are not at all like a distinct tribe, and preten-

ding that they are is merely a way of concealing from them and from ourselves that we are responsible for their ongoing oppression. Examples of this approach may be found in writings on children's rights (Freeman, 2001); and in Burman (1994).

Green: *Childhood is discursive*

And yet surely, political action cannot achieve the impossible. If our very definitions of childhood are loaded, initiatives at the political level may be little more than tokenism. For, it may be argued, we do not either perceive or experience "childhood" directly. To make sense of what we experience we need frameworks of meaning, and those frameworks are inevitably drawn from our cultural-historical setting. It is said that the special significance of the number seven influenced Isaac Newton – always fascinated by the mystical significance of numbers – to discern exactly seven colours in the broken beam of light thrown by his prism. If he had described (say) six or ten named colours in the spectrum, we would (in the Newtonian west at least) find it "natural" to see six or ten also.

The point is that we can only work with patterned expectations, scripts, formulas, ways of setting forth, and these things are constructed through dialogue. They are "intersubjective." We acquire or "appropriate" ways of looking at the world from our social interaction. Childhood is thus constructed through talk, writing and similar processes. Striking examples and supporting arguments may be found in the writings of the Stainton Rogers (1992) and of Walkerdine (1995) as well as Burman (1994).

Blue: *Childhood is a structural component of society*

On the other hand, perhaps talking about "discourse" is a distraction – an over-intellectualisation of some rather mundane facts. Putting issues of discrimination aside also, childhood may simply be a necessary component of industrialised or pre-industrial society – a demographic phenomenon (Qvortrup, 1994). When we consider the role of adult workers (either industrial or agricultural) we do not feel the need to explain the meaning of adulthood. If new workers need to be produced (via biological reproduction), and need to acquire some skills before participating in the work-force, then childhood is simply necessary.

This idea can be understood in a functionalist sense, as for Qvortrup, or a Marxist sense. Oldman (1994) has explored the ways in which much adult work (especially in the case of a large number of professions) relies on the supposed needs of children. Teaching, and hence the training of teachers, and hence the research into children's development which is applied in teacher training, all depend on the exploitation (in a Marxist sense) of children as a "class." Children's needs are defined in ways that support and appear to justify the relevant profession. (Child care and welfare professions among many others need to be added to the teaching professions in this context – teachers are merely the most obvious of such "child-workers"). Childhood is no more than a structural consequence of human society.

Indigo: *Childhood is phenotypical*
The structural approach might again be too scientistic, treating childhood as unified and objective when it is not. It might be said that there are different types of childhood – not an infinite number but a significant range. Different languages around the world have different expressions for what the English language calls a "rainbow" and yet all refer to the same thing. In the vocabulary of biology, one might say that what we call childhood is the variable expression or manifestation (phenotype) of some deeper causal structure (genotype). The point of this analogy would be that childhood can only be expressed through the very processes that make it diverse and yet it is still "the same" at a deeper level of analysis.

Another version of this approach may perhaps be indicated in the cognitive developmental theory of Rogoff (1990). For Rogoff, children growing up in different cultures are subject to enculturation into vastly different ways of thinking. Children grow up to be culturally diverse in their thinking as well as in their language and behaviour. Yet, says Rogoff, the same basic processes of "guided participation" apply universally. This notion of guided participation or "apprenticeship" by which children are drawn into their local culture is closely related to the ideas of Vygotsky (Van der Veer and Valsiner, 1991).

Yet another version is a more historical one. In the study of the history of childhood, there is an important debate between what has been called the "big bang" theory of Aries (Jenks, 2001) – the claim of a sudden emergence of childhood in modern times – and the alternative "steady state" theory in which stress is laid on the continuity of treatment of children across the centuries. At different times in history, it may be argued (Hendrick, 1997), childhood has taken different forms and yet it has always been in some sense recognisably "childhood."

To adopt this approach would be to think of childhood as something that is inherently variable yet far from chaotic. The three alternative versions of this approach themselves, *as a set of alternatives,* make the general point. For it to make sense that there are three (or more) different ways of illustrating the same idea (that childhood is a phenotype), there must be some underlying unity to the idea.

Violet: *Childhood is performative*
Perhaps all the above approaches are misconceived. Childhood, it might be said, is surely not predetermined even in the sense of there being a range of options. Childhood is simply what children do (English grammar is not adequate to the sense at this point). It is "performed." There are few explorations of this approach at present, although some suggestions may be found in the various contributions to Holzman and Morss (2000). This would be as it were to see the rainbow as performance art, as a great installation, an "event" or "happening."

Moving beyond the visible (to humans) spectrum, we could perhaps add to our repertoire of seven alternatives, the *Infra-red* (we are all children) and the *Ultra-violet* (childhood does not exist). The point is that the social spectrum captures or at least hints at the richness of the actuality of childhood, whereas the thinking of naturalism and of socialisation is hopelessly impoverished. If we agree that thinking reflectively about childhood is worthwhile at all – and any commitment to research into early childhood seems to presuppose this – then surely we would not wish knowingly to narrow our vision.

Conclusion: Narrative, childhood, and the personal dimension

What brings people to these issues of the nature of childhood is professional involvement in the lives of young children. All of those people must think it appropriate that adults should in certain circumstances take responsibility for "other people's" children (I have scare-quotes around the term because of reservations about the idea of children being "ours" in the first place). Teaching, including early childhood teaching, includes such "looking after" although it also includes more. We all agree further, I take it, that it matters *how* people do that looking after. We agree that it is right for adults to think with care and humility about how they carry out this role, and therefore that it is right for other adults to be concerned about how those adults carry out that role.

Thinking with care and humility means being prepared to think critically – to ask difficult questions whether of oneself or of others, or of the literature, or of the "system." What everybody agrees about – whether it's all the experts, or all the parents, or all the community – may not be right. There always may be other ways of thinking about things. And if we want to encourage or even merely not to obstruct the creativity that we like to associate with early childhood, surely we should model that creativity as best we can. This means being prepared to go outside the safety zone. It means being prepared to respond to difficult questions – like "Why are you doing that?" or "Why are you doing it that way?" It may include saying or doing things that everyone around us thinks is weird or even threatening.

If this makes any kind of sense then we may need to ask what we should do with the idea of "narrative". Do we pull it inside our comfort zone, "recognising" it as what we've been doing all along? Or do we take a risk and allow ourselves to be drawn out, extended, taken in unknown directions – to be prepared not to know the end of the story before it begins? It is often said that young children enjoy hearing the same story again and again, reassured by the predictability of an ending. But surely it is we adults who are most committed to the sense of control that comes with familiarity. There seems no better explanation for the continuing authority of the orthodox psychology of development.

That continuing authority – the dominance of developmental thinking – is best illustrated by the reaction one gets to challenging it. Of course every performer and writer (not least the academic) has a story to tell, probably in a bar, about her or his struggles against an uncomprehending world. The spectator sees most of the play so it may be that the developmental approach, with the broader naturalistic outlook of which it is a part, really is on the wane. If so the idea of narrative will have played a significant role in the refreshing of the *zeitgeist*. Most significant of all might be if those most centrally and directly involved with early education were to recognise their own knowledge and act on it (Cannella, 1997).

Developmental statements, whether used in a curriculum document, research report, or in casual staff-room or household conversation, have the potential to do harm. If nothing else, they get in the way of more thoughtful and more particular comments. They are banal and impoverished. Whoever it is we are speaking about – not least, young children in an early education setting – they surely deserve more from us. Neither age nor "stage" should be considered adequate as the basis for decision-making about children's needs or welfare. One way or another, the story must move on.

References

Baker, B. (1999). The dangerous and the good? Developmentalism, progress, and public schooling. *American Educational Research Journal* 36/4 pp 797-834.

Bradley, B. (1989). *Visions of Infancy*. Cambridge: Polity Press.

Burman, E. (1994). *Deconstructing Developmental Psychology*. London: Routledge.

Cannella, G. (1997). *Deconstructing Early Childhood Education*. New York: Plenum.

Freeman, M. (2001). The child in family law. In J. Fionda (Ed.), *Legal Concepts of Childhood*. Oxford and Portland: Hart Publishing.

Hendrick, H. (1997). *Constructions and reconstructions of British childhood*. In A. James & A. Prout (eds) *Constructing and Reconstructing Childhood: Contemporary issues in the sociological study of childhood.*(2nd Edition) London: Falmer Press.

Holzman, L. & Morss, J.R. (eds). (2000). *Postmodern Psychologies, Societal Practice, and Political Life*. New York: Routledge.

James, A. (1993). *Childhood Identities*. Edinburgh: Edinburgh University Press.

James, A., Jenks, C., & Prout, A. (1998). *Theorizing Childhood*. Cambridge: Polity Press.

James, A. & Prout, A. (Eds.). (1997). *Constructing and Reconstructing Childhood: Contemporary issues in the sociological study of childhood.* (2nd Edition) London: Falmer Press.

Jenks, C. (2001). Sociological perspectives and media representations of childhood. In J. Fionda (Ed.), *Legal Concepts of Childhood*. Oxford and Portland: Hart Publishing.

Lee, N. (2001). *Childhood and Society: Growing up in an age of uncertainty*. Buckingham: Open University Press.

Morss, J.R. (1990). *The Biologising of Childhood*. Hove: Erlbaum.

Morss, J.R. (1996). *Growing Critical: Alternatives to developmental psychology*. London: Routledge.

Morss, J.R. (2002). The several social constructions of James, Jenks, and Prout: A contribution to the sociological theorization of childhood. *International Journal of Children's Rights* 10/1, pp 39-54.

Oldman, D. (1994). Childhood as a mode of production. In B. Mayall (Ed.), *Children's Childhoods: Observed and experienced*. London: Falmer Press.

Opie, I. & Opie, P. (1959). *The Lore and Language of Schoolchildren*. Oxford: Clarendon Press.

Prout, A. (Ed.). (2000). *The Body, Childhood and Society*. New York: St. Martin's Press.

Qvortrup J. (Ed.) (1994). *Childhood Matters*. Aldershot: Avebury.

Rogoff, B. (1990). *Apprenticeship in Thinking*. New York: Oxford University Press.

Stainton Rogers, R. & Stainton Rogers, W. (1992). *Stories of Childhood*. Hemel Hempstead UK: Harvester Wheatsheaf.

Tolkien, J.R.R. (1993). *The Lord of the Rings*. London: Allen and Unwin.

Van der Veer, R. & Valsiner, J. (1991). *Understanding Vygotsky*. Oxford: Blackwell.

Walkerdine, V. (1995). Subject to change without notice. In S. Pile & N. Thrift (Eds.), *Mapping the Subject*. London: Routledge.

II

NARRATIVES IN PRACTICE:
Exploring the
narrative of
the playing child

[7]

Basic development:
Developmental education
for young children

Frea Janssen-Vos

Introduction

This chapter aims at providing the reader with some basic information about 'Basic Development' and its youngest offshoot: 'Startingblocks'. References to further information may be found in the bibliography.

In 1988, a project was commenced that intended to make a significant contribution to the upbringing and education of young children. Our most important motivation was, and still is, to help improve the education of young children. The reason for this was the integration of nursery education and primary education into the new primary school, which was accompanied by a number of practical changes, not all of which had been anticipated or planned. There was a need for a practice-theory that would provide an answer to the question of how schools would be able to realise continuity and cohesion in the education of children from four to eight years of age, the early years of the primary school.

As a result of collaboration between various disciplines, a theoretically underpinned educational concept, a curriculum for practical improvements and an innovation strategy are now available. The early education project group of the APS (national institute for school improvement) accomplished the development tasks. The Alkmaar College of Higher Education and Teacher Training (staff-members also formed part of the APS project group) explored the significance and practicability while working with teachers and developed initial strategies for professionalisation and school improvement. The Free University of Amsterdam (Van Oers) has made theoretical contributions and further developed the theoretical concept, drawing from a socio-cultural perspective. Many people working in primary education have shared their experiences with us, so that the concept and curricula became theoretically and practically reliable.

Currently, an estimated 10 % of primary schools are working with Basic Development in the early years of Dutch primary schools, while the developmental approach is being extended to the intermediate stage and the upper grades. Together with preschool playgroups, a number of schools have started an implementation programme that focuses specifically on young children in high-risk groups. Within this context, an extension of Basic Development has been produced, aiming at children from 2 to 4 years of age. This pedagogical plan is called 'Startingblocks of Basic Development'.

In the following, some of this project's central points are briefly introduced:
- theoretical principles of developmental education;
- characteristics of Basic Development, the play based curriculum for early education in primary school;
- characteristics of Startingblocks, the pedagogical plan for preschool education in playgroups.

Theoretical principles

The educational concept underpinning the curriculum and working strategies is based on neo-Vygotskian theories. The following aspects of these theories are particularly relevant for education of young children (Janssen-Vos & Van Oers, 1998):

Zone of proximal development

Central to Vygotsky's developmental theory is the idea that children develop and learn in interaction with others, by participating in (adult) social-cultural activities. Adults can stimulate children's development by offering them the appropriate help in social-cultural activities in which the children wish to be involved.

For Vygotsky, the concept of the zone of proximal development was related to the notion of imitation (see Van Oers, 1999a). Vygotsky also indicated that two levels occur in children's development. One is indicated by the actions that a child is already able to accomplish by itself. He refers to this level as the actual level of development. But this level only represents part of a child's development potential. What else the child is able to do becomes clear in the activity when it receives social guidance for its performances. This activity area is referred to as the zone of proximal development.

Interpreted in this way, a zone of proximal development may be described as a sociocultural activity in which the child wishes to participate and can participate in a meaningful way, but which it is not yet independently able to accomplish. To be able to do this, the child needs the help of someone else, who takes responsibility for those parts of the activity that the child itself has not yet mastered. Reading aloud to children, who are not yet able to read themselves, is a good example of an activity that forms such a zone of proximal development for young children. The child wants to read too, but is not able to figure out the text by itself. Therefore the adult, or another more knowledgeable partner, takes this part of the activity for his or her account. By reading together in this way, the partner not only forms a model for the child, but the desire to learn is also aroused in the child.

According to Vygotsky, the only good form of learning is, in fact, that learning which is ahead of development (as in the above-mentioned example: learning to read independently) and that creates a new zone of development (reading with the adult who decodes the text) (Vygotsky, 1978, p.87). It is clear that Vygotsky's educational philosophy was forward-looking.

Leading activities

Vygotsky not only attached much importance to the part played by adults in development processes; he considered the part played by children to be just as important: "The child must act itself, the teacher should only guide the activity and provide direction" (Vygotsky, 1926/1991, p.118). He emphasised, therefore, the necessity to work from the child's own skills and interests, as development can only become meaningful to a child if this is the result of an endorsement or transformation of that child's own abilities: that which it already can and wants to do.

Leont'ev, and later El'konin, further developed this idea by elaborating the notion of 'leading activity' (El'konin, 1972). The gist of this theory is that children display a great preference for a certain type of activity at different points in their development. Activities that are in line with their actual interests, on the one hand, and that also appear to play a special role in their total developmental process, on the other hand.

Based on these 'leading activities', El'konin identified stages in development. He argued that educational activities are the most conducive to the stimulation of development, if they are embedded in the leading activity that the child is involved in at that particular point in time. During the primary school period, two consecutive activities are regarded as 'leading'. For children from approximately the age of 2 play activity is the most frequent, and 'leading' in the development process. Initially, the manipulative play with objects dominates; this play activity is gradually extended in role-playing in which children imitate the actions of adults in social-cultural activities ('shopping', for example). In the main, the role-play is characteristic of 3 to 6 year old children. This play activity gradually evolves into a conscious (productive) learning activity, which gains the upper hand during the ages of approximately 7 to 12. In the learning activity, learning to learn itself is the leading principle of activities. This manifests itself in the children's questions when they ask for correct answers, for procedures, and for problem solving strategies. They consciously want to find out how things work. The learning activity in this sense of the word emerges from the play activity, in which children initially 'make believe'.

During the transitional process from play activity to learning activity, role play is probably an important factor, as all of the new qualities necessary for the learning activity already reveal themselves in it: communication and negotiation with partners, the use of cultural instruments (writing, numbers, diagrams, etc.), reflection upon actions and meanings, making plans and agreements, obeying rules, etc. Important empirical support for these principles was already suggested in the eighties by Russian researchers (Venger, 1986; Podd'jakov & Michailenko, 1987; El'konin & Venger, 1988).

This theory is particularly valuable for the concrete application of the notion of the zone of proximal development. As a matter of fact, new possibilities for action and mediational means can be meaningfully introduced within such a leading activity. Strategies for the stimulation of new learning processes (in the zone of proximal development) must, therefore, be sought in play activity. However, such learning processes must meet two criteria:

- They must contribute to the optimisation of the play activity itself. What children learn can only be useful to them, if they can see this learning as a contribution to their ongoing play. That is to say: the children's play must increase in value, a value that they themselves attach to it.
- The learning processes to be initiated must prepare children for their future participation in the activity that is to become 'leading' in the next developmental period. For young children this means that the learning processes concentrate on enhancing motivation and on precursors of the productive learning activity.

Learning processes that comply with both of the above-mentioned criteria may be regarded as developmental. However, they do not occur automatically or spontaneously; children must be helped to meaningfully enter into these learning processes. The efforts that teachers make to achieve this are characteristic for developmental education.

Developmental learning processes
Which learning processes are conducive to development, for participation in the learning activity? A first note is that the 'learning' concept, in this context, should not be regarded as the result of knowledge transmission, but as a productive process of knowledge construction, that is founded on discourse and the critical comparison of various meanings, ideas and methods of solution (Van Oers, 1987). As such, the learning activity is a semiotic activity, in which pupils explore and attribute meaning to the relationships that exist between rules, actions and signs accepted in our culture. From a young age, children learn that the 'signs' used by adults (such as gestures, actions and language) have certain meanings. During development, semiotics (the theory of signs and their meanings) expands to include more symbols, such as diagrams, the written language and symbols for quantities and numbers. In essence, learning activity is all about pupils constructing the meaning of these (language) signs and other symbolic representations (images) in their discourses with others. This process, in turn, requires a certain level of development in terms of communicative skills. This view is now quite widely supported by researchers (see, amongst others, Davydov, 1988; Wertsch, 1897; Moll, 1990; Forman et al, 1993).

In the development of pupils, the transition to the phase in which the learning activity becomes 'leading' is characterised by an increased self-regulation of the learning process. That is to say that children find learning interesting for the learning itself. Learning activity therefore supposes the presence of a learning motive that has become independent (El'konin, 1972); it is no longer bound to a role-play activity. This implies that developmental innovations are also required in the sphere of motivation. Learning from now on is more and more self-motivated and self-sought learning for learning's sake.

Briefly, three factors have been indicated that form the psychological foundation for meaningful participation in the productive learning activity: the semiotic function, communication skills and the learning motive. These qualities can be stimulated via the (early development of) play activity, by using a developmental strategy in which the teacher and the child together create a zone of proximal development.

Developmental education

On the basis of these principles concerning development and learning, the concept of 'developmental education' has taken shape with increasing clearness. Its core can be characterised, in summary, by the following points of departure:

- education undertakes systematic attempts to make optimal use of the developmental possibilities which children already possess;
- education strives for a broad personal development, encompassing motivational and emotional development, social, communicative and meta-cognitive competencies, including specific skills;
- education focuses on participation in social-cultural activities that are personally meaningful for children, and that are or become significant to them;
- education depends on the part played by teachers, who adopt the role of the children's partner and help them to carry out activities; teachers so mediate between children's needs and meanings, on the one hand, and cultural reconstruction on the other hand.

Basic Development

Both the theoretical principles and the characteristics of the existing situation in schools offer starting points for a play based curriculum that can contribute to fundamental improvements in early education. The curriculum consists of 'building blocks' that teachers can use to give form to a developmental practice.

The building blocks can be specified as (Janssen-Vos, 1997):

- the core activities;
- the educational objectives and learning processes;
- the teacher's roles;
- activity-oriented observation, registration and evaluation.

Core activities

This theory of 'leading' activities and developmental learning processes have brought us to determine five core activities, which we consider essential in early education of all 4 to 8 year old children:

- Play activities: movement play, manipulative play and role-play.
- Constructive and expressive activities: making products with creative materials, construction materials, building materials and coincidental materials and techniques.
- Conversation activities: interactions and conversations between teacher and children in the small and the large group, and in other activities in circle-time.
- Literacy activities: initial literacy in play activities, functional reading and

writing with children's own narratives and texts.

- Numeric-mathematical activities: mathematical actions in play activities, mathematical cognitive operations and mathematisation in social-cultural contexts.

The play-based character of the curriculum reveals itself in these core activities: they all emerge from play. Constructive activity, for example, finds its roots in the joy of handling things, objects and matter the child finds within its reach: sand, water, bricks, buckets, sticks, paper, nails, glue. These initial manipulative and experimental activities with objects lead to role-playing on the one hand and to making constructions or compositions on the other. The constructions are accidental at first; the children are mainly experimenting, trying out what the materials can 'do'. It doesn't really matter whether the constructions fall apart or not; the process makes it an enjoyable action, not the result. In this stage the child often happens to recognise by accident the product as a house, a car, a shopping basket, or a tree. It also occurs that adults or other children draw the child's attention toward the product: "Hey, this looks like a Christmas tree"! Once attention for the product is caught, the child intentionally starts making certain things; constructing objects that fit in with other activities, and establishing contents that include more children (thematic activities about busses and trains), or objects that have a special conventional meaning.

The play character of the constructive activity expands to the learning activity. This transformation reveals itself when children are no longer satisfied with a very global design of their plans and products, and become interested in correct constructions; 'make believe' is taken over by a sense of reality and by a growing interest in the surrounding world. The children tend to ask more questions about the constructions, look out for examples and instructions in books and work schemes, estimate the necessary amount and size of materials and plan the construction process in advance. This developmental process does not take place spontaneously; the transition from experimental play activity toward intentional and planned constructions largely depends upon the role of the adults/teachers. Together with the children they create zones of proximal development in which they promote and stimulate this process. In order to organise the aimed at developmental process, the teacher keeps in mind the above mentioned stages as a potential 'developmental perspective' of this core activity.

Activity settings
The core activities must be linked up with relevant contents or themes that form the social-cultural context of learning. Because activities are always about something, the value of an activity for children is not only determined by their actions, but particularly by the content and how this relates to the child's motives and interests. Children play about shops, vets, the fairy-parties; they construct houses, railway tracks or equipment for a birthday party; they read and write about the circus, the new house next to the school, or the beautiful-things museum. Activity and content together ensure emotional involvement, and meaningful and developmental activity settings. Basic

Development prefers thematic activities that are designed for a period of several weeks in order to guarantee coherence and continuity in the children's activities and learning process.

It needs to be stressed that themes and core activities are not prescribed or completely planned beforehand. The manuals offer the guidelines and examples of good practice, which can help teachers with designing thematical and integrated activity settings. Teachers use a design model to plan activity settings for a period of 4 to 6 weeks, in which they link thematic content to each of the core activities (see also figure 7.2 below). Moreover, the thematic activities are not to be planned in a fixed way, but are meant to grow out in the course of time. Children's accomplishments, their experiences during the performance, and the teacher's intentions give form to the concrete contents and activities. It thus happens that some thematic activities gradually change as they progress. This kind of open and dynamic planning puts special demands on day-by-day reflections and planning, and on a practical registration strategy.

The thematic core activities have been extensively elaborated in various documents for teachers, to be used as a source of inspiration and as a guideline. The descriptions not only provide examples of educational activities, but also indicate how teachers can use these activities to systematically support and stimulate the development intended. Therefore, each description of the core activities provides information about:
- the developmental value of the activities and their potential contribution to the developmental and learning processes (the objectives);
- the development of the core activity itself, as well as the processes that are stimulated through these (communication and language, for example), outlined in 'developmental perspectives';
- the possible educational activities, and related content and themes;
- the assisting roles of teachers, related to points for attention in observation and evaluation.

Educational objectives and learning processes

The above-described characterisation of developmental learning processes provides indications for important objectives of early education. They are: cultural participation, social development, motivational development and communication skills. Such intentions can effectively be stimulated in the context of play activities (Van Oers, Janssen-Vos & Schiferli, 2002).

The aimed at broad personal development and specific knowledge and skills have been represented in a circle diagram, in the form of three concentric circles (see figure 7.1).
- In the centre: basic conditions of all developmental processes, like well-being, curiosity and self-confidence.
- The middle-circle: aspects of a broad personal development, focussing upon social, communicative and meta-cognitive competencies (self-direction, reasoning and problem solving, for example).

- The outer circle: specific skills, amongst others in the field of the motor system, perception, language and concept formation.

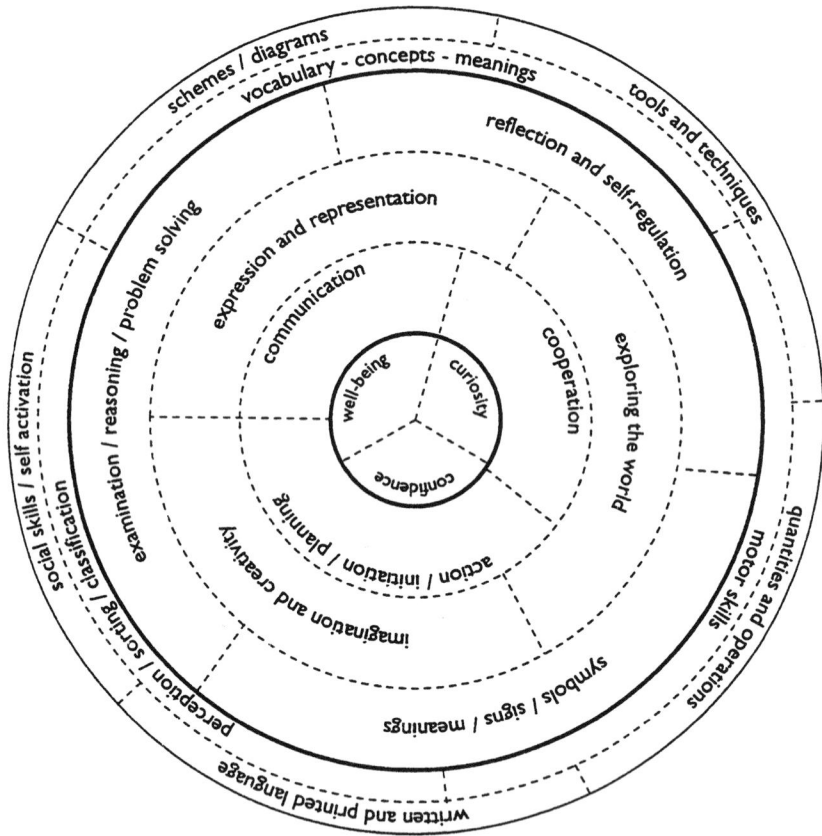

Figure 7.1: *The circle diagram with the aims of Basic Development*

These objectives guide the actions of teachers, when they design a curriculum. In this process they take account of each of the three areas (i.e. centre, middle and outer circle), and their interrelationships. In theory, it should be possible to cut slices from the circle, each of which covers part of the circles.

The core activities intend to promote the aimed at developmental and learning processes. Constructive activities, for example, can meet children's need for play, experimenting and a sense of achievement, and thus support basic characteristics. They offer experiences in the areas of planning and reflection, of communication and cooperation, of exploring the world, and of symbols, symbolic representations (broad development). The accomplishment of constructive activities asks for certain skills and techniques, like fixing parts and using scissors, or estimating, measuring and counting the number of bricks. The core activities offer most of all very stimulating and meaningful learning contexts, because children wish to take part in them and doing so, meet the needs of social, communicative and cognitive skills.

Within these objective areas, the learning processes that promote progress towards the conscious learning activity become clearly visible. They form the leitmotiv in the developmental course of young children, i.e. in the development from play activity to conscious learning activity. This leitmotiv is of particular importance because it offers a clear prospect of continuity and cohesion in the developmental and learning process within the age group of 4 to approximately 8 year olds. This vision on continuity may be used to overcome the traditional fissure between nursery education and primary education. This viewpoint on learning and learning activity also draws attention to three developmental dimensions that contain the psychological precursors that form in due time the psychological foundation for the conscious learning activity:

- *Communication:* being able to establish contact with others, exchange thoughts and 'negotiate' about ideas, feelings, wishes; using language and other means of communication.
- The *semiotic function:* understanding rules and 'signs' and their meanings, which are encompassed in our culture, in our language and our behaviour, and in the symbolic signs (such as the written language, numbers) and in schematic representations (such as maps and models). When meaningfully embedded in play activities, even these 'abstract' elements can be part of young children's daily life (see also Egan, Chapter 2).
- The *learning motive* and specific interests (the pupil wanting to know, understand and be able to; being curious about how things work; aiming at acting 'exactly' and at acquiring the abilities to do so). These psychological qualities constitute a self-directing ability, which enables children to hold on to their plans, and to persevere in the solution of questions or problems that occur when acting out their plans.

By means of the core activities and of two 'intermediaries', children's learning and development may be stimulated and supported in the direction of the aims: teachers in their role as assistant for the performances of children; and the close observations of the children's actions and developmental potentials.

(1) The teacher's roles
Participation in core activities, however, does not guarantee that the desired developmental processes will actually occur. Purposeful guidance is necessary for progress in these activities. Guidance that is conveyed by the teacher's actions is, in fact, the heart of the developmental strategy in Basic Development.

In Vygotskian terms, the teacher's role is characterised by the term 'assisting performance'. The teacher and the children create together a zone of proximal development, that is an activity (activity setting) in which children want to participate and are (almost) able to participate at their actual level of development. As a consequence of this participation new possible actions come within the children's reach. By participating in such joint activities, the teacher helps to ensure that the activity is performed well, and, by doing so, can add new experiences, knowledge and skills. In a shop game, for example, where the teacher helps by playing the part of a customer (thus serving as a model of language and role actions), by asking questions that stimulate a child to think about the prices in the shop, by handing out commercial, 'special offer' brochures (new impulses), or by teaching children how to write out a price list.

Providing guidance is a matter of 'mediating' between potentials and needs of children on the one hand and specific educational aims on the other. This is the reason why teachers do not merely await children's initiatives, nor rely on spontaneous developmental processes. They encourage development; they anticipate, as it were, future developmental processes, because they have clear goals in mind, which they try to achieve in a goal-oriented and systematic way. Yet, this always occurs on the basis of children's motives, meanings and the contributions made by the children involved.

The role of assisting performance entails a number of tasks for teachers:

- teachers design and plan activity settings, which are in line with the actual development and motives of the children;
- they engage children into choosing and planning themes and activities and help them to take initiatives and make plans;
- they participate in the activities, so that, in interaction with children, they can assist in such a manner that development and learning are promoted;
- they introduce an educational organisation that makes it possible to play and work with children in small-group settings, in an interactive manner;
- they observe children's activities and reflect upon them, so that information is available to plan future activities as well as the required assistance;
- they ensure a systematic cycle of designing and planning the curriculum, its execution, reflection and evaluation. Reflection and evaluation are aimed at children's developmental progress as well as at the teacher's educational-methodical actions.

To be able to fulfil this role well, teachers can employ different resources and methodical means. These are concentrated in 5 'didactic impulses', which help to deepen and to broaden children's activities and to add new abilities and skills, all in a systematic and structured way.

The first impulse is *orientation* on joint activities. The teacher likes, for instance, to engage children in activity settings about traffic and means of transport. She reads a picture book with the children and invites them to tell about their experiences with transport and with cars, bicycles or motorbikes. Her intention is twofold: she wishes to prepare the children for future activities and to encourage them to express their ideas; and she wants to hear about their actual interests, experiences and knowledge on this subject.

The way many children tell enthusiastically about their bikes brings her, amongst others, to plan a bicycle workshop and a bicycle factory.

Illustration 7.1: The bicycle shop (Photo: Willibrordusschool)

During the following days and weeks the teacher organises several activity settings in which children take part, independently or with the teacher. In the joint activities the teacher reflects on the children's activities and decides what kind of assistance they need at that moment. Her resources are the following impulses:

Adjust and deepen the activity (impulse 2). She notices that children who want to make a bike from a construction set are quarrelling about the materials and roles. She intervenes by asking them about their individual wishes and plans and helps them by offering ideas for a joint plan and for collecting the necessary instruments.

Broaden the activity (impulse 3). Other children have chosen to draw all kinds of bicycles. When they tell that they are finished, the teachers invites them to tell about their drawings and guides the conversation in the direction of the functions of printed objects. Children mention art exhibitions, advertisements and magazines, and storybooks about children's adventures with bicycle trips. Thinking these options over the teacher helps the children to create new (core) activity settings: making stories and designing books for the factory showing different kinds of bikes and describing the bikes' details (measures, colours, material, costs).

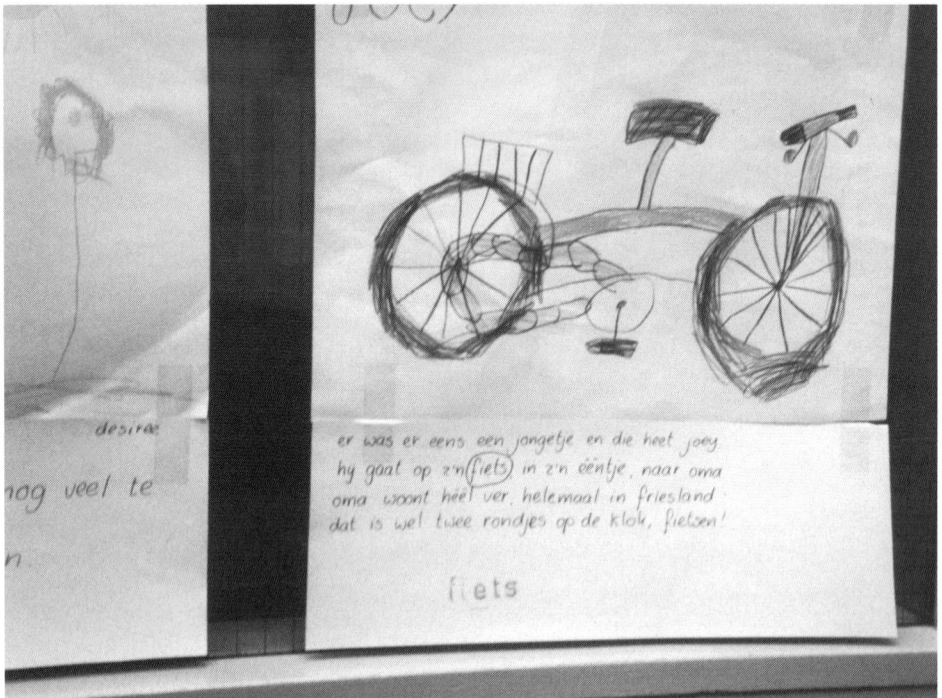

er was er eens een jongetje en die heet joey.
hy gaat op z'n (fiets) in z'n eentje, naar oma
oma woont heel ver, helemaal in friesland
dat is wel twee rondjes op de klok, fietsen!

fiets

Illustration 7.2: A story about a bike

The story says: *"Once upon a time there was a little boy named Joey. He was riding on his bike to his grandmother, she lives very far away, in Friesland. It takes two times around the clock to get there by bike".*(Photo: Willibrordusschool)

Finding teaching opportunities (impulse 4). In all activities the teacher looks out for meaningful teaching opportunities, offering children assistance in the acquisition of knowledge and skills that improve the activity. The children in the bicycle workshop, for instance, show her what they are repairing and how they do that. One of the girls tells she likes to make a seat on the bicycle for her baby-doll. The teacher encourages her to explain how it must look like, and to tell what material she needs for the construction. She also suggests her to draw a model of the seat and to show in the drawing how it must be fixed on the bike. When the girl shows her the schematic representation after a while, the teacher asks her to explain certain elements to her and to the other children in the workshop. They all agree that it is very clear and that the model must have a place in the workshop so that more seats can be produced for future clients. It is the first time that this girl made a schematic representation of an object and its construction.

Reflection (impulse 5). During the activities the teacher encourages the children to reflect on their actions, their experiences and thoughts. Often this reflection also takes place afterwards, in circle time, when children tell others about their play and work,

Illustration7.3: Constructive activities with the teacher's assistance.
(Photo: Hanneke Verkleij)

show what has been made or done, and invite others to think about possible extensions or continuations. The teacher assists children in this reflection process.

Beside this overall strategy, domain-specific didactic guidelines are part of the curriculum documents. Examples are to be found in guidelines for language development and second-language development, play development and literacy development.

(2) Action-oriented observation, registration and evaluation

Related to the curriculum strategy, an observation strategy has been developed. It is documented and described in a manual called 'Horeb' (Janssen-Vos, Pompert & Schiferli, 1998/200 1). A fundamental assumption of this observation strategy is that actions to be assessed have to be embedded in activities that are meaningful for the child. Hence, the observation strategy is curriculum-bound, which means that it is directed at the broad developmental characteristics and specific skills, and embedded in the core activities and related to the teacher's roles.

Teachers find in the Horeb-manual the instruments for systematic and interrelated planning, reflection and evaluation. For instance, schemes and instruments for the design and planning of thematic (more or less long-term) activity settings (see figure 7.2, and chapters 8, 9 and 10 for further elaboration).

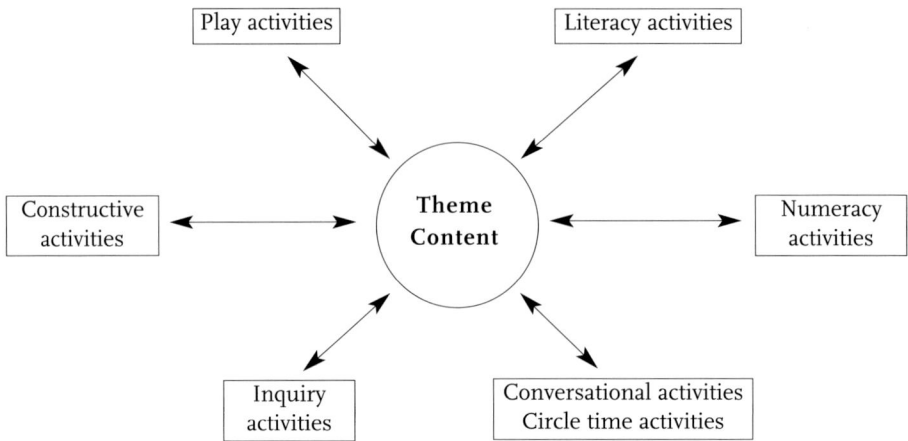

Figure 7.2: The 'web-scheme' for designing themes and activities

Other instruments are the observation models, linked to each of the core activities. They focus the teacher's attention on the development of the core activity itself, as well as on the related learning processes. Teachers use these models for planning and for evaluation purposes. Logbooks are used for day-by-day planning, observation and reflection (more about this can be found in chapter 8). Observations of individual children's performances are registered in individual diaries and portfolios, producing assessments of authentic actions. The objective of the diary keeping is the construction of an overall record of each pupil's development on a nearly day-by-day basis. Practice experiences demonstrate that specific training in using the instruments is necessary. In the beginning teachers need time in order to learn to work with the process and instruments. Their confidence is sometimes unstable, under the influence of external scepticism about the validity of this observation strategy. However, a small scale intervention study demonstrated that systematic assistance of teachers in writing logbooks about their planning of play and teaching, and in writing diaries about the individual children's development, strengthened the self-confidence and observation quality of teachers when they were working in accordance to this approach (Van Oers & Holla, 1997). In another longitudinal study an analyses was made of the teachers' diagnostic abilities in the domains of literacy and numeracy. The pupils' literacy development was assessed with standardised tests, and the results of these tests were compared with the teachers' independent criterion-referenced judgement of their pupils' literacy development (with the Horeb observation models). The teachers' judgements proved to be valid and reliable (Van Oers, 1999b).

Startingblocks of Basic Development

On a national level, attention is more and more focused on the special needs of 'children at risk': children with developmental problems, and children that fall behind in their education due to their language, social and cultural background. In the debate about 'effective programmes' for children at risk, a play-based curriculum takes a special position. Instead of focussing on isolated language training, developmental education points out the profits of play activities for successful performances in the later school life and society. As has been mentioned before, a play-based curriculum aims at the promotion of cultural partnership, social and communicative skills, semiotic activity and motivational development; all create a sound context for language and cognitive development (Van Oers & Janssen-Vos, 2002). Children at risk need, just like all children, teachers who are capable of creating meaningful activity settings that are meaningful and educationally relevant for the children involved. The effects on children with special needs depend even more on the specific qualities of the teachers in promoting the (specific) learning processes in this context, in a way that meets the specific needs of these children.

Regarding these points of departure, a precursor has been developed for under-fours who need special care and developmental support: 'Startingblocks of Basic Development', a play-based curriculum for play groups (Janssen-Vos & Pompert, 2001). Startingblocks is (of course) based on the same theoretical assumptions as Basic Development, and consists of the same 'building blocks'. However, this time focused on children from 2 to 4 years of age, and on the care takers of these young children.

In comparison with Basic Development, emphasis is placed on those elements that apply to care and education of these very young children. Experiences in several play groups make clear that no strict lines exist between interests and abilities of toddlers and young pupils. That is why a considerable overlap occurs in the curriculum materials for the preschool and for the early years in primary schools. In this manner, the perspectives of the entire developmental and learning process remain in sight, and an alignment and collaboration between both institutions can be worked on in practice. In this way, Startingblocks is inextricably linked to Basic Development.

As regards the objectives aimed at, emphasis is put on the establishment of a good foundation: conditions for an active and involved participation in activities, the promotion of social and communication competencies, the stimulation of (first and second) language acquisition and the promotion of initial literacy. The core activities consist, in any event, of play activities: movement play, manipulative play, simple role-play and constructive play, and activities involving stories, books and texts. Daily actions and routines (clearing up, taking care of each other, eating together) are also regarded as an important source of joint actions and communication. The developmental perspectives of the core activities have been adapted to perspectives for preschool groups.

The preschool educators work in the same developmental way as their colleagues in primary schools. Their developmental roles also have been elaborated in guidelines for design and planning of (thematical) activity settings, assisting and explicit guidance in joint activities (by means of the five didactic impulses mentioned earlier in this chapter), a sound educative organisation and systematic observation and reflection. For this case, a Horeb-manual provides the strategy and instruments for observation, registration and evaluation of Startingblocks for playgroups (Janssen-Vos & Pompert, 2001). In this way a continuous curriculum line and -strategy has been established in the education of young children from approximately 2 to 8 years of age: from Startingblocks through Basic Development. The narrative of 'Developmental education' continues in the upper grades of primary schools and in secondary education. The outlines of the strategy have been drawn and the first curriculum sources and instruments are ready to be used.

References

Davydov, V.V. (1988). Problems of developmental teaching. *Soviet Education*, Vol. XXX, nr 8, 9, 10.

El'konin, D.B. (1972). Toward the problem of stages in the mental development of the child. *Soviet Psychology*, 10, 225-251.

El'konin, D.B, & Venger, A.L. (1988). *Osobennosti psichičeskogo razvitija detej 6-7 letnego vozrasta* [Characteristics of psychic development of 6-7 year olds]. Moscow: Pedagogika.

Forman, E.A., Minick, N., & Stone, C.A. (Eds). (1993). *Contexts for learning. Socio-cultural dynamics in children's development*. Oxford: Oxford University Press.

Janssen-Vos, F. (1997). *Basisontwikkeling in de Onderbouw* [Basic Development in early Education]. Assen: Van Gorcum.

Janssen-Vos, F. & van Oers, B. (1998). Basisontwikkeling: een Vygotskiaanse strategie voor ontwikkelingsstimulering [Basic Development: a Vygotskian strategy for development stimulation]. In: A. Harpman, H. Veenker & G. Pol (red.), *Praten, denken, doen. Taal- en denkstimulering van 0- tot 6-jarigen* (pp. 183-202). Alphen aan den Rijn: Samsom.

Janssen-Vos, F. & Pompert, B. (2001). *Startblokken van Basisontwikkeling. Een goed begin voor peuters en jongste kleuters* (Startingblocks of Basic development. A good start for toddlers and infants]. Assen: Van Gorcum.

Janssen-Vos, F., Pompert, B., & Schiferli, T. (1998/2001). *HOREB. Handelingsgericht Observeren, registreren en Evalueren van Basisontwikkeling* [Activity oriented observation, registration and evaluation of Basic Development]. Utrecht: APS.

Janssen-Vos, F., van Oers, B. & Schiferli, T. (2000). Eén voor één maar niet alleen. Een ontwikkelingsgerichte pedagogiek voor jonge (risico)kinderen [One-by-one but not alone. A developmental pedagogy for young children at risk]. *Tijdschrift voor Orthopedagogiek*, 39, 300-312.

Moll, L. (Ed.). (1990). *Vygotsky and Education. Instructional implications and applications of socio-historical psychology*. Cambridge: Cambridge University Press.

Oers, B. van (1987). *Activiteit en begrip. Proeve van handelingspsychologische didactiek* [Activity and concept]. Amsterdam: VU University Press.

Oers, B. van (1999a). Teaching opportunities in play. In: M. Hedegaard & J. Lompscher (eds), *Learning Activity and development* (pp 268-289). Aarhus: University Press.

Oers, B. van (1999b). Quality of diagnostic teaching abilities in early education. *European Early*

Childhood Education Research Journal, Vol. 7, nr 2, 39-51.

Oers, B. van, & Holla, A. (1997).*The Milestone: an implementation of developmental education.* Case-study report for the European observatory of innovations in education and training. Parijs/Amsterdam: INRP/VU.

Oers, B. van & Janssen-Vos, F. (2002). Startblokken voor een goed begin. Ontwikkelings-gerichte omgang in de voorschoolse periode [Startingblocks for a good start. Developmental interaction in the pre-school period]. In: B. van Oers, F. Janssen-Vos & T. Schiferli, *Jonge kin-deren in risicosituaties. Enkele bijdragen vanuit de ontwikkelingsgerichte pedagogiek aan theorie en prakijk* (pp. 9-24). Utrecht, Academie voor Ontwikkelingsgericht Onderwijs/APS.

Oers, B. van, Janssen-Vos, F. ,& Schiferli, T. (2002). *Jonge kinderen in risicosituaties. Enkele bij-dragen vanuit de ontwikkelingsgerichte pedagogiek aan theorie en prakijk.*Alkmaar/Utrecht: Academie voor Ontwikkelingsgericht Onderwijs/APS.

Podd'jakov, N.N. & N.Ja. Michailenko. (1978). *Razvitie myšlenija i umstvennoe vospitanie doškol-nika* [Development of thought and cognitive eduation of infants]. Moskow: Pedagogika.

Pompert, B. & T. Schiferli (1998). Samen Basisontwikkeling invoeren [A joint implementation of Basic Development]. *School en Begeleiding,* (September)15, nr 4, 9-11.

Tharp, R. G. & R. Gallimore (1988). *Rousing minds to life. Teaching, learning and schooling in social context.* Cambridge University Press.

Venger, L.A. (Red.). (1986). *Razvitie poznavatavel'nych sposobnostej v processe doškol'nogo vospita-nija* [Development of cognitive skills in infant education]. Moscow: Pedagogika.

Vygotskij, L.S. (1926/1991). *Pedagogičeskaja Psichologija.*Republished and edited by V.V. Davydov. Moscow: Pedagogika. (Translated as: L.S. Vygotsky, Educational Psychology. Boca Rata (Florida): St Lucie Press.

Vygotsky, L.S. (1978). *Mind in society.* Cambridge, Mass.: Harvard University Press.

Wertsch, J.V. (1987). *Vygotsky and the social formation of mind.* Cambridge, Mass: Harvard University Press.

[8]
Teaching as a joint activity

Bert van Oers, Frea Janssen-Vos, Bea Pompert, & Trudy Schiferli

A pedagogy of voices

One of the exciting challenges of today's educational science is the problem of dealing with the multiplicity of perspectives and the related narratives about humanity and human development. Once we recognize that every human being views the world from his or her own personal perspective, we also have to accept the obligation of confronting the different narratives - or 'voices' to use the modern semiotic language inspired by Bachtin. With regard to education, this acknowledgement sharply articulates the need for a pedagogy of voices, as Aronowitz & Giroux (1991) already argued: a pedagogical approach to education that accepts the pluriformity of voices, that calls for a serious collaboration of all participants, precludes automatic hegemony of one voice, and that opens up the possibility of voices merging together in a constructive and non-oppressive way.

The work reported in this chapter is one result of an attempt to analyse and improve educational practices in school from this perspective of the pedagogy of voices. It is our conviction that such an approach should not just lead to another narrative about early childhood development in the classroom. This approach should also reflect how we carry out our own work at the innovation in early childhood education. In the construction of our approach a number of people from different professional backgrounds are working together: teachers, innovators, teacher trainers, school counsellors, and academic researchers. So there is a multiplicity of voices involved here and all members of this group share a deep belief in the developmentability of the child, as well as an awareness of the educators' shared responsibility for the child's welfare as a human being, now and in a future society. A common notion in our work, then, is the concept of *developmental education*. This concept refers to a theoretical view on education that tries to promote the development of children by evoking cultural learning processes in a way that makes sense to the children themselves, as well as by seriously taking into account the developmental characteristics of the children involved. One of the basic assumptions of the theory is drawn from the works of Vygotsky/Leont'ev/El'konin and says that in the present state of sociocultural development, basically, young children relate to their cultural environment in a playful way. This starting point pictures the young child as *a playing child* that gets access to sociocultural activities of its community by playing (see chapter 1). So actually, our work investigates the implications and applications of the narrative of the playing child for the innovation of early childhood education.

From this point of view we will focus here on teaching activity and analyse the act of teaching as a cultural activity, particularly teaching in early education. After a brief introduction on how we see the role of the teacher in a teaching activity, we will discuss some examples of teaching as a joint activity, where different views ('narratives on early years education') merge together. In the last part we will reflect on how this might contribute to the innovation of early education practices.

The role of the teacher in a teaching activity

The growing body of knowledge about children's development has made clear that the course of children's development strongly depends on the kind of interactions in which they have been involved. Vygotsky already stipulated the developmentability of children and the essential role of the adult (or more capable peers) for the promotion of children's development. According to Vygotsky, good education promotes the development of children. This can be achieved by engaging the children in cultural activities, and helping them perform and appropriate new actions embedded in that activity (see for example Vygotsky, 1978). Through their interaction children and adults construct a shared cultural activity as a context for the performance of those actions that the child already masters. But this very same activity is also a context for new actions that the child cannot yet carry out on his own: for the accomplishment of these new actions the child needs assistance. Such activities constitute a zone of proximal development. Basically, a zone of proximal development is an activity setting imitating some cultural activity in which the adult initially is in charge of the actions the child himself cannot yet perform (Van Oers, 1995, 1996). When the child eventually takes over the responsibility for these actions, this may lead to the appropriation of new actions that contribute to the children's development. As Tharp & Gallimore (1988) already pointed out, the concept of assistance is essential for the understanding of the zone of proximal development and for the learning and teaching that may occur within this zone (see also Tharp, 2001).

This recognition of the zone of proximal development as a joint enterprise based on cultural activities and on distribution of responsibilities and psychological functions, has a variety of educational consequences. In this chapter we want to explore the meaning of this approach for the analysis of teaching in early education.

To begin with, the reader may have noticed that we do not identify 'teaching activity' with 'a teacher's activity'. We begin with the assumption that teaching is a meta-personal cultural activity system, in which a teacher may play a prominent role, but in which she/he is not the only actor. 'Teaching', as we know it today, is a cultural-historical product, built up by many generations of teachers, educators and academics. The enactment of the cultural teaching activity by a teacher at any one moment in a particular classroom is always the joint product of different actors. We can distinguish at least three forms of collaboration with the teacher, which make teaching a joint activity:

- *Collaboration of the teacher with other teachers* in a team in order to plan or improve education at school; this interpretation of the concept of 'teaching as a joint activity' relates to an appraisal of teaching as a social process in which teachers as a team act as agents, to improve their individual teaching in the classroom; see for example the work of Smyth (1991);

- *Collaboration of the teacher with innovators*: in this case the teacher works together with someone outside the school staff in order to find ways to innovate and improve teaching on the basis of new concepts and values. It should be emphasized here that this should not necessarily result in a top-down approach in which an innovator drops a new concept in the school, and subsequently observes from the outside to see if the teacher implements the idea correctly! In order to realize teaching as a joint activity, the innovator should accept responsibility for the quality of the teaching, seriously assist the teacher involved, and reflect on the teaching as well as on her/his own activity. See for example the work of Tharp & Gallimore (1988). By participating in such innovative activity the teacher becomes more of an innovator;
- *Collaboration of the teacher with pupils*: for their teaching, teachers obviously need pupils; pupils are actually co-actors in the teaching process; from the point of view of teaching as a joint activity, the role of the teacher in the classroom is seen as an assistant of pupils, aiming at the improvement of the pupils' proficiency as participants in cultural activities (like reading, writing, mathematizing, drawing, constructing, singing, etc). With respect to teachers of the youngest children, we contend that teachers ought to participate in the play activities of the children and try to spot around for teaching opportunities which contribute to the quality of the play itself, as well as prepare for future developments of the child (see Van Oers, 1994; 1999; Janssen-Vos & Pompert, 1993; Pompert & Janssen-Vos, chapter 9; see also Rogoff, et al. (1993) on 'guided participation').

It is important to note, that in all these forms of teaching as a joint activity the same dynamics are at work. In each case there is a form of collaboration between participants who contribute to a shared activity from different perspectives and who are dedicated to harmonizing the different voices involved. In each case a zone of proximal development is constructed in collaboration.

In this chapter we shall focus more particularly on the second and third of the above-mentioned forms of teaching as a joint activity. Below a strategy will be described that demonstrates how an innovator participates in the teaching activity of a teacher in order to find ways to implement the concept of developmental education in the first years of primary school (in the Netherlands ages 4 – 8). The strategy shows how the innovator tunes her actions to the level of development of the teachers involved. Thus the innovator shares the responsibility for the quality of teaching with the teacher. An example will illustrate how a teacher/innovator collaborates with pupils in their play and tries to contribute to the play activity by helping the pupils to appropriate new means of organizing special parts of their mutual activity. Finally, we will reflect on possible contributions of this approach to teaching for the realization of those aims and objectives that we think are significant for the early grades of elementary school.

The role of the innovator in a teaching activity

Developmental education is to be seen as an innovative narrative on educational practices for (young) children. Teachers who want to improve and renew their practice according to this educational concept, need to appropriate the related underlying theoretical views about learning and development, as well as new ways of thinking and interacting with children (see Tharp et al., 2001). However, it should be repeated here, this is definitely not meant as a top-down process of teacher training. Actually, the challenge is how to reconcile the teacher's own views of teaching, learning and development with those of the intended innovation.

Hence, any attempt at innovating actual teaching activities has to deal with the problem of the complex relationship between theory and practice, thinking and acting. To tackle this problem, adequate communication strategies and counselling methods must be developed in order to collaborate productively with the teachers involved. In our approach we took a Vygotskian perspective and reasoned from the assumption that both for the children and for the teachers the learning processes must be conceived of as a qualitative development of human activity on the basis of cultural attainments and personal sense by the learner (see Van Oers, 1996). Hence, the teacher's professional learning has to be founded on the two dimensions, i.e. personal sense and involvement in the innovation, and the objectives implied in the planned innovation (intentions of the educational concept).

As a consequence of this view, our implementation strategy is based on the assumption that the innovator and teacher are jointly responsible for the improvement of the teaching activity in the teacher's practice. They work together to produce a kind of practice that they both find satisfying.

In this way the innovation strategy can be described as a mutual learning process in which the contributions of both the innovator and the teacher are taken seriously and equally valued.

Example:

In a school the staff has chosen to improve the quality of the play activity in the infant department. In their opinion, this requires (among other things) that the teacher gets involved in conversations with small groups of children after their play activity. The entire school staff i.e. the class teacher, the internal counsellor and the innovator, all contribute and co-operate in order to attain this goal. The innovator supports co-operation by means of class consultation and feedback. Problems are analysed during these discussions and each person contributes to the improvement of the activities in the classroom according to her/his capacity.

The innovator must avoid prescribing innovative changes. In order to attain really new insights in the teaching activity, all participants have to discuss their actual situation in comparison to the new concepts. With regard to the developmentability of the child, the following issues are important to discuss with teachers (compare Janssen-Vos, chapter 7):

- children's active involvement;
- children's making sense of activities which stimulate higher order abilities such as problem solving, co-operation, reflecting, self-regulation, communication and reasoning;
- real social-cultural activities that form the heart of the new curriculum, especially play activities in which broad developmental aims, and specific knowledge and skills are integrated;
- teacher's role as mediator within the activity settings.

One of the innovator's tasks is to cooperatively create contexts and situations in the school in which she/he can encourage and support the desired improvement in a clear and concrete way. This requires joint activities such as:

- proposing new classroom environments;
- designing and planning activity settings;
- registering children's performances;
- guiding and modelling children's activities by intervening (like a teacher);
- activity-orientated observation;
- reflecting on daily teaching activities.

The innovator and the teacher work together in these activities: analysing and reflecting with the help of the conceptual framework of developmental education. Within these joint activities the most important challenge is to reflect on the teacher's practice as well as on the fundamental concepts of the teacher.

In our work with teachers we became aware of the necessity of tuning in our intervention to the developmental characteristics of the teachers and their level of involvement. In our assistance strategy we usually distinguish a number of successive phases in a teacher's development with respect to the use of several conceptual tools. We will discuss our strategy below, describing the main phases as well as the most effective tools in each of the phases[1].

Stages in teacher development
PHASE 1
In the first phase the teachers are expected to recognise basic elements of developmental education in their own teaching-actions and their own practice. The innovator uses two diagrams as tools in the discussions of the teachers' reports on their teaching activity. Video-recordings of their teaching-activities, photographs, and works of the children are used as means to support the conversation and reflection. In this phase the main goal is to discuss with each other one of the main dilemmas of teaching,

---

1. Recently the strategy has been elaborated further into a more detailed innovation strategy focussing on both teacher development and school development. The basic pattern is similar to the one described here.

namely the concept of learning as the directly instructed acquisition of knowledge, versus learning as a personally meaningful constructive process in the child. The balance diagram is used for recognising and analysing this dilemma in the teachers' own practices.

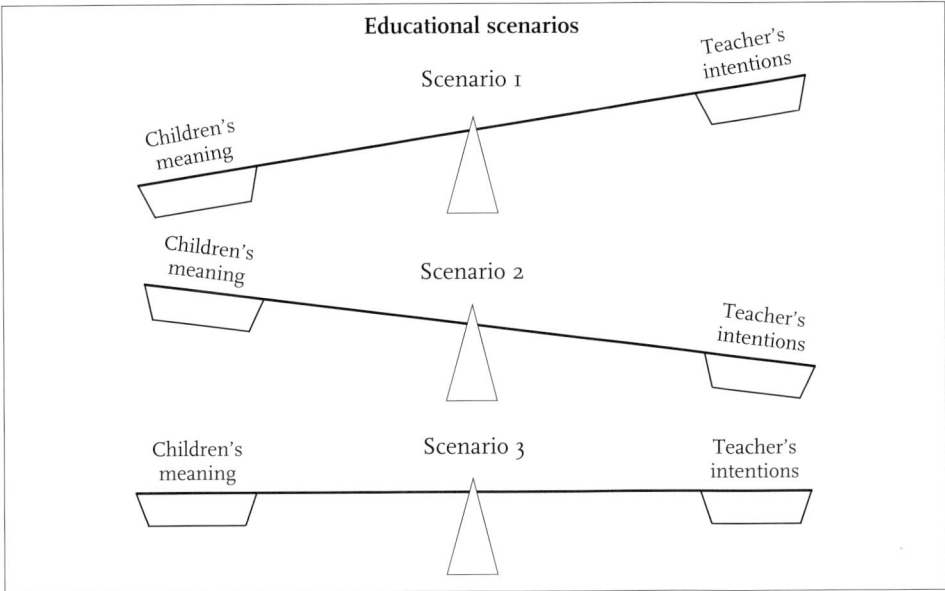

Figure 8.1: *Balance diagram*

The dilemma is schematically represented by balance 1, in which the objectives of education are fixed and consist of knowledge and skills. These objectives dominate the course of learning. In balance 2 the autonomous learning and children's capability are seen as the main motors for learning and development. Balance 3 shows the balanced situation that is advocated by the concept of developmental education: the dynamic balancing of educational objectives and the children's own motives and meanings.
The following diagram is used to discuss the design of the meaningful activity settings with the teachers:

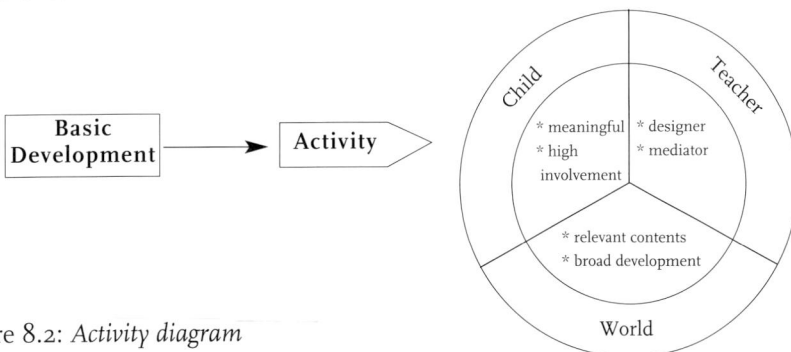

Figure 8.2: *Activity diagram*

The theoretical narrative of 'Developmental Education' is based on an activity theoretical approach (Vygotsky, Leont'ev). According to this approach, teachers should learn to reflect on the quality of the children's activities. Points for reflection are:

- the child's involvement and making sense of the activity;
- the teacher's design of meaningful activities;
- the teacher's mediating role in the pupils' way of dealing with cultural activities and its implied meanings;
- the social-cultural characteristics of the activity and their contribution to the broad developmental aims.

Teachers' acting obviously doesn't change immediately as a result of such discussions. It should be taken into account at this stage of teacher development, that the teachers may still use their old rhetoric and directive-formal ways of teaching, rather than real developmental teaching strategies. Characteristic for this stage of teacher development is their ability and willingness to reflect on classroom activities in terms of the developmental education view without necessarily practicing this view in their daily classroom work.

At this point of the development, the teacher and the innovator decide together not to move on immediately to the next phase but to reflect a bit deeper on the teacher's development. Together they decide which activity will be developed further and which bottlenecks, within this activity, should be tackled in their future collaboration.

PHASE 2

In this phase we see teachers moving from an aloof reflection on classroom activities towards real implementation of some elements of developmental teaching in their own classrooms. In this phase the teacher actually designs and implements developmentally appropriate activities. In order to establish this level of functioning we proceed from one or two core activities (like play, construction, conversation, mathematics or reading and writing) that will be carried out by the teacher in her classroom. All activities are conceived of as joint activities between teacher and pupils. The main instructional aim of these activities is the improvement of the quality of the pupils' participation in the selected core activity. That is to say:

- enhancing the children's ability to make sense of the activity setting, as well as their involvement in it;
- stimulating children's own initiative and decision-making abilities;
- clarifying the social-cultural nature of the activity.

The teacher must learn to participate in these activities in such a way that the developmental value of the activity increases. The interaction between the teacher and the children is directed at establishing a zone of proximal development. The children's current learning abilities should be extended and broadened. This starts out by assessing the quality of the pupils' participation in the activity, and by identifying the actions that they cannot yet do on their own. As the teacher carries out these latter parts of the activity, he/she gains an insight into how new possibilities arise and gradually come within the child's reach. The innovator analyses and reflects on these teaching activities with the teachers. Gradually teachers become aware of the importance of their role as a designer, a mediator, and an interactor with children. The following three diagrams (figures 8.3, 8.4, and 8.5) are used in a further exploration of these aspects.

To be able to participate in the child's development, it is necessary that the teacher manages classroom activities with many opportunities for new experiences and actions and with possibilities for construction. By so doing, the joint activity between teacher and pupils establishes a zone of proximal development. A simple diagram is used in the discussions about possible organizational changes in the classroom practice.

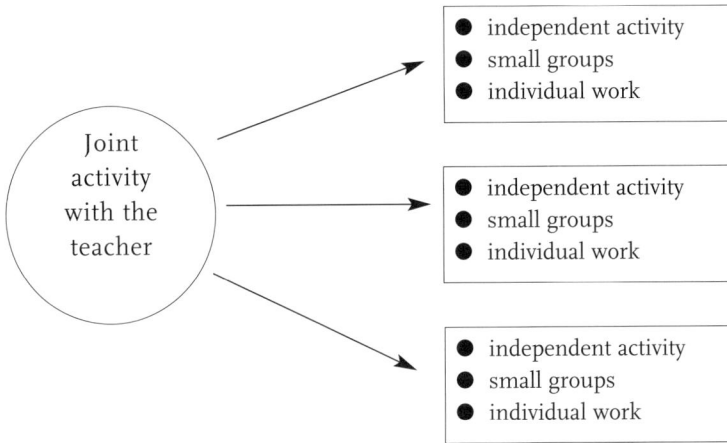

Figure 8.3: *Diagram of organization*

This diagram clearly shows the complexity of the teaching activity, and at the same time stipulates the teacher's main organizational problems. When learning to work according to this design, teachers have to overcome their urge to be everywhere at the same time. Instead of constantly running around the classroom, they have to get engaged in one group's activity, while other children are acting independently or in small groups. This is an essential condition for the improvement of developmentally appropriate ways of guiding instructional conversations.

One of the most complicated teaching skills within developmental education is to participate in the activity and at the same time reflect on the interactions. Teachers have to play a double role (Van Oers and Pompert 1991). On the one hand they have to take part in pupils' activities, and on the other hand they must be able to distance themselves from the ongoing activities so that they can evaluate the interaction and propose qualitative changes in their own approach. This differs from what most teachers usually do, namely to assess the results of the children's independent activities and evaluate these performances in a static way.

Within developmental education the teacher's mediating role has to become visible. To help teachers with this new way of reflective teaching, we provide a triangle diagram as a tool for the teachers' reflections:

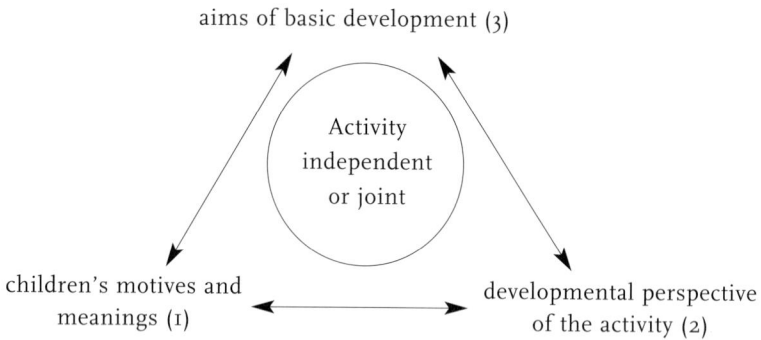

aims of basic development (3)

Activity
independent
or joint

children's motives and
meanings (1)

developmental perspective
of the activity (2)

Figure 8.4: *The triangle diagram*

Reflection on the selected core activity and on the part taken by the teacher may be guided by the following questions:
- how does the child respond to the activity, the participation, meaning making, use of language?
- how should the child carry out this activity in the near future?
- what is the contribution to the child's general development (in terms of problem solving abilities, self-regulation, and reasoning abilities)?

For the gradual improvement of the mediating role of the teacher in all her classroom activities, the teacher must develop competence in activity-orientated observation. This is where phase 3 begins.

PHASE 3
For daily planning and assessment the teachers record their ideas and observations in a personal journal. This record is an important companion to their innovative activity. It functions as a record of their growing understanding of children's development and it documents the teachers' process of active decision making. The main objective of this phase is that teachers learn to analytically reflect on their own role as an educator. The teachers learn that their registrations should be more than mere reports of past events, but these should entail consequences for future pedagogical actions, especially with regard to children who need help.
For these registrations they learn to employ the following tool:

	Plans	Reflections

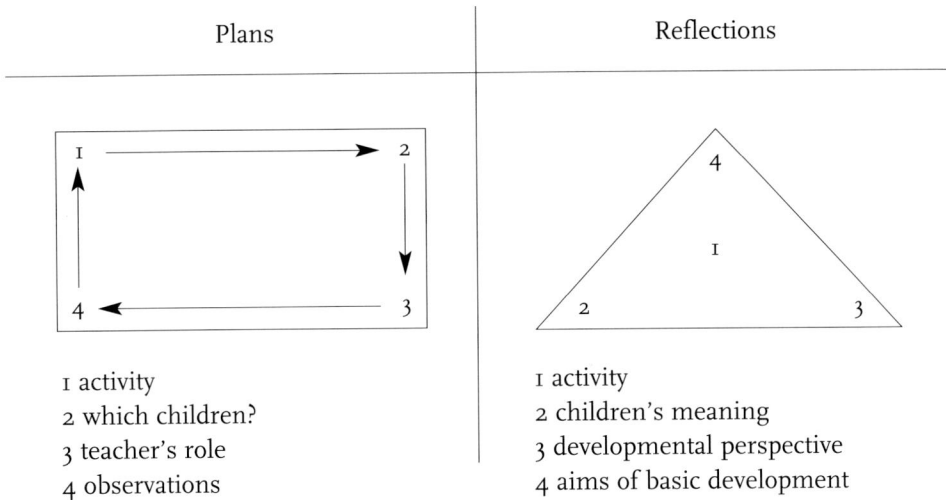

1 activity
2 which children?
3 teacher's role
4 observations

1 activity
2 children's meaning
3 developmental perspective
4 aims of basic development

Figure 8.5: *Illustration of the logbook layout*

In the left-hand column teachers describe their plans and in the right-hand column a brief description is made of their reflections and decisions for further activities. On the planning side four aspects are written down: which activity is being accomplished, which children are involved, the teacher's role, points of observation. At the end of the day teachers use the triangle diagram to evaluate and to draw conclusions for further actions.

In this phase two aspects are important. The teacher must learn to observe joint activities and evaluate them systematically. The teacher and the innovator look closely at the results of the teaching activity in relation to the learning and development of the children. The results for the teachers themselves must also be highlighted: which characteristics of teaching as joint activity have been realized? In collaboration with the teachers the innovator registers all relevant elements of teaching as a joint activity. Particularly, the quality of the following teacher activities is assessed:
- providing adequate material;
- selecting and designing meaningful social-cultural activity settings;
- transforming the related activities into a zone of proximal development;
- the organization of working in small groups;
- activity-orientated observation, registration and evaluation.

In this phase the classroom observations should provide clear examples of these activities. All participants have to approve of the result in this teaching-activity.

In the next section we will describe an exemplary case of such a class consultation and illustrate how an innovator participated in a teaching activity, collaborated with children. By doing so, the innovator collaboratively created one possible example of developmental teaching for the teacher.

An innovator's intervention: The Nintendo Racetrack

The teacher in this case is an experienced one. She is working with a group of children aged 4-6 years. In terms of the stage-model of innovation processes (as described in the previous section), this teacher is moving from phase 2 to phase 3. She is already able to design and select developmentally appropriate activities for the children. She is very good at creating a stimulating learning environment. When we visit her classroom, she is working on the improvement of constructive (play) activities, especially focussing on her own double-role.

Her questions are:

- Can I participate in constructive (play) activity and deepen the process of meaning making of the children?
- Can I discover teaching opportunities that may contribute to the quality of the constructive (play) activity and at the same time prepare for future developments of the children?
- Can I reflect on the joint activity and make decisions about next steps in selecting/designing constructive (play) activities?
- Can I evaluate that joint activity in terms of the individual development of the participating children?

She seems uncertain about her own possibilities and those of the children. The teacher and the innovator then agree that the innovator would carry out some activities in the classroom and work with the children. The innovator would join in with the constructive (play) activities of the children, while the teacher is observing. While doing so, she uses the triangle diagram (see figure 8.4).

A description of one of these activities

Kevin, Job and Stefan are busy in the building area. They are working intensively. They use multifunctional rectangular and oblique blocks, and coloured chocks and toy-cars. They make a racetrack that they call "Nintendo". For more than an hour they are trying to get it exactly as they want it. They constantly talk about their ideas, change and improve it by knocking down what they first built, and are building it up again.

> A hot, dangerous lava-well was placed on the corner of the right-angled track. They all agreed that the cars had to avoid the lava-well; otherwise you were out of the game. They built an obstacle with two chocks, which the cars had to pass, without collisions. They made several ski-jumps and a route on which the cars could return.

Then the innovator enters the scene. She begins by saying "What a fantastic track you have made. It is a very exciting one, I see". This remark did the trick. The boys enthusiastically start to explain and show how the cars have to try and proceed via the ski-jumps, avoiding the obstacle and the lava-well. They explain their construction in a very involved and precise way.

Then the innovator makes the following suggestion: "I think it is such a good track that we should save it. What do you think, can you draw the Nintendo racetrack in such a way that other children could use your drawings to rebuild this exciting racetrack?" They all agree immediately and after deciding that each of them should make his own drawing (making one drawing together is too difficult, they conclude). They fetch pencils and large sheets of paper.

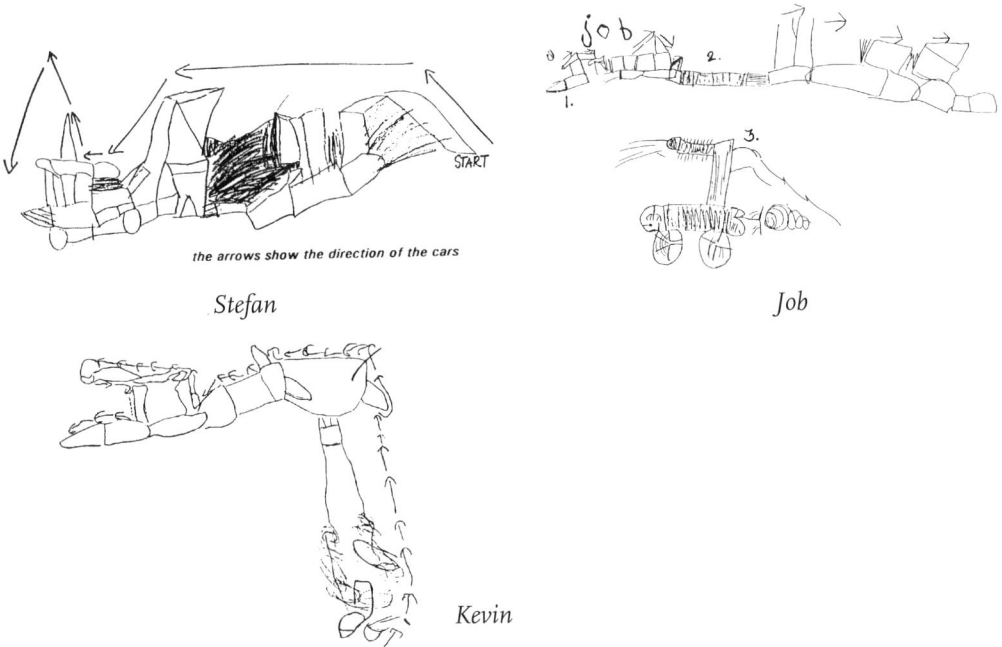

the arrows show the direction of the cars

Stefan

Job

Kevin

Figure 8.6: *The drawings*

Stefan finishes his drawing easily. The shaded coloured part is the lava-well. After finishing his drawing he turns to the innovator and says: "I have a problem. When other children use my drawing, how will they know in what direction the cars have to go?"

The innovator: "Do you think it is a good idea to use arrows?" Stefan agrees and gives instructions to the innovator for placing the arrows and says: "Write START for me at the beginning".

Kevin is working very intensively at his drawing. He is carefully mapping the track onto his paper and makes a clear reconstruction of the angle. When the innovator places arrows on Stefan's drawing, Kevin also starts drawing arrows on his. When he is finished, he begins explaining about the track and the drawing. He makes a kind of narrative about it, saying that the real name was "Lava-track tectif". He also gives the playing rules, regarding:
- where to start
- falling into the lava means you are out
- when you have finished without accidents, you may start again.

Job starts drawing at point 1 (see figure 8.6) and works very meticulously. At point 2 he has serious problems. From his perspective the lava-well is at the back. Job asks, "How should I draw this?" He and the innovator discuss the problem and together they look at the angle from above. Finally Job draws a shaded coloured part with extra space. After solving this problem, he finishes his drawing very quickly. Later he adds the arrows and the car (3).

Afterwards the teacher and the innovator used the triangle diagram to analyse the activity and they came to the following conclusions:
- Constructing the racetrack was a meaningful activity for the boys. They really wanted to make something special. The racetrack must be exciting and challenging. The boys' language was goal-orientated and they negotiated about their intentions, plans and rules.
- When the innovator encouraged them 'to save' the track for rebuilding (also by other kids) they immediately wanted to co-operate. Their drawings got a communicative function.
- Intervention by the innovator made it possible for the three boys to reflect on the interrelationship between the real track and their drawings.
- These interventions were welcomed by the boys and they turned the activity into a zone of proximal development for them, where new actions could be appropriated.
- The innovator used different types (means) of assisting performance. She:
  - suggested making a drawing;
  - gave them feedback on their performance;
  - offered mediational means, such as arrows and key-words ("START");
  - modelled certain actions: looking from above to make a good map.

Actually the innovator's suggestions were adopted by the children as an enrichment of their play.
After 10 days the innovator showed the boys the drawings again. She and the teacher wanted to find out:
- if the boys wanted to 'read' their drawings;
- how they tackled that problem;
- if they could rebuild the racetrack on the basis of these drawings.

The boys recognised their own drawings immediately. Stefan also recognised Kevin's drawing. Each of them pointed out on his own drawing: the starting point, the lava-well, the corner, the coloured obstacle, and the ski-jumps.
They reacted enthusiastically to the innovator's suggestion that they may rebuild their track from their drawings. They used Job's drawing and started at point 1. However, when they had to make the angle, their problems started. They didn't agree with each other about the lava-well and the precise place of the obstacle. The innovator then suggested that they could use the photographs that were made during the first session. They also used Kevin's drawing, for they agreed that his showed the angle and the

place of the lava-well in the best way. At the end they all accepted the innovator's suggestion to compare their rebuilt track with their original drawings.

Results

The results of these activities can be specified differently for the children, the teachers, the innovator, and for the concept of developmental education.

For the children:

The boys showed a fascination not only for building the racetrack but also for making a representation, reading their drawings and using drawings and photographs for rebuilding.

They realised a high level of reasoning and problem solving within these constructive play activities.

In the months following these activities they continued to make drawings and schemes. E.g. Job made several maps of a castle he built.

For the teacher:

The teacher indicated that these activities made it very clear to her that she had to join in the constructive (play) activities in order to nudge the children's development. She also reported that her teaching practice changed a lot in the months following. She used the diagram from figure 8.2 to describe her own professional growth and how she established concrete changes in the group. Moreover, she returned to her initial questions and notified that she had really made progress.

For the innovator:

For the innovator the main result is the positive effects of her assistance on the development of the teacher. In the following period she used this kind of assistance more and more with teachers who were moving from phase 2 to phase 3 and experienced a noticeable acceleration in the teachers' implementation process after periods of more intense co-operation in the classroom.

For the concept of developmental education:

The Nintendo-activities also made a modest contribution to some parts of the theory on play-activities and adult intervention. Van Oers compared our present findings with the outcomes of earlier research that he did in schools on semiotic activity of young children in play (see Van Oers, 1999). Our data thus contributed to the growing body of evidence showing that

- young children can be involved in semiotic activity, within play-activities, when they accept the functionality of the semiotic tools, that is to say in our case:

    making drawings for rebuilding
    using photographs for rebuilding;
    inserting symbols in the drawings

- the development of semiotic activity to a great extent depends on the active participation of the teacher. She has to create a new type of activity in co-operation with the children, in which she models the structure of the ongoing semiotic activity.

The teacher's perspectives: Basic Development

So far we have considered the joint efforts of teachers and innovators to promote, support and increase developmental processes of young children. This focuses on the strategic side (rather than the content) of the innovation process. However, the notion of teaching as a joint activity also presupposes negotiation between teacher and innovators as to the content and aims of (early) education. Actually, we assume that there must be an intrinsic relationship between the aims and contents of education and the strategy of implementation.

The teacher's mediating role in the classroom consists of the preparation of relevant activity settings and subsequent participation in the activities. She/he continuously has to mediate between: the children's motives, interests, meanings and actual developmental stages, the core activities and their developmental perspectives, as well as the aims or objectives of Basic Development (see Janssen-Vos, chapter 7). The teacher has to create a dynamic balance between these aims and contents and the children's own motives and meanings. The triangle diagram (figure 8.4) helps teachers to reflect upon their role and enter into a dialogue about it.

In finalizing our chapter we need to say a few words about the contents and aims of early education that the innovator tries to achieve in the innovative collaboration with the teacher. Basically, these contents and aims are core objects of negotiation between teacher, pupils and innovator. We will discuss the aims and content of early education at the level of developmental contexts (development of leading activities), and at the level of specific educational objectives within these contexts.

Development of leading activities

Young children's development is largely dependent on their active participation in meaningful activities and on the adult's modelling and supportive interactions. Consequently, we need to know what kind of activities are in principle meaningful and developmentally appropriate for young children.

In Vygotskian theory, developmental stages are defined in terms of leading motives and activities (El'konin, 1980). Play is the leading activity and motive at the ages of about 2/3 years to 7/8 years, but it must be noted that this does not imply just free play. In every play there is a cultural tendency that promotes the children's actions and that calls for help from more knowledgeable others in order to improve or expand the play-bound actions. Moreover, in order to promote children's development even further it is important to foster the precursors of the productive learning activity that emerge already during the role play. Productive learning activity will become the leading activity and motive after the age of 7. From that age, the children tend to be motivated for and interested in the learning activity itself. According to this theory, teachers should organize social-cultural activity settings that can contribute to the quality of the play-activity, as well as support the development from play towards the future learning activity (see van Oers, 1999).

The curriculum "Basic Development' suggests and elaborates five core activities that we assume to be relevant in this respect: play, construction, conversation, literacy (reading and writing), and mathematical activities (see Janssen-Vos chapter 7, Pompert & Janssen-Vos, chapter 9; Fijma, chapter 10). Within these core activities, teachers construct zones of proximal development in which children are not only challenged to improve their play activities, but which also evoke new learning motives and invite children to explore productive learning activities. Teachers spot for teaching opportunities in the child's play, as we could see in the Nintendo racetrack, where the teacher/innovator suggested making a plan of the racetrack and co-operated in the negotiations necessary to achieving this.

Educational objectives

Core activities help to establish developmental contexts and zones of proximal development for the pupils. Within the context of these developmentally relevant activities more specific educational objectives can be aimed at.

As to the issue of educational objectives, developmental education takes the position that short-term knowledge and skills alone offer insufficient opportunities for optimal development. Instead, a broad pedagogical view on aims or objectives is essential. According to the 'Basic Development' curriculum (as was presented in the previous chapter), we differentiate between three categories of educational objectives. In this case study we can clearly recognize the fundamental conditions for development and learning: well-being, self-confidence and curiosity. Secondly, a broad personality development contains attitudes and abilities that are of a long-term nature and impregnate the children's actions entirely. Reference can be made here to objectives in the area's of communication, negotiation, verbal exchanges, making plans, imagination and creativity, the attitude of exploring the social, cultural and physical world. A broad personality development, finally, cannot take place without acquiring essential skills. So, in the third place, specific skills belong to the educational objectives as well. In the "Nintendo case study" these objectives pertain to the domains of motor skills (drawing), language (vocabulary, communicative pragmatics), perception (perceptual analysis of two-dimensional representations), cognitive skills (e.g. comparing different symbolic re-descriptions of one situation), and social skills (collaboration, creating agreement, togetherness).

A balance between meanings and motives of children at the one side, and educational objectives at the other, comes within reach by means of this core activity. A variety of aims or objectives can obviously be stimulated through this core activity.

The Vygotskian framework as we used it here in our work with teachers confirms the conviction that early education has above all a pedagogical mission and concerns the children's fundamental, basic development. It also sheds a new light on assisting young children to learn. Instead of training in prerequisite learning skills preceding the actual learning processes in the subject matter areas, attention is paid to higher order skills which children can learn to perform within meaningful, social-cultural activities in which they want to act, and can do so with the assistance of others. But the same goes for the teacher. By participating in innovative activities with innovators and researchers the teacher is coached into a new developmental track leading to developmentally appropriate teaching. It is in such innovative practices where a new pedagogy of voices can develop and where we tried to investigate the ins and outs of the narrative of the playing child.

Finally it is the teacher who always plays the crucial part in the concrete innovations, but the teacher can only do this -as we tried to show in our chapter- in close communication with others (pupils, other teachers, innovators, researchers). Therefore the teacher must acknowledge that her/his teaching is essentially a joint product of many agents, evolving gradually over time.

References

Aronowitz, S. & Giroux, H.A. (1991). *Postmodern Education*. Minneapolis/Oxford: University of Minnesota Press.

El'konin, D.B. (1980). *Psychologie des Spiels*. Moskou/Köln.

Janssen-Vos, F. (1997). *Basisontwikkeling in de onderbouw* [Basic Development in the early years in primary school]. Assen: Van Gorcum.

Janssen-Vos, F. & Pompert, B. (1993). *From play activity toward learning activity. Developmental perspectives in early childhood education*. Paper for the third European Conference on the quality of Early Childhood Education. Kriopigi, Greece.

Oers, B. van. (1992). Ontwikkelingsgericht onderwijs in de onderbouw: contouren van een cultuurhistorische onderwijsvisie [Developmental education with young children: outline of a cultural-historical approach]. In B. van Oers & F. Janssen-Vos (Eds), *Visies op onderwijs aan jonge kinderen*. Assen: Van Gorcum.

Oers, B. van. (1994). Semiotic Activity of young children in play: the construction and use of schematic representations. *European Early Childhood Education Research Journal*, vol. 2, no 1, 19-33.

Oers, B. van (1995). How to define the zone of proximal development? *Studi di Psichologia dell' Educatione*, 14, nr. 1,2,3, 157-165.

Oers, B. van. (1996). The dynamics of school learning. In: J. Valsiner & H-G. Voss (Eds.), *The structure of learning*. (pp. 205-229). New York: Ablex.

Oers, B. van. (1999). Teaching opportunities in play). In: M. Hedegaard & J. Lompscher (eds.), *Learning activity and development* (p. 268-289. Aarhus: Aarhus University Press.

Oers, B. van. & Pompert, B. (1991). Kijken naar kleuters: ontwikkelingsgericht observeren [Observing young children: a developmental perspective]. *Vernieuwing*, 1991, (September), (50), nr. 7, 3-8.

Rogoff, B., Mistry, J., Göncü, A., Mosier, C. (1993). *Guided Participation in Cultural Activity by toddlers and caregivers*. Monographs of the Society for Research in Child Development, Vol. 58, no 8.

Smyth, J. (1991). *Teachers as collaborative learners*. Milton Keynes: Open University Press.

Tharp, R.G., & Gallimore, R. (1988). *Rousing minds to life. Teaching, Learning, and schooling in social context*. Cambridge: Cambridge University Press.

Tharp, RG., Estrada, P., Dalton, S.S. & Yamauchi, L.A. (2001). *Teaching transformed. Achieving excellence, fairness, inclusion and harmony*. Boulder: Westview Press.

Vygotsky, L.S. (1978). *Mind in society*. Cambridge: Harvard University Press.

[9]
From narrator to writer. Promoting cultural learning in early childhood

Bea Pompert & Frea Janssen-Vos

Introduction

Children grow up in a literate world, with all kinds of printed messages and culture-bound narratives. They have a lot of experiences that have to do with literacy in everyday life. They wish to be involved in activities such as singing songs, making up stories, reading books and newspapers, or watching TV-programmes. Lots of everyday outdoor activities also contain literate experiences, like shopping, a visit to the park or parking the car. Actually, it is almost impossible for young children not being influenced by the literate characteristics of our culture (Van Oers, 1999b).

This implies that young children are, in a way, already literate when they enter school. The question, however, is how schools can create good practices which elaborate on the already obtained capacities, and which deepen and extend children's understanding and involvement. It is not a matter of whether young children should be involved in literate activities or not. It is a matter of when and how!

The national school reform in the Netherlands in 1985 resulted in an integrated primary school for 4 to 12 year olds. The reform meant to promote continuity in development and education; the start of cultural learning processes should no longer be fixed at a particular moment in the year. Rather, education should harmonise with actual developmental levels of the children.

Nevertheless, after almost 10 years of integrated primary education the discussion about learning to read and write is vivid as ever. There are teachers who are still convinced that the early years should be devoted predominantly to the social-emotional development, and that activities like exploration and play are much more important than cognitive development. Other teachers admit that children need some kind of support in order to make a good start in group 3 (in the Netherlands for 6 year olds). These teachers find a kind of 'compromise' by introducing pre-reading training programmes in the last few months before the children enter group 3. The main reason why some teachers feel that they hardly have another choice is the persistence of class teaching in group 3. Moreover, the widespread use of highly structured reading methods in group 3 reinforces the opinion that (these kinds of) learning activities are not appropriate for the younger children.

With Basic Development we are able to break through this stalemate. We can show that there is a better approach in developmental and school-learning matters when we start from another narrative on child development. With this narrative we can help teachers to put new ideas into practice. Partly by making an appeal to their common sense: do not we all know that, at a very early age, children want to participate in activities which are part of their surroundings; that toddlers and infants love to scribble messages on their drawings; that at a very early stage they recognise printed language, want to be read to, recognise titles and some subtitles in television programmes and so on. We can all observe this, once we are really interested in what engages young children; and once we are willing to stimulate activities like this in school. This common sense attitude is an essential starting point, but it needs to be supplemented by a practice-theory which helps teachers to recognise the value of children's play activities, and by which they can decide in what direction these activities should be developed.

We do not intend to discuss our developmental approach in detail in this chapter and refer to chapter 7 in this book and to other publications (e.g. Janssen-Vos, 1997; Janssen-Vos and Pompert, 1993).

Rather, we would like to explain this concept at a concrete level, particularly with regard to the matter of learning to write. We would like to go into the practical implications of Vygotskian principles and pay attention to matters like the following (Vygotsky, 1978):

- how can children's activities such as play be organised in order to make them culturally significant, developmental contexts that prepare for later successful school learning?
- how must adults organise the settings and interventions in the child's play activities? First, we will explain the place of a cultural activity like writing in our curriculum Basic Development. Then we will pay more detailed attention to major aspects of educational processes: the meanings children attach to writing; the developmental perspectives of writing activities; activities that are potentially appropriate and the teacher's interventions. We will conclude by addressing the issue of teacher's qualities and recounting some of our classroom experiences in working with teachers who want to improve their practice.

Writing in Basic Development

In Basic Development, the progress from play activity toward learning activity is seen as one coherent process (see Janssen-Vos and Pompert, 1993). Cultural learning finds its starting-points in play activities. Therefore, we give cultural learning like written language a substantial place in the Basic Development and advance the thesis that writing is utterly relevant for young children indeed. But the activities we have in mind must bear some distinctive characteristics to make them developmentally valuable.

In the first place we think of activities which are familiar to the children and to which they can attach meaning in their own way. An example to clarify this characteristic:

A teacher plays in the sweetshop with Stefan and Glenn. She encourages them to make notes of her orders. They value this as an attractive idea, but Stefan says that he is not yet able to write. The teacher then suggests doing the writing for him. Stefan reads the order and takes care of a perfect delivery. Then he makes the words 'dummies' and 'spek' with letterstamps. Glenn is as interested as Stefan, but he acts differently. First, he sells the teacher the things she asks for, and after that he writes this 'order' down. Then he makes the word 'snoep' (sweets) with letterstamps.

As a second characteristic we like to mention that writing activities in Basic Development are significant social-cultural activities with an accent upon the real communicative functions of written language. This implies that, from the very beginning, young children should pick up writing as a communicative activity by which people reason, argue, solve problems or pour out their heart by means of written symbols. We think that isolated training in specific skills does not contribute to this understanding, whereas 'comprehensive' activities do, like making a shopping list, writing a letter to grandma or a story about a day's outing with the group. The activities we have in mind are part of the child's reality and daily life.

In the third place we want to refer to the development of the activities themselves as an important characteristic. The children's involvement in certain writing activities is in itself not enough for a successful literacy development. It is the actual quality of these activities in the light of the further development in the direction of cultural learning that count (Van Oers, 1999a, 1999b). This means that teachers are always after opportunities to improve the activities. They fulfil a mediating, developmental role in joint activities with the children by bringing in elements that deepen and broaden the children's part in the activities and that stimulate the children to emulate these literate activities. By taking over the elements the teacher brings in, the child develops its writing activities.

These specific characteristics show that the developmental value of writing activities as well as the developmental opportunities they offer are largely dependent on the way the teacher manages the classroom activities. What should teachers know, do, think, to make writing activities worthwhile? How can they ensure that children become motivated and skilful writers?

The meaning children attach to writing

The teacher, who wants to guide children's activities in a particular direction, needs to be aware of the meaning the child attaches to these activities. Only if the teacher understands the child's own intentions, motivation or interpretation, she or he can choose the most appropriate interventions.

The fact that writing does have meaning for most young children can be concluded from all kinds of observations. In everyday situations children are active writers in their own way. They become curious about the functions of writing if they get the chance to participate in everyday social activities like making a shopping list with your father or mother, or making notes in your diary just as your mother does. Susan shows us what writing means to her in the following example. Susan's friend is ill and she has made a beautiful get-well postcard for her. Susan tells her grandmother in detail where her friend's name and address should be written down. Grandma must do the

Photo:
Hanneke Verkleij

writing: 'because I cannot write yet', Susan says. Then she dictates: 'Write there: love from'. After that she adds her own name and tells grandma: 'Now you write your name too so she knows it is you' (Pompert, 1994).

Susan has something to say, and she is aware of the function of putting her message into written form. But many more examples can be found of narratives in connection with writing. We notice this for instance when children draw pictures in response to certain events. Like Marco who draws a cat and adds the following text: *the cat lies down – the cat eats catfood - the cat looks outside – the cat has its birthday – the cat is asleep – end.*

Because play is for young children most important, many of their stories are related to play activities. In a group of four- and five-year-olds, the children had the opportunity to play in a pet shop for weeks. This resulted in a variety of meaningful (literate) activities:

- stories about what can be bought for what kind of animals;
- making telephone calls in the shop, calling customers;
- waiting one's turn and having social talks;
- sending bills;
- setting prices of items;
- making up names for the shop.

Sometimes it was the teacher who did the writing for the children; sometimes the children did it themselves.

Role-play is very important for young children because in their roles they can represent their ideas about reality in a very concrete way. The roles are realistic for the children and they promote more expanded sociocultural activities. These activities engage children in writing. After all, a real doctor writes prescriptions; a powerful policeman writes tickets; and a waitress always takes the orders on a writing pad. So you pretend to be a writer in hospital, traffic or restaurant play.

But at a certain point young children also want to be conventional writers, as adults are. There comes a moment when they are no longer satisfied with their own scribbles and invented ways of writing. More and more they integrate conventional rules in composing messages and syllables, they chose certain words and require the correct way of spelling. For such accomplishments they turn to adults for help. Then they ask questions, like:

- would you mind writing it properly for me, so I can copy it?
- should I write it like this?
- is this a good sentence?

Meanings like this, however, do not arise automatically. Much depends on the way in which adults handle children's initiatives. Do they only tolerate initiatives, or do they encourage children to participate in writing activities?

Moreover, teachers should be up to develop the children's meanings so that children's meanings gradually come closer to the meanings our society attaches to cultural activities such as writing and its tools. A nice example of the importance of the adult's role was shown by the teacher of a group of young Turkish-speaking children. This teacher had never before stimulated any writing activities: 'I have more than enough work teaching them to speak Dutch', she said. 'Writing is really impossible!' But after some time of collaboration with this teacher (following the strategy described in chapter 8), she invited children to participate in writing activities: letters for Santa Claus, stories about their play and recipes for biscuits and cakes. This caught on very well with the children. They wanted to write themselves and had lots of stories to tell to the teacher who wrote them down. The oral language skills were reinforced by the writing activities.

Developmental perspectives of writing activities

Not only the meaning children attach to writing activities determines the teacher's interventions. The second angle is given by the teacher's knowledge of the developmental process of writing. How does development of writing take place; what lines can be sketched? Having insight in this process the teacher will be able to value present activities in the perspective of further development.

In Basic Development a general developmental perspective constitutes the guiding principle. Development from play activity toward learning activity is the perspective that holds for early education in general. This principle clearly applies to the development of writing, as early stages in writing are closely related to the child's play motives. Play activities give children the opportunity to use language in order to direct actions and to reflect on ideas. For instance: 'No, it doesn't go like that in a shoeshop. You have to try them on first and then you buy them.' These oral forms of language have provable effects on children's writing (Pellegrini & Galda, 1993). When children expand this kind of play in the direction of thematic role-play, they become increasingly engaged (Vygotsky, 1978; Dutton, 1991) and the use of written language can be meaningfully employed.

In our work we have found ample evidence of this. Young children are enthusiastic writers, playing waitress, doctor, counter-clerk in the postoffice. We notice they attach meaning to their scribbles when they say: 'It says here....', although they cannot yet use the conventional symbol system. Scribbles that look alike can have quite different meanings. The precise meaning is determined by what the child says during or about the play activity. The scribbles Jerry writes for instance when he is making up a list of the things he has to do today, are like the ones he uses when writing a recipe for witches' soup. He knows, however, exactly what the note says.

Fig.9.1 Jerry's list of things he has to do today. The teacher writes what Jerry reads (from top to bottom): getting dressed, having breakfast, playing with Esther, going to school, having lunch, cycling, parking my bicycle, locking my bicycle, entering school, playing.

So play activities and the child's stories create important contexts in the further development of written language in the period of 4-7 year olds. In this developmental process we distinguish three stages:

Stage 1. I know that I write
In this stage children name their writings as a message or report, just as a drawing or a gesture stands for something. However, they do name drawing and writing as distinctive activities: 'I have written this and this is my drawing'. Children scribble without attaching specific meanings to the different words, letters and sounds. Following Vygotsky (1978, p. 106, chapter 8) we name the child's first scribbles as symbols of the

first order. The symbol directly refers to the object or action. The spoken language does not yet serve as a link between them. Yet, as a result of verbalised reflections on their writings by more knowledgeable others, there is a growing comprehension that written language is a reflection of spoken language. We recognise this first stage in the example of a four-year-old boy telling the teacher a story about a tiny hexagonal figure he had drawn: 'This is the house where I live. With my mum and dad. The house is in Amsterdam. My mum and dad tried to find it for a long time.' The boy dictates a story to the teacher about his own room in the house. He understood the written text very well and, together with the teacher, he was able to reread the text.

Stage 2. I write scribbled messages
In this stage the notion grows that writing is a different way of saying things. The relation between spoken and written language is named explicitly. At the same time, distinctive details in the child's scribbles emerge. They also distinguish types of writings: 'This is a letter, a very long one'. Or: 'This is a shopping list' (see also Newman, 1985). Scribbles look more and more like conventional numbers and letters; and in scribbled messages real, familiar letters are given a place. Like in Ilse's recipe for witches' soup, in which she uses letters of her own name (fig.9.2). Writing remains connected with the child's stories, which arise out of play and the corresponding actions and role dialogues.

Fig.9.2. A recipe for witches' soup

Stage 3. I want to be a real writer
More and more the children understand writing as an 'adult' social-cultural activity in which they want to participate. They begin to understand the fixed relation between a certain sound and symbol. In their texts they experiment with spelling on their own and use all the letters they know. But gradually writing things correctly, in accepted, conventional spelling, becomes important for them. This becomes manifest when children ask questions like: 'Is this how you write it properly? Can you write it down correctly for me?'

Insight into the graphical organisation of a text also emerges: the child writes from left to right and from the top of the page to the bottom, it uses interpunction and starts a new sentence at a new line. More and more texts are provided with a certain intention and the corresponding form. This can be seen in letters with the name or signature underneath; or in stories that start with a title and finish with a recognisable end. Also in this stage, play activities remain important sources for writing and children even use their self-made scripts to act out stories (see Mc Lane, 1990).

These three stages show in what dynamic perspective writing activities should be directed. The stages originate from activities in which writing is not essentially present: play activities and narrative activities. In other words: children need to be good (role) players and narrators in order to become writers.

It is important that teachers should be aware of the fact that writing activities originate from activities that have a much wider significance than writing itself. This knowledge makes them sensitive of the impact of play and stories and gives them the opportunities to expand the quality of these activities. They also need insight in the early stages in the writing process itself, to be able to recognise the indicators of transition to further development.

Teachers express this need themselves, like one of our teachers who said: 'I want to be able to promote the development in writing of my children, just as I can in play and constructive activities.'

Meaningful writing activities

Teachers, who understand the development of writing, know how to create educational settings that stimulate children to go through this process. Again we emphasise the fact that play activities and narrative activities form the core of settings in this respect. Teachers create activity settings in which:

- children have the opportunity to explore writing by writing themselves, in their own way;
- children undertake role play activities and can act as writers;
- children and teacher cooperate in writing.

a. Exploring writing

An inviting and stimulating environment is a prerequisite for writing, i.e. an environment in which writing fulfils a communicative function, and that provides an abundance of writing stuff, as well as ready-to-use letter material. There is always plenty of time and room for writing. In the read-and-write corner children can write texts, stories, letters, lists or little books (Christie, 1991).

Activities are always accompanied by verbal interactions between children and between the teacher and children, individually or in small groups. The teacher stimulates children to talk about their activities and about events or objects that occupy them. The teacher encourages this, not only by being sensitive to what is in the child's mind but also by talking about activities herself. Along with the narrative aspects, teachers invite and encourage children to undertake writing activities. The teacher 'radiates' the expectation that children will start to write, so to speak. Very important in this respect are the teacher's attitudes. They read children's writings respectfully and seriously. The writings are made functional, whenever possible. For instance by answering a letter, or commenting on a text; by illustrating, printing and pinning up texts.

Last but not least, teachers serve as important models: they write a lot when children are present and involve children in it. We observed many inspiring examples of this model function of teachers in:

- messages to parents;
- the 'letter of the week' written to an absent classmate;
- writings in the class-diary;
- text boards pertaining to certain themes;
- semantic maps in connection with play activities;
- book reports;
- art notes.

b. Play activities

Play activities that provoke writing should meet some important conditions.

To begin with, the situation should encourage different kinds of writing activities. A well-equipped house corner is an example of such a situation, where several play ideas evoke writing activities:

- making shopping lists, which especially makes sense when there is a shop in the classroom as well;
- writing letters and postcards;
- writing messages to housemates or taking notes when making a telephone call.

Other examples of situations that are especially inviting for writing activities are shops, a travel agency, post office, school or restaurant.

A second condition is that children are allowed plenty of time to explore the play situation as well as the writing activities. They need to explore the situation and materials and to experience the various activities before initiatives in the area of literacy or writing can occur. Besides that, play situations are more comprehensive: they involve more than writing alone, of course. According to their own needs and developmental levels, children have the opportunity to determine the most appropriate activities. In most cases very young children are more interested in manipulating the materials and in role-playing than in using the situation and equipment for writing. But as experience shows, the children who are familiar with the writing possibilities of the available equipment and who see examples from peers and teachers, tend to be interested in writing themselves very soon. For older children for that matter, the opposite applies: they can still be very interested in exploring manipulative activities in a play situation. We observed this in a group where a shoe shop was set up for some time. Only in the second and third week some of the older children started to write price labels, bills and receipts.

Other experiences show that the more children have the opportunity to undertake writing during play, the more they are active in coming up with new ideas and stories for play situations. In a group where children were very familiar with play situations like a sweet shop, a shoe shop and Santa Claus, a new situation is created: a witch corner where children can make all kinds of magicians' potions. Many children appeared to assume from the start that they would (eventually) write down what they were going to do and make.

These examples stress the important role of stories. Not only stories from books or stories told by the teacher serve as a spur to play initiatives and situations. Children have their own stories that lead towards play and writing. Often new stories originate from play that has taken place. Children tell them to each other, act them out and write about them, mostly in co-operation with the teacher. We found an interesting example in a group of children playing in a flower shop for some time. In the role of shopkeeper a couple of children made a pricelist and a sign with the opening hours of the shop. Next, they demonstrated other children how they should use the list and the sign.

This communicative activity, showing other children the meaning and function of written messages, is extremely important because it marks the transition to cultural learning. After all, the list and sign acquire a stable function, just as in everyday reality.

c. Writing with the teacher

Children, who want to put their stories on paper, cooperate with the teacher. They dictate their story to the teacher, as it were. The teacher takes care of (parts of) the writing and thus, as a model, supports the child in gaining insights that are necessary in order to become a writer, like:

- what you think can become a story and that story can be written down;
- what has been written down can be read;
- what has been written, survives;
- a text is made up with words and sentences.

It is not only the writing the teacher takes care of; she or he also supports revising, editing and publication of children's stories for peers in their own group and for readers in other groups. If children know that their work will be read and discussed by others, their motivation for intentional writing grows (McLane, 1990). We experience this in our work, especially in group three (6 year olds) where teachers work with children's texts and stories instead of lessons out of a writing method (see Knijpstra, 1994; Knijpstra et al., 1997).

An example of such 'distributed writing' is the following. Every week a teacher makes a newspaper with the children and she says: 'Formerly I used lessons to teach the children to write. Correcting mistakes was a great problem for me because I did not like to mark mistakes, but I could not leave it as it was either. Now the children write in their notebooks first. We correct together and subsequently the child makes the final text for the newspaper. Never before a group of mine has achieved so much. And what is even more important: they are enthusiastic and motivated writers. The slower pupils as well!'

The teacher's interventions

Above we mentioned the importance of the cooperating role of the teacher. This general role probably indicates more adequately the nature of interventions than a mere summing up of various actions like:

- inviting children to participate in activities;
- encouraging to talk about their activities and about their stories and thoughts;
- showing or teaching how to use certain materials, instruments or techniques;
- asking questions;
- bringing in new ideas and materials;
- assisting in difficult aspects of a task;
- reflecting on and evaluating the activity.

In developmental education, the contexts in which the interventions take place are as important as the various interventions themselves. The context is especially characterised by two aspects we mentioned before: the meaning children attach to certain activities, and the developmental perspectives of the activity (see also chapter 8). In a continual reflection on both aspects while working with the children, the teacher is able to choose the most appropriate interventions. The central questions in this reflection are:

- what kind of activity settings should I create in order to offer optimal developmental opportunities for the different children in the group?
- in what activities of which children shall I participate today and in what way? We have illuminative examples from our teachers that clarify the coherence of interventions in the context of meaning and developmental perspectives.

Marco's cake.
Marco asks the teacher, Jetty, to bake cakes with him. 'Yes, I'd like to', the teacher says, 'but later, because I am busy with this group at the moment. Why don't you make a start and I'll join in after a while?' That is all right for Marco and he returns to the corner where one can make beautiful cakes of coloured clay, with all kinds of decorations, boxes and wrapping paper. Ten minutes later, he taps the teacher on her shoulder and says: 'You can also give me your order for a cake, you know.' The teacher likes the idea and with the class-assistant, Marjolein, they place an order. Marco fetches paper and pencil and the ladies place their orders; he writes these down (fig. 9.3). The teacher says: 'I am not sure about this. Are you sure we really get two different cakes?'
Marco goes off, coming back again with a newly written order (fig. 9.4). To the teacher he says: 'Can you please write it all correctly for me Jetty?' 'All right', Jetty says, 'but you have to read to me what exactly is written.' Marco points out and reads: 'Cream cake for Marjolein, cheese cake for Jetty'. Reading the last sentence he adds: 'This says: ready tomorrow'. The teacher writes this down for Marco (fig. 9.5). 'Now I can do it all by myself', Marco says and starts writing again (fig. 9.6). In the afternoon Marco seems to have his plans made. He picks up his last order and goes to the read-and-write corner. With cut-out letters he makes the word cream cake very precisely and

then he sticks a paper cake next to it. The next days Marco and other children are baking many cakes and many orders are written.

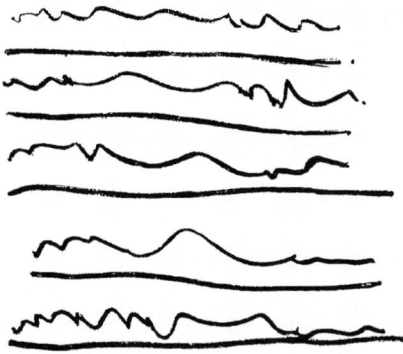

Fig. 9.3. The first order for cakes

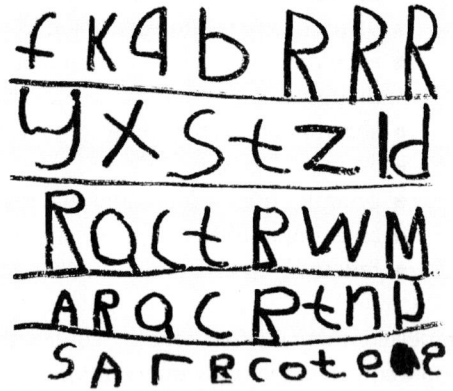

Fig. 9.4. The second order

Fig. 9.5. The teacher writes for Marco

Fig. 9.6. Marco's third written order

This writing activity opens new possibilities, not only in written language. The teacher introduces other recipes and children's cooking books. The bakery in the classroom is expanded with a shop and shopwindow with a rich assortment of bread and pastry. In order to offer the children ideas for their role-play, the teacher takes them to visit the local bakery.

This example shows the way in which Marco's teacher succeeds in evoking further development of the writing activity:

- The teacher joins in with the meaning Marco attaches to the play activity: he

is the baker who writes the orders precisely in order to bake the right cakes for the right persons.
- She participates in the activity, plays a role, and brings in new elements as a part of the activity itself. We recognise two important interventions in this respect: her response to the first order: 'I am not sure about this'. And her request to read the second order aloud. These interventions result in an obvious development of the writing activity.
- The teacher demonstrates how to write.
- She gives Marco time to go on with his activity at his own pace.

A significant point of attention in these interventions concerns the child's motivation. It is important that the child remains motivated to continue the activity meaningfully, and that he still enjoys it.

In Developmental Education, teachers are not merely awaiting children's initiatives in starting writing activities. They take initiatives themselves as well and play a very active role regarding children who need impulses for further development.

Doctor Bobby

We present another example of a teacher who works in special education with children having learning difficulties. This teacher introduced play activities in order to create meaningful learning situations. In this context she also introduced a variety of literacy activities. Before, most children would not engage in these activities by themselves and had built up a vast aversion against anything having to do with reading or writing. This is the way this teacher currently guides and directs her children's activities.

Bobby is playing doctor; he is 7 years old and did not succeed in learning to read or write in regular primary education. The teacher plays the patient and comes to the doctor's surgery. She suffers from a sore, squeaking knee. Doctor Bobby examines her with his stethoscope and bends and stretches the knee carefully. 'There is a bacterium in your knee', he decides. 'Oh dear', the patient says, 'could you possibly write that down for me because I am afraid I'll forget that'. 'Sure', the doctor says and he draws the bacterium, making a B next to it. Then the conversation goes on about what should happen next. Doctor Bobby knows it all: 'You should eat potatoes and take vitamin C'. That too is written down. The patient asks whether she should eat anything else, upon which the doctor answers: 'Yes, not the wrong pills'. And he draws the pills that should not be taken, putting a cross through them (fig.9.7).

With such interactions the teacher is able to acquire insight into the way the child understands and performs writing in joint activities.

In our in-service assistance of the teachers, we stimulate them to reflect on their actions and observations, and we assist them in this process with our model for observation and assessment (see Chapters 7 and 8 for further explanation). This model supports them in analysing the children's activities and in determining their developmental potentials.

The teacher's recorded reflections tell us that Bobby:
- participates well and enthusiastically in role play;

●⃝ Ọ⃛ → B

Aı D A P/S
vint mie n A C

Fig. 9.7. Doctor Bobby's notes. (from top to bottom): There is a bacterium in your knee; you have to eat potatoes and vitamin C; don't take the wrong pills

- has sufficient knowledge about going to the doctor, and about suffering from something, doctor's actions etc. in order to play his role;
- can give reading and particularly writing a functional place in the context of the play;
- uses symbols and diagram (bacterium and wrong pills);
- uses conventional spelling;
- makes use of writing letters as well as capital letters A, B en C.

On the basis of this analysis she considers subsequent adequate activities for Bobby. She plans the activity settings and her own contribution as she writes:

- continue this type of play activities; also in different play settings;
- use schemes and models also in other activities;
- stimulate to copy correct texts, writing or using letter materials;
- stimulate written language: own stories, messages, letters.

The teacher's qualities

In Developmental Education great demands are made on teachers. In the previous paragraphs we explained what teachers should know and do in order to promote the children's development in the direction of cultural learning. In the case of the development of writing they:

- are able to examine the meanings their children attach to writing activities;
- recognise the developmental aspects of writing and using functions of written language;
- have a variety of significant writing activities at their disposal;
- are able to put several strategies and interventions into practice.

It is an interplay of knowledge and skills, which are closely related and lead to a situation-specific teaching style. 'Teacherproof' programmes that prescribe educational settings or dictate appropriate teaching methods offer no solutions, because in those

Photo: Hanneke Verkleij

cases it is always the teacher who constructs the programme and who decides what interactions will be most adequate in what situations. Continual reflection on the activity and on the form and function of writing therefore is a steady constituent of the teacher's responsibilities.

These demands refer to a teaching style that is also known as responsive teaching. Responsive teaching is characterised (Stremmel, 1992):

- by the fact that (both) adult and child collaborate in structuring the situations which offer opportunities for cultural valued activities;
- by the amount of guidance a teacher gives the child: just enough to perform a task;
- and by the input of a repertoire of alternative interventions instead of assuming that there is one preferable method or strategy.

All this appeals to a large amount of effort and professionalism of teachers. Teachers need support for the appropriation of these qualities. That is where our responsibility as innovators and counselors starts. It is our task to put principles of developmental education into practice by assisting teachers in performing their role as responsive teachers, and to use play as a context for learning to write.

We have developed and explored settings and strategies to be used in teacher training, in-service training and teacher counselling. Providing curriculum documents which give teachers the opportunity to study the educational ideas and in which they find suggestions for activities with children, is one aspect. Such written material is not nearly enough. Therefore, accents are put on working with teachers in courses, seminars and on the job.

In cooperation with the teachers we put all energy in three elements of the teacher's role:

- exploring and examining the children's needs and meanings in general and concerning writing in particular;
- understanding and recognising the writing process and the developmental perspectives;
- learning to reflect on children's activities and upon their own actions and interventions.

A distinctive characteristic of responsive teaching is that teachers need to be able to reflect on action and to decide on action (Stremmel, 1992). We are not pursuing automatically performed actions; neither do we think teachers can act properly if they need a time out to study their books and notes on the spot before being able to choose the appropriate activities or interventions. Therefore, we try to make the necessary information as brief and as logical as possible. The earlier section about the stages in writing can serve as an example. Instead of providing teachers with all available and interesting information about writing theory and practice, we reduce them to a few points of attention. If these can come to function as a kind of common sense knowledge, we are convinced that teachers can really put them into practice.

Again, we are aware that the demands we put on teachers are not simple. But fortunately the experiences of the last few years confirm that the direction we chose was the right one. And what is very important, it seems that teachers appreciate their role of responsive teachers. Experience shows that teachers become very active and interested if they get the support to come closer to their children, to understand them better, to establish a better relationship and to improve the children's development. The experienced results of our work with teachers are encouraging and promising. We would like to give some examples of teachers' reactions:

This for instance is what Marco's teacher told us in an interview:

> 'I used to encourage the children who were nearly six to write their names because I thought they were old enough to start writing. That is what parents expect too. But now, my children start to write as soon as they enter school. They need it in their play. And we make stories, we write about the books we read, we make books ourselves all the time. All children are involved in writing activities which they see as important; they make progress regardless of their ages.'

Bobby's teacher talks about the progress in literacy development the group as a whole made:

> 'Because this way of working with children is still relatively new for us, we do not dare completely abandon the regular reading methods yet. But we work through them with great leaps. Because of many years of experience in special education, I know that my children need a lot of time to finish the prescribed programme. Now I notice that they are much faster and that they have more understanding of what they read. Two of the children reached a level that had never been attained before. I am convinced that this

is caused by our new way of working; the children really enjoy it!' (Schoonhoven, 1993)

About Bobby she says:

'When Bobby arrived in my group, he only knew a couple of the words that occurred in the method. Now, after a year, he reads fluently and he understands what he reads. Converted into didactical age he progressed from two to fifteen months. He also shows much progress in correct writing. The assistance supplied by the speech therapist during the last couple of years, can be stopped now. She says that Bobby got rid of his language delay.'

Other teachers who stimulate writing from play activities mention large points of profit (Pompert and Van Zanten, 1994). Successively they refer to:

- the increase of the children's motivation to write;
- the potentials in functional writing; children apply what they can do in several (play) contexts;
- working in small groups, the teacher is able to pay attention to individual children, who profit from this.

Comparable experiences can be seen in some multi-ethnic groups in the large cities in our country (see Knijpstra, 1994; Knijpstra et al., 1997). Not only the experienced teachers, but also beginning teachers book successes.

Teachers, who participated in our courses and are putting Basic Development into practice, reveal their experiences. A teacher working in group 3 told us:

'Because of writing in play activities, the children seem to be much more critical about the usual language lessons. They want to do it correctly and want to know why they are doing certain exercises. Even the slower readers and writers.'

Two teachers, who organised an animal shop in their classroom, say:

'A couple of children we were worried about, regarding their literacy development, benefited from the shop enormously. They wrote a lot of orders and bills, and made books about what happens in an animal shop. After some weeks, we observed them writing in all kinds of situations. They showed an amazing growth.'

Two other teachers mention:

'In our grocery shop a lot of literacy initiatives arose. Some children made price lists. Stories were written about how a price list should be made and used; and other children read those and started to act them out.'

The deputy head of a multi-ethnic school, who is working with the young children, recalls:

'I never realised that our children are capable of doing all this. Now I regard their potentials quite differently.'

Our impression is that teachers, who are successful, are the ones with particular skills:

- They are able to cooperate with the children in such a way that writing activities are not only meaningful for children and functional, but at the same time exciting and challenging. Expansion of the activity can occur at any moment.

- They can give feedback on the children's writing products in a way that encourages children to continue their activity.
- They are able to make adequate planning decisions.

Small-scale scientific research confirms our experiences that teachers are capable to implement developmentally appropriate play-based literacy activities. If they succeed in doing so, their children score even higher on reading and writing tests than children from programme-oriented classrooms (Harskamp & Suhre, 2000; Suhre 2002).

References

Au, K.H. (1993). *Literacy instruction in multi-cultural settings*. Orlando: Harcore Publishers.

Christie, J.F. (1991). *Play and early literacy development*. New York: State University of New York Press.

El'konin, D.B. (1972). Toward the problem of stages in the mental development of the child. *Soviet Psychology*, 10, 225-251.

Dutton, H. (1991). Play and writing. In: N. Hall & L.Abbott (Eds.), *Play in the Primary Curriculum* (pp. 45-60). London: Hoder & Stoughton.

Harskamp, E. & Suhre, C. (2000). *Praktijkbrochure Ontwikkelingsgericht lezen. Lesportretten en leerresulaten* [Practice brochure developmental reading. Class vignettes and learning outcomes]. Groningen: GION.

Janssen-Vos, F. (1997). *Basisontwikkeling in de onderbouw* [Basic Development in early education]. Assen: Van Gorcum.

Janssen-Vos, F. & Pompert, B. (1993). *From play activity toward learning activity. Developmental perspectives in early childhood education*. Paper for the third European conference on Early Childhood Education. Utrecht: APS.

Janssen-Vos, F., Pompert, B., & Vink, H. (1991). *Naar lezen, schrijven en rekenen. Ontwikkelingsgericht onderwijs* [Toward reading, writing and mathematics. Developmental education]. Assen: Van Gorcum.

Knijpstra, H. (1994). Migrantenkinderen leren methodisch eigen teksten lezen [Migrant children learn to read own texts methodically]. *De wereld van het jonge kind*, 21, 10, 300-308

Knijpstra, H., Pompert ,B., & Schiferli, T. (1997). *Met jou kan ik lezen en schrijven. Een ontwikkelingsgerichte didactiek voor het leren lezen en schrijven in groep 3 en 4* [I can read and write with you. Developmental teaching didactics for reading and writing in group 3 and 4]. Assen: Van Gorcum.

McLane, J.B. (1990) Writing as a social process. In: L. Moll (ed.), *Vygotsky and education* (pp. 304-318). Cambridge: Cambridge University Press.

Newman, J. (1985). *The craft of children's writing*. Portsmouth, NH: Heinnemann.

Oers, B. van. (1999a). Teaching opportunities in play. In: M. Hedegaard & J. Lompscher (Eds.), *Learning activity and development* (pp 268-289). Aarhus: University Press.

Oers, B. van. (1999b). Four year olds growing up in a literate world. In H. Colberg-Schrader & P. Oberhuemer (Hrsg.), *Qualifizieren für Europa. Praxiskulturen, Ausbildungskonzepte,*

Initiativen (pp 61- 73). Baltmannsweiler: Schneider Verlag.

Pellegrini, A.D & Galda, L. (1993). Ten years after: a re-examination of symbolic play and literacy research. *Reading Research Quarterly, 28,* 163-175

Pompert, B. (1994). Schrijver worden in de onderbouw [Becoming a writer in the first primary years]. *De wereld van het jonge kind,* 21, 10, 312-318

Pompert, B. & Schiferli T. (1993). *Spelen en leren op school* [Play and learning at school]. Tilburg: Zwijsen.

Pompert, W. & van Zanten, P. (1994). Hoe verder in groep drie ? [How to continue in group three ?]. *De wereld van het jonge kind,* 21, 10, 327-331.

Schoonhoven, E. (1993). *De ontwikkeling van MLK-kinderen door rollenspel* [The development of children with learning difficulties through role play]. Internal publication. Alkmaar: Hogeschool Alkmaar.

Stremmel, A.J. (1992). *Responsive teaching: a culturally appropriate approach.* Internal publication. Blacksburg: Virginia Polytechnic Institute and State University.

Suhre, C. (2002). *Praktijkbrochure ontwikkelingsgericht leesonderwijs. Functioneel lezen in de groepen 3 en 4* [Practice brochure developmental literacy education. Functional reading in group 3 and 4]. Groningen: GION.

Vygotsky, L.S. (1978). *Mind in society.* Cambridge: Harvard University Press.

Whitehead, M.R. (1990). *Language and literacy in the early years.* London: Paul Chapman.

Mathematics learning
in a play-based curriculum.
How to deal with heterogeneity?

Niko Fijma

Introduction

The relevance of education lies in its capacity to improve a child's broad development and enhance his or her abilities to participate in cultural activities. Education is not just a preparation for fulfilling a specific role in a culture. It should also create a community of permanent learners, in which the participants (the pupils and their teacher) actively reconstruct their cultural heritage. In schools, pupils already participate in cultural activities, thereby learning to participate in an increasingly competent way and, at the same time, renewing the very activities in which they participate (Bruner, 1996). The process of continuing and renewing relevant meanings occurs in 'negotiations of meaning' between the participants in an activity. It is a process of collaborative meaning-construction, in which heterogeneity is required and discourse is essential. Within this process, learning is seen as an expansion of an activity, based on the improvement of actions or the acquisition of new actions in the context of that cultural activity (Van Oers, 1996a). Education is an attempt to build up joint activities that also provide a context for acquiring significant knowledge and skills.

The formation of such education demands that the teacher is capable of working in a developmental way. Important qualities required are:
- to design relevant activities in co-operation with the pupils;
- to organise these activities in a way that is of interest to the pupils and contains relevant cultural meanings;
- to participate in these activities as a partner in the negotiation of meaning;
- to spot and create teaching opportunities to help pupils in further developing their actions and abilities (Van Oers, 1999);
- to gain insight into the pupil's development and to link this to hypotheses on an adequate follow-up.

Our work as teacher-trainers is based on a Vygotskian conception of development and education. The teachers involved in our training activities have adopted the concept of developmental education as a basis for their teaching methods. The theoretical approach has been elaborated into a curriculum strategy for the junior classes of primary school, called Basic Development (Janssen-Vos, 1997; see also chapter 7).
From this Vygotskian perspective the teacher:

- finds it important that pupils participate in relevant cultural activities;
- wants the pupils to be actively involved in their own learning activities;
- knows that only activities that make sense to pupils offer the best chances for their development;
- sees him / herself as a partner in the development of the children; within the activities the teacher fulfils the role of a more competent partner;
- emphasises broad development as a major educational goal.

In this chapter I will give an example of a teacher of the junior primary classes of the Juliana school in the Dutch town of Schagen, who seeks to work in a developmental way, also for teaching mathematics. Nan, the teacher, works with 24 pupils in group 2/3 (5 to 6/7-year-olds). From the early nineties Nan and her colleagues have been implementing Basic Development with the assistance of our external supervision and support. Previously her work with the children in mathematics lessons was structured by programmes with uniform day-by-day curriculum planning, meant for all the pupils at the same time. In those days, programmatic continuity was taken as continuity in the subject materials rather than as continuity experienced by the pupils themselves. The sequence for acquiring knowledge and various skills is determined from a content analysis of the domain of mathematics. Hence, the curriculum for mathematics just focuses on transmitting basic knowledge and skills, while no role is awarded to the pupils as partners in the dynamic process of curriculum construction (Pinar *et al.*, 1995).

The transmission approach of mathematics teaching is problematic for two reasons:
- *heterogeneity* is not adequately dealt with: how to cope with the differences between the children?
- *personal meaningfulness* is not seriously accounted for: how to learn mathematics in a meaningful way (Van Oers, 1996b)?

Nan, however, does not want to isolate mathematics; she tries to connect it with relevant contents and other activities in the classroom. In a diverse mix of activities she creates opportunities for every child to receive the teacher's assistance in a context of intense, responsive, and sustained dialogue (Tharp et al., 2000).
Besides, she considers learning mathematics as an activity of mathematising whereby problem solving, schematising different solutions, expressing solutions with the help of symbols, and comparatively negotiating available solutions are basic elements (Freudenthal, 1991). In this perspective (early) mathematics learning is closely linked to language and the formation of language, based on mental constructions. As such this approach is obviously narrative (see Burton, 1996, and chapter 4 of this volume). These are the starting points that form Nan's practice for teaching mathematics and that regulate her actions. From her pedagogical perspective Nan tries to integrate mathematics learning into her pedagogical perspective by adopting a developmental strategy (Fijma and Vink, 1998). Mathematics learning related to meaningful contexts

and embedded in other activities is desirable for the younger pupils, because it appeals to the pupils as agents and therefore gives a better guarantee for broad, meaningful (mathematical) development. Nan therefore does not want to programme the children's activities with a day-to-day package of mathematics. Determining the package to be offered to the pupils is a matter to be dealt with by the teachers themselves. They know what their pupils require in accordance with the pupils' current questions, motives and abilities. They try to ensure the (integrated) mathematical development of their pupils through targeted planning for the long term as well as for the next day. In this respect, her proposal for activities links with the children's interests, motives and abilities on the one hand, and offers opportunities for realising the teachers' own educational goals on the other hand. Activities are always linked to real life contexts and themes, and the teacher accordingly develops a thematic proposal for a period of six to eight weeks.

An essential strategy for the sensitive planning of the educational process is the teacher's careful observation of her pupils. The systematised and purposeful application of the teacher's educational approach is supported by working with an observation manual, called 'HOREB' (activity-oriented observation, registration and evaluation of basic development). This observation strategy is based on the idea of continuous guidance in meaningful activity settings (Janssen-Vos, Pompert and Schiferli, 1998). The following aspects of the teachers' activities are supported by the HOREB tools:

- design a range of meaningful activities;
- actively observe intensive interactions of and with children;
- guide the activities in such a way that they get added value for the children and are in line with the teacher's intentions.

HOREB has three means that offer support in this respect (see also chapter 8 of this book):

- the *book of activities*, which offers teachers starting points and means for designing and planning a range of activities;
- the *logbook* in which they write their short-term plans and their reflections on the implementation of these plans;
- a *children's diary* in which they categorise the data that show the children's developmental steps and enable the teacher to evaluate the developmental progress these children make. Observation models for the various activities serve as tools for the teacher for monitoring and expanding these activities.

I will explain this procedure by means of the theme 'Kings and Queens', which was scheduled in Nan's group in the autumn of 1999. Finally, I will indicate some benefits of this approach.

Designing and planning the range of activities

A theme covers a longer period. This is necessary because, in this way, there will be many opportunities to appropriate theme-related actions, knowledge and skills. Children need time to 'become acquainted' with a theme in order to be able to take more initiatives themselves and to continue building on the theme together.

For the period from mid-September to the beginning of November 1999 Nan drew up a plan for the first theme of the school year: 'Kings and Queens'. By means of a scheme derived from HOREB the goals, meanings and possible activities of the theme were explored. This general preparation is given a place in the book of activities and looks like this:

THEME PREPARATION
Theme: Kings and Queens

September – November 1999
Group 2/3 (5 to 7-year-olds) Nan, Julianaschool in Schagen, the Netherlands

Choice of theme:
- There are many young pre-school children who are attending school for the very first time; start with play activities whenever possible.
- Fairy tales usually involve kings and queens and are the stories that young children are familiar with.
- During this period 'Prinsjesdag', the day of the Dutch Queen's speech, takes place.

Goals:
- Work on the well-being of the pupils (be emotionally free, be curious and confident) during the first six weeks. We want to give each child the feeling 'of being a king or queen', so that they feel at home quickly and can work confidently within the new group.
- Learn to work and play together, become familiar with functional numeric, reading and writing skills. Become curious about these functional activities in the context of play.
- Develop the rules of the group and learn to apply them.

Children's meanings:
- Tell and play familiar fairytales /stories /books / rhymes (containing kings and queens).
- The magic of the world of kings and queens (castles /crown /footman / clothing etc.).
- Many children know the Dutch royal House of Orange (television /coins /stamps etc.)

Contents:
- What do you know about kings and queens?
- Which fairy tales about kings and queens do you know? Which books/stories?

- What would you like to do if you were king or queen?
- Sub-themes are: castles, gemstones, being polite (rules of behaviour), family / relatives and 'Prinsjesdag', and other subjects that are put forward by the group.
- Books to be used:
  - Koningin Beatrix (Queen Beatrice)
  - Ik wil patat (I want chips)
  - Koning Bobbel (King Bump)
  - Various fairy tale books
  - Poems and songs

The range of activities

After these initial steps, Nan worked on the theme and linked it with relevant activities. These involved the following core activities that are important to achieve the goals of Basic Development:

- play activities;
- constructive and expressive activities;
- conversational activities;
- reading and writing activities;
- investigative activities;
- mathematical activities.

Each of these activities will be elaborated below. In addition to this list of activities, the teacher considers how to start the theme.

In her book of activities she writes the following:

RANGE OF ACTIVITIES FOR THE THEME: KINGS AND QUEENS

Period: 13 September - 5 November 1999
Group: 2/3

Play activities:
- Role play: The Queen's office, a corner of the house, puppet play
- Motion play with the following songs:
  - Queen, what time is it?
  - The king's crown.
  - Good morning queen.
  - Rodereel.
  - King, may I cross the street?
  - There is a castle in Holland.
- Games: Make and play the castle game.
  Catch fishes (numbers and letters) in 'the castle pond'.

Constructive and expressive activities:
- Make a throne in the classroom ('story throne', a throne pupils may sit on for telling their story)
- Make and decorate your own magic mirror

- Make your own princess skirt.
- Make your own family tree.
- Design your own jewellery.
- Build a castle garden on the small building table or with sand / water.
- Build castles in the large building corner.
- Make gemstones from mosaic materials.

Conversational activities:
- Talks on planning the activities and discussion afterwards.
- Tell about the pupils' own projects.
- Read aloud or tell a story on the story throne: books, picture books, poetry.
- Informative discussions about the different contents.
- Make word fields with: castle; king; coach.
- Puppet show.
- Ask the queen questions (entrance hall).
- Story table (puppets and objects to play the story of a book).

Reading and writing activities:
- In this theme all letters are offered. Word fields, word cards, make and put down their own texts.
- Stamp or paste together key words from their own texts.
- Writing song texts and word fields with the computer (also to acquaint children with the computer).
- Copy or type poems and rhymes.
- Key words: the kiss, the house, the wheel, the garden, the pen, the book, the shoe, the school, the jester, the treasure.
- All children have their own letterbox with letters they know well.
- All children have their own notebook in which they write or draw.
- Familiarise them with reading strategies (like making use of the pictures) in small groups by letting them read texts they have put together themselves and by discussing the pictures.
- Copy word fields.
- Read together and discuss books / if so desired, write about books.
  The children themselves read books.
  Little golden books.

Mathematical activities:
- Make the castle game and play it with one or two dice; mathematical actions involved: synchronised counting / practise counting sequence / number sequences / structure quantities / arrow language.
- Queen what time is it?: synchronised counting / time.
- Make and count the stingy king's golden coins.
- Treasure hunt: geometry / coordinates.

- Numbers for the castle rooms: understanding numbers and their meaning.
- Draw maps of buildings and assignments: measure / geometry.
- Make and read diagrams.
- Recognise numeric symbols in the fish game.
- Keep the office diary: days of the week / weekly routine / perception of time.
- Make a calendar ('Prinsjesdag' on the third Tuesday in September).
- Make a princess skirt: measuring activities / sequence of numbers / compare quantities.
- Jewellery / shapes: geometry (triangle / square / rectangle) and arrange them.
- Work in the mathematics exercise book: to practise / especially blocks one and two.

Investigative activities:
- Admire the gemstones with a magnifying glass and copy them on paper.
- Magnets (castle ponds): what do they do?
- Coins / stamps: collect / describe and compare them.

Other activities:
- Visit to the town's tower (castle ruins).
- Conclusion with, among other things, a puppet show.
- Final party (state banquet) to conclude the theme.

Planning for individual pupils

With regard to the mathematical activities Nan indicates which mathematical aspects are dealt with. For this purpose she uses the mathematics textbook as a resource and, in this way, 'guards' the basics. Not every child, however, develops in accordance with this line and she therefore decides that a number of children will be given special attention during the coming period. This demonstrates how she deals with the heterogeneity in the group.

A more detailed planning of the activities takes place during the theme's implementation phase. The teacher uses her logbook for this purpose. Within the phase of general planning, the teacher also plans each theme for a number of individual pupils. For the theme 'Kings and Queens' she does this for Brian and Moreno with regard to mathematics. Brian is a vulnerable pupil who has considerable difficulty with counting, among other things. Moreno, on the other hand, is quite advanced in the field of addition and subtraction. Nan wants to keep him interested in mathematical activities. She carefully follows an activity approach and holds on to the narrative of the playing child.

The following schemes represent her plans for these two third-grade pupils:

Special attention plan

Name: Brian   Period: Sept. - Nov.1999
Points of activity   *Reflection*

Points of activity	Reflection
Which special activities do I want to undertake?	*Progress of the activities*
Game activities • fish game • Queen, what time is it? • castle game	
What do I observe while guiding (which impulses, help)? • doing a lot of things together and showing things • one jump is one count • focusing on solving things together • adding new counting methods and learning to arrange	*How did I assist?*
What results do I have in mind? • learning synchronised counting to 20 • becoming capable of recognising and writing numeric symbols • becoming more self-confident • adopting a problem-solving attitude	*What results / benefits did this have?*

Points of special interest for follow-up:

Special attention plan

Name: Moreno	Period: Sept. - Nov.1999
Points of activity	*Reflection*

Which special activities do I want to undertake?	*Progress of the activities*
Game activities	
• treasure hunt	
• drawing maps	
What do I observe while guiding (which impulses, help)?	*How did I assist?*
• stimulating working together and completing things	
• reflecting and orientating together on determining a new activity	
What results do I have in mind?	
• mathematics should become / remain challenging	
• learning to make representations (maps)	*What results / benefits did this have?*
• exploring / structuring sequences of numbers up to 100.	

Points of special interest for follow-up:

Implementation of the theme

From mid-September, all kinds of theme-related activities are dealt with during the daily play-work periods. The following are some examples resulting from all these activities, particularly with regard to mathematics. We followed Nan's guidance of Brian and Moreno in this respect. During these seven weeks she plans her guided activities for the two boys, specifically focused on possible follow-up activities. In this way, she wants to gain better insight into the learning processes of these pupils. Of course, mathematics is not the only issue she works on. She conducts basically the same teaching strategy with all pupils in all areas of the curriculum.

Brian is enthusiastic about the castle game. In cooperation with other children and the teacher a castle was copied as realistically as possible. It looks beautiful! Paths have been laid in the castle gardens, with arrows indicating directions. The children turned it into a game. Sometimes you have to go back a few places and at other times you move up at least five places, just like a game of snakes and ladders! Who is the first one to be back at the castle: the king or the queen?

Moreno picked up Nan's suggestion to make a treasure map and wants to make a second one with coordinates that point to the treasure. A few other children also find this very interesting. Nan wants to start working with Brian and Moreno and considers what she wants to know and do (on Thursday 7 October).

Daily plan and reflection in the logbook

The logbook is a means for short-term planning. Teachers use it to contemplate their own actions and to (continue to) focus on the individual development of the pupils. The logbook is simple in shape and comprises two sections: the range of activities offered / the plans on one side and a report / reflection on the other side (see also chapter 8, figure 8.5). Nan plans her joint activities with (small groups of) pupils under the heading 'guidance' in her logbook. At the end of each day she reflects on these joint activities and draws her conclusions for follow-up activities. She registers this under 'reflection / follow-up' in her logbook.

Her logbook of Thursday 7 October looks as follows:

Thursday 7 October 1999

Plan

- Circle:
  - the king who lost his crown
  - counting (blocks / silent counting)

● Play-work times:	- make a castle room	Dax, Remco
	- castle game	Lonneke
	- treasure island	Esmee
	- label words	Katja, Laura, Lois
	- small building table	Juliet
	- office game	
	- computer (text)	Brian, Remco
	- sand table	
	(The other children are free in choosing their activities)	

- Afternoon circle:
  - letter game

Guidance	Reflection / follow-up

• Brian with the castle game
  - observation point: synchronised counting
  - my role: play together / assist
	1. He really enjoys it and has almost mastered synchronised counting. Last week he failed to do so.
	
	Brian counts the dots on both dice all the time. He does not quite understand all number images. When asked to continue counting, he can only do it with my help.
	
	follow-up: do together number images, dice and continued counting.
	N.B. He has played Bingo with Niko and recognises numeric symbols 1 up to 10!

• Moreno together with Esmee, Lois and Janiel
  make treasure map and determine coordinates
  Moreno can explain his work to the other children: how does he do this? does he find it interesting?
  my role: if necessary, help him to listen to others.
	2. Moreno explains things in a calm and firm manner. The others accept this. I did not have to assist. He produced two treasure maps himself.
	
	follow-up: add texts to the maps and a list of coordinates, if possible.

This day's logbook shows clearly which points of special interest Nan uses. In the planning component she indicates each time:
- which activities she is going to undertake;
- for which pupils these actvities are meant;
- which observation points she applies;
- what her role will be in the activities.

In the section 'reflection / follow-up' she considers:
- the progress of the activities;
- the meaning these activities have for the pupils;
- observations she considers indicative for possible proximal developments.

On the basis of these reflections she draws conclusions for a possible range of follow-up activities.

Evaluation of development

While working on this theme there will be moments when Brian and Moreno receive focused guidance. As a result, Nan knows exactly which follow-up activities these boys require. If there are important developmental moments to be observed, she writes this down in these children's diaries; in the course of this theme she wants to help the two boys to achieve something in their (broad) mathematical development, therefore she makes a list of results for them upon the completion of the theme.

At the end of the theme period she first reflects on the 'special attention plan'. She considers the planned activity points and writes down the following:

Special attention plan

Name: Brian	Period: Sept. - Nov.1999
Activity points	Reflection
Which special activities do I want to undertake?	Progress of the activities
Game activities ● fish game ● Queen, what time is it? ● castle game	Brian joined in enthusiastically He increasingly works together in a focused manner and chooses more consciously (no longer 'wanders'!)
What do I observe while guiding (what impulses, help)? ● doing a lot of things together and show things ● one jump is one count ● focusing on solving things together ● adding new counting methods and learning to arrange	How did I assist? It is difficult for me to understand Brian / to grasp his 'track'. Sometimes I go too fast for him. I will pay extra attention to this with a view to his self-confidence.
What results do I have in mind? ● learning synchronised counting to 20 ● becoming capable of recognising and writing numeric symbols ● becoming more self-confident ● adopting a problem-solving attitude	What results / benefits did this have? ● succeeded in synchronised counting to 20 ● he recognises numeric symbols up to 10, beyond 10 the numbers 12-13-14 are difficult (pronunciation); ● writing symbols is difficult for him (motor dysfunction) ● he is more confident ● he no longer cries!

Points of special interest for follow-up:
- practise on writing numeric symbols
- recognise numeric symbols beyond 10 with the aid of the structure of numbers

Special attention plan

Name: *Moreno* **Activity points**	Period: Sept. - Nov.1999 **Reflection**
Which special activities do I want to undertake?	*Progress of the activities*

Game activities
    ● treasure hunt
    ● draw maps
	Moreno really wanted to join in and was also a support to others

What do I observe while guiding (what impulses, help)?
    ● stimulating working together and completing things
    ● reflecting and orientating together on / determining a new activity
	How did I assist?
	I basically offered suggestions and helped him to get started. I noticed that he can do a lot by himself. Perhaps I should let him take the initiative more often and then 'negotiate' so that it becomes clear what and how things need to be continued.

What results do I have in mind?
    ● mathematics should become / remain challenging
    ● learning to make representations (maps)
    ● exploring / structuring sequences of numbers up to 100.
	What results / benefits did this have?
	    ● Moreno is enthusiastic and open to 'new' things (i.e. coordinates)
	    ● he makes drawings and maps, not always two-dimensional
	    ● he knows the sequence of numbers up to 100 and the structure of numbers up to 100.

Points of special interest for follow-up:
- make accurate drawings / maps > reflect on it together
- continue counting to 100 (add an empty line of numbers?), also with extra attention for divisions up to 10

These forms are added to the children's diaries. For each child in the classroom there is a diary in which the details of their individual development are registered.

The teacher has an observation model available for each core activity. These models have five categories:
- meanings and motives;
- developmental perspective of the activity;
- development of language and thinking;
- broad development;
- specific knowledge and skills.

The observation model (icluding these categories) offer the teacher starting points for concept-driven evaluation of the pupils' development.

Nan puts the forms 'special attention plan' in Brian's and Moreno's diaries. She makes notes of the planned joint activities during this theme phase. These notes involve 7 October, 18 October and 2 November. Finally, Nan summarises a few things focused on Brian's and Moreno's future development.

Brian A.

CHILDREN'S DIARY
Mathematical activities

7 October	His synchronised counting is constantly improving (fish game) and he recognises the numeric symbols up to 10.
18 October	His synchronised counting up to 20 is really good! He enjoys his own development. Brian is also starting to recognise numeric symbols up to 30.
2 November	He is beginning to understand the structure of numbers up to 20. Writing the numeral symbols is difficult for him

N.B. See 'special attention plan' period September – November 1999. Brian's skills have improved substantially. It is important that he has become much more confident, he has learnt to work together with others and his behaviour has become more direct He really wants to improve himself in mathematics.

Moreno J.

CHILDREN'S DIARY
Mathematical activities

7 October	Moreno has made two treasure maps with coordinates. He finds it very interesting and understands it well. He also helps others.
18 October	He made a drawing plus a diagram and text for his lorry. He produced it (almost) independently and in a dedicated way. He recognised shapes (circle–square–rectangle).
2 November	Moreno worked with the bars up to 100. His number orientation (sequences and structure) up to 100 is fine. He does his additions himself, also beyond ten, and does it by counting up

N.B. See 'special attention plan' period September – November 1999 Moreno is very interested in mathematical activities and has many skills (counts to 100!). He is investigative, but has to learn to reflect on his results such as drawings / maps. Cooperation with me is necessary in this respect (in order to 'negotiate').

Benefits for the pupils and for the teacher

A few years ago, Nan used to work from mathematics books with her third group pupils every day; each child worked on the same page. Mathematical activities were 'separated' from the theme, unlike, for example, reading-writing activities. This caused more and more 'friction', with Nan as well as among the children. The current working methods are much more appealing to Nan and to the pupils. Mathematics now is a functional tool for problem solving. Mathematics has become much more interesting for both parties.

What are the differences compared with a few years ago? Summarised:

For the pupils:

- they can 'progress' and experience continuity; they learn through transformation of participation
- contexts and goal-orientated activities are important for learning
- mathematics is experienced as being functional
- the connection with the rich, day-to-day reality is preserved
- mathematical activities themselves become increasingly interesting.

For the teacher:

- mathematics education in meaningful contexts
- cross-reference of mathematical subjects / subject areas ("mathematics across the curriculum")
- cohesion between broad and specific goals
- focused on 'the growth' of children / flexible planning
- cohesion with other activities

In this classroom, learning mathematics is connected with the pupils' personal motives and interests. In this way, learning mathematics is more like constructing a 'text' that was commonly experienced and understood (Burton, 1996). The 'narratives' that children build up regarding their problem solutions and about 'mathematics' is seen as an important outcome of this way of working with children. The knowledge and skills acquired do not only have a cultural aspect (the subject of mathematics) but also a personal aspect because it is not 'imposed on' the pupil, but it is the result of working together actively in meaningful activities. The pupils are also given a responsibility for their own learning process. The teacher knows this will lead to better results for the pupils and she also has the tools available to give shape to mathematics education in this way. The teacher is capable of stimulating each individual's learning processes adequately within a learning community. Essentially, the teacher and the pupils share commitments of that community.

We have seen in Nan's classroom, that there is no direct mechanical mathematics instruction left. "Mathematics is there to be experienced and to be enjoyed, just like reading, writing, doing handicrafts, drawing, singing, breathing, as part of integrated education", to quote Hans Freudenthal (Treffers, 1992).

But mathematics education within a coherent range of activities is also desirable in groups three and upwards (seven years and older). In this respect, teachers are fortunately not left empty-handed, because the educational-pedagogical concept of Basic Development and the teaching methodology of realistic mathematics offer an ample basis and, as a result, a firm foundation. Consequently, it is a requirement for sound mathematics education focused on integrated mathematical development that you should know your pedagogical concept and know the subject (mathematics and its history)! Teachers should familiarise themselves thoroughly with the subject and sources (such as mathematics programmes). They should know:

- that mathematics in essence is a problem-solving activity, and as such related to language
- that the use of relations and the representation of reality are important mathematical features
- which subject areas with corresponding core objectives are being distinguished
- which key teaching points and interim targets are dealt with in this respect
- that technical mastery of arithmetical operations is not the main or only outcome of mathematics education; mathematical narratives are important as well
- that heterogeneity in a classroom can be a source for individual development, if the teacher manages to deal appropriately and sensitively with each pupil's meanings and interests.

References

Bruner, J.S. (1996). *The culture of education*. London: Harvard University Press.

Burton, L. (1996). *The implications of a narrative approach to the learning of mathematics*; paper for the conference 'The Growing Mind' in Geneva, Switzerland.

Fijma, N. &. Vink, H. (1998). *Op jou kan ik rekenen* [I can count on you]. Assen: van Gorcum.

Freudenthal, H.F. (1991). *Revisiting Mathematics Education*. Dordrecht: Kluwer.

Janssen-Vos, F. (1997). *Basisontwikkeling in de onderbouw* [Basic development in junior primary classes]. Assen: van Gorcum.

Janssen-Vos, F., Pompert B. , & Schiferli T. (1998). *Handelingsgericht observeren, registreren and evalueren van Basisontwikkeling* [Activity-oriented observation, registration and evaluation of basic development]. Utrecht: APS.

Oers, B. van (1996a). The dynamics of school learning. In: J. Valsiner & H. G. Voss (Eds), *The structure of learning processes* (pp. 205-228). Norwood, NJ: Ablex.

Oers, B. van (1996b). Learning mathematics as a meaningful activity. In: L. Steffe, P. Nesher, P. Cobb, G. Goldin & B. Greer (Eds), *Theories of mathematical learning* (pp. 91-115). Hillsdale, NJ: Erlbaum.

Oers, B. van (1999). Teaching opportunities in play. In: M. Hedegaard & J. Lompscher (eds), *Learning activity and development.* (pp. 268-289). Aarhus: Aarhus University Press.

Pinar, W.F., Reynolds, W.M. Slattery P., & Taubman P.M. (1995). *Understanding Curriculum: an introduction to the study of historical and contemporary curriculum discourses.* New York: Peter Lang.

Tharp, R.G., Estrada, P., Dalton, S. S., & Yamauchi L.A. (2000). *Teaching transformed: achiev-*

ing excellence, fairness, inclusion, and harmony. Colorado: Westview Press.

Treffers, A. (1992). *Terug naar de toekomst; reken-wiskundeonderwijs voor de basisschool* [Back to the future, mathematics education for primary school] 1972-2002. In: F. Goffree, A. Treffers and J. de Lange, *Rekenen anno 2002* (pp. 11-35) [Mathematics in the year 2002]. Culemborg: Technipress.

[11]

Institutional contexts and language use in classroom conversations in the early grades

Eelje F. Dijk

The narrative

The word *narrative* can be used to refer to a story people tell about, for example, educational practices (see chapter 1). In this chapter, I will focus on a *narrative* about the organisation of 'effective' whole classroom conversations. These conversations are dialogues between teacher and pupils in which the pupils are stimulated to use language actively and abundantly. The *narrative* can be summarised as follows: *'conversational strategies like questioning (e.g. open questions) and revoicing should stimulate pupils' active language use during whole classroom conversations'*. However, in the realm of educational practices, such strategies, mostly deliberately applied by the teacher, do not always result in the desired active language involvement of the pupils during classroom conversations. Teachers and educators may attribute the low involvement to the pupils; they have a small vocabulary, they are not very fluent in their language use, or they are not used to being engaged in such dialectical whole classroom conversations. There is, however, more than that. A teacher can steer a conversation in a certain, not always intended, direction without being aware of it. Also, the educational philosophy of the school can influence the kinds of conversations that occur between a teacher and the pupils. In my view, a classroom conversation is not just an isolated activity. The conversation is embedded in the culture of a classroom, a lesson, a school, an educational system, a society. I refer to these aspects as the institutional context in which the conversations take place. In that context, we can possibly find an explanation as to why the conversational strategies of the teacher do not always enhance active language use of the pupils, as the *narrative* assumes.

In this chapter I address this question by presenting a small classroom analysis based on my observations during whole classroom conversations. By using a multifaceted model, I attempt to show that this problem must be studied within the social-cultural context. Finally, we formulate a new narrative on classroom conversations

Theoretical orientation

The theoretical orientation of my study has three main parts. The first part is a concise theoretical overview of Vygotsky's theory and an expansion of his ideas. The second part describes the Vygotsky-based approach to (early childhood) education in the Netherlands, called Developmental Education (and Basic Development). Finally, the third part consists of a few theoretical notions of language use, which I call here conversational strategies.

Vygotsky
The study presented in this chapter is primarily based on the ideas of Vygotsky and his school. The social context and the role of language are two important principles underlying the Vygotskian framework. The social context is a crucial condition for development, because it is essential for the acquisition of mental processes. In joint activities, children improve their mental processes by using them in interactions with others (classmates, teachers). Language plays a central role and is itself a mental tool that children acquire in most joint activities. Language enables logical thinking and learning new behaviours. The role of the teacher in these joint activities can become clear by defining a key concept of Vygotsky's theory. This key concept is the *zone of proximal development* and is defined as *'the distance between the actual developmental level as determined by independent problem solving and the potential development as determined through problem solving under adult guidance or in collaboration with more capable peers'* (Vygotsky, 1978).
As you can see, Vygotsky claims that learning processes start on the interpersonal level, thus in the social context, but he also acknowledges that eventually their function will become a quality of the individual himself. In order to articulate the social aspects of individual qualities, I have placed this Vygotskian framework in a broader social cultural dimension by incorporating some ideas of Wertsch, Cole and Gauvain.

Sociocultural theory
According to many psychologists, human memory, perception and cognition cannot function without an active agent. This agent executes the mental processes. If we consider agency only as a property of the individual himself, then this individual is positioned in a historical and cultural vacuum. The influence of sociocultural factors seems to be denied. Wertsch et al. (1993, 1998) have applied a sociocultural approach to agency and claim that human agency extends beyond the skin. Agency is considered a property of a dyad or a small group rather than of a single individual. This conception of 'agency' directly also entails the notion of mediational means.
In the sociocultural approach to human agency, a distinction is usually made between four levels where development of the agency is involved. The ways individuals enact a mental process depends upon the phylogenetic, sociogenetic, ontogenetic and microgenetic development of the agent. Cole (1998) also describes levels in his research on the relationship between cognitive development and formal schooling. He emphasises the fact that a complete theory of human development must take into account changes which occur, at times simultaneously, on four historical levels: the development of the species (phylogenesis), the development of human beings or culture (sociogenesis), the development of individuals (ontogenesis) and the development of particular psychological processes (microgenesis). These levels are intertwined in a complex manner.

This broader sociocultural perspective on the functioning of an individual can also be found in the ideas of Gauvain (1998). Gauvain uses the concept of developmental niche in her study of the cognitive development of young children in relation with culture. According to this concept, each development is embedded within a sociocultural context. By participating in sociocultural practices that are meaningful for us and have personal significance, we can appropriate the tools of the culture we live in. Besides, these practices reflect the values and beliefs of that culture. Through participation we can appropriate the ways of thinking and problem solving that are meaningful within that culture. In this way, cultural values and beliefs will also guide and shape children's cognitive activities. To be able to understand, for example, what a child is doing while solving a problem, it is important to study that activity in relation with the sociocultural practices in which the child has learnt the problem-solving skills (Gauvain, 1998).

Developmental Education
Developmental Education is the name for the Vygotsky-based approach to education in the Netherlands (see for example van Oers, 1997; 1999). The most important characteristics of this educational approach are (see also Janssen-Vos, chapter 7):

- developmental education is first of all aimed at promoting children's identity development.
- developmental education is aimed at expanding and deepening children's current abilities. Children's development is not based on imposing new qualities in a forced manner, but on growth of their current abilities. In this process the zone of proximal development plays an important role.
- developmental education assigns an important role to the so-called leading activities. A leading activity is a specific type of interaction between the child and the environment that is most beneficial for developmental accomplishments. Playing is the leading activity for children aged 4-7 and productive learning is the leading activity from 7 years of age. From this developmental educational perspective, the development of children aged 4-7 must be seen as a coherent whole. In this period the transition from play to productive learning occurs. Therefore children have to develop the motive for learning during their play activities to be able to participate successfully in later learning activities. Besides, they need to develop their social competencies to be able to engage successfully in a group.
- developmental education is aimed at organising social cultural activities (and contents) that have meaning and personal significance for the children. Teachers have the responsibility to enhance the educational value of these activities and therefore it is necessary that the teachers participate in the children's activities.

Based on this approach, a curriculum strategy has been designed in the Netherlands for the early education for children aged 4-7, called Basic Development.

Basic Development

As mentioned earlier, the main educational aim of Developmental Education is to promote the children's identity development. The same applies to Basic Development. In addition, there are other important aims of this curriculum strategy. The fields in which these aims are embodied can be divided into three main categories and are described in the curriculum strategy as a system of concentric circles (see Janssen-Vos, Chapter 7). These three categories are basic feelings (self-confidence, curiosity, involvement etc.); broad developmental activities; and specific knowledge and abilities (taking into account the children's actual individual abilities). This whole system is meant to provide the teacher with guidelines for designing appropriate educational activities in the classroom (see Janssen-Vos, 1997). In general, the activities that are most beneficial for developmental accomplishments for young children (aged 4-7) are play activities, construction and expression activities, read-and-write activities, mathematical activities, and conversational activities. These activities are considered core activities in the early educational classroom practices.

Thus, a classroom conversation is more than a verbal joint activity for children aged 4-7. It is a specific type of interaction between the child and the sociocultural environment, which leads to particular developmental accomplishments. The interaction between the teacher and the pupils within this activity is crucial. In this interaction the teacher creates zones of proximal development together with the pupils. Within these zones the teacher must support the interactions by using certain conversational strategies, like *revoicing* and *questioning*. I will elaborate the latter point in the next paragraph.

Conversational strategies

In classrooms where the organisation of the educational (joint) activities is based on the concept of Developmental Education, the role of the classroom teachers is crucial, especially with regard to their language use. The teachers use language explicitly in the form of the so-called conversational strategies to promote the interaction processes in the classroom, and particularly to make use of the child's own language and language abilities. They can employ for example the strategy of revoicing (O'Connor & Michaels, 1996), which means something like articulating and re-uttering a pupil's utterance within a classroom conversation. *Revoicing* can have different functions: clarifying the content or relevance of the utterance, aligning different positions toward the topic of conversation, introducing something new, repeating the utterance to emphasise the importance of it, and relating the utterance to educational aims. The pupils themselves can also adopt this strategy and by doing so they learn to clarify thoughts and utterances, to summarise them and to understand that their ideas and intentions are not always clear to others and vice-versa.

Questioning is another conversational strategy teachers can use in classrooms to enhance the pupils' language during conversational activities. This conversational strategy is rather complex, because it includes a variety of strategies. In typical educational practices, teachers ask the questions. A distinction can be made between the so-called known answer questions (closed questions) and the questions that do not anticipate one right answer (open questions). Theoretically spoken, closed questions have several disadvantages. Teachers can control and structure (see Edwards & Mercer, 1987) the conversations at the expense of the pupils' active participation in the interactions; closed questions do not optimally promote the language development of the pupils. They don't seem to be appropriate for use in classroom conversations that are organised according to the concept of Developmental Education, due to their focus on mastering fixed school knowledge, rather than personally meaningful problem solving with the help of language. Open questions, on the other hand, seem to promote the active use of language by the pupils, to stimulate pupils to give their own opinion, and to enhance their conversational and social skills. Open questions challenge pupils to participate in a 'language game' that aims at meaningful problem solving by applying their own insights, discussing divergences, and looking for consensus. Under the appropriate conditions, open questions trigger a more playful way of dealing with language and may stimulate the new genre of inquisitive discursive learning. As such, teaching on the basis of open questions allows pupils to use their imagination and to act on their own interests and meanings. This evidently fits in with the pedagogical narrative of the playing child.

The attitude of the teacher is very important in this respect. For example, he or she is responsible for appropriate understandable language input during classroom conversations, for giving enough space and time for discussion, and for enhancing the pupils' active and critical participation (by being an active participant and responsive listener and by promoting pupils' initiatives).

Methodology

To analyse the role of the conversational strategies of the teacher in early education, I used a multifaceted model. This model is based on the ideas of at least four important researchers: Cole, Wertsch, Hicks and Wells. All of them conduct their studies within a Vygotskian perspective and try to expand this perspective by placing it within a broader sociocultural stance.

Hicks (1996) studies children's classroom learning from a Vygotskian perspective and emphasises the role language plays in this process. Her study focuses on the social activity of journal writing and she uses a multifaceted model for 'contextual inquiries'. She claims that participants in sociocultural activities are engaged in various social discourses, at times simultaneously. The general framework of her inquiries comprises the following levels (for more detailed information I refer to her publication):

Level 1:   refers to the sociocultural and historical context of social activity;
Level 2:   refers to the course of the activity itself;
Level 3:   refers to the contribution(s) of the individual child to the activity from his or her own developmental level;

Level 4:   refers to the development of the child over time.

I left out of consideration the fourth level of Hicks' model, because this level is not relevant to my research, due to the relatively short time for my classroom observations. An adapted version of this framework (three levels) in combination with the four levels of development described by Cole and Wertsch led to my model for the analysis of language use in classrooms.

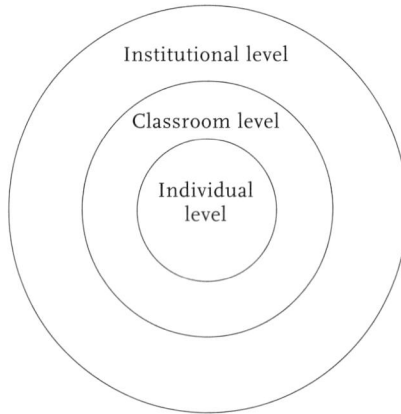

Figure 11.1: Levels of analysis

The data for my study are drawn from video-recorded observations in classrooms where the educational environment is organised according to the concept of Developmental Education. The classroom conversations in 2 combined classes (Year-3 and Year-4; 6-8 year-olds; 2 teachers) were the focus of this study. These conversations were held as part of a language-oriented project of the National Centre for Language Education in the Netherlands. Together with the qualities and abilities of the classroom teachers, these situational features can be situated on the first level of my model. On the second level, I focused on the language used in the conversations and particularly on the conversational strategies of the teachers. Studying the influence of the teacher's language use is relevant to the microgenetic development of the conversation. This development is embedded in the sociocultural context (institutional level) and must be studied within that context. On the third level, I studied the individual contributions of pupils to the conversations. The analysis on the third level indicates that pupils are engaged in various contexts, at times simultaneously, within an activity. That way, the third level touches both the microgenetic and the ontogenetic development of the conversations within the sociocultural context and the context of the classroom activity (institutional and classroom level).

1- The INSTITUTIONAL LEVEL or sociocultural historical context
On this level we address, for example, the question What is the broader sociocultural context in which the conversational activities are embedded?
Within this level, we could look at the school and the classrooms as institutions and analyse the theoretical assumptions on the basis of which for example a teacher enacts. I call this the microgenetic dimension of the institutional level. We could also look at the sociogenetic dimension of this institutional level, that is the classroom activity.

2- The CLASSROOM LEVEL
In this analysis we study the activity of classroom conversations and address for example the question What happens during classroom conversations?
Within this level, we could look at the influence of conversational strategies, like revoicing and questioning, on the course of the conversations. I call this the microgenetic dimension of the classroom level.

3- The INDIVIDUAL LEVEL
On this level we study the contributions an individual child makes to the conversation(s). When we analyse within this level the contribution(s) a child makes in reaction to others or in relation to the subject of the conversation, I call this the microgenetic dimension of the individual level. A spontaneous contribution of an individual child without any relation to the subject or reactions of others is studied on what I call the ontogenetic dimension of the individual level.

For my analysis of classroom conversation, I have divided the conversation fragments into smaller sequences to clearly structure the analysis. In this way I hope to find out how the teacher stimulates the pupils' language use. Which conversational strategies does he use? How often does he use these strategies compared to the pupils' language use? For this analysis, I used some of the ideas of Wells (1999).
Wells' research project focused on the role of language use in joint activities within a Vygotskian perspective. Wells calls the smallest unit of analysis a move, for example, a question or an answer. The smallest unit for analysing discourse in a functional manner is broader, and consists of both a question and an answer. This is what Wells calls an exchange. Often such an exchange also comprises a third follow-up move. This three-part exchange structure is called the IRF-sequence. In its prototypical form: an Initiation (I), usually a teacher question, is first followed by a pupil's Response (R), and then by a Follow-up move (F) from the teacher in which he or she provides some form of feedback to the pupil's response. Wells further makes a distinction between nuclear exchanges and bound exchanges. The so-called nuclear exchanges can stand alone, which means that they can contribute new content to the conversation. A bound exchange on the other hand is in someway dependent on a nuclear exchange and cannot stand alone. The unit that consists of a nuclear exchange and any exchanges that are bound to it, is what Wells calls a sequence. According to him, the sequence has the greatest functional significance in studying the role of language in joint activities. I

used the division in sequences to keep my analysis functional with a view to answering my research question. It is difficult to define the boundaries between the different sequences. In my analysis, a dependent initiation move, which in Wells' terminology would be a part of the bound exchange, is called a follow-up move. This is due to the purpose of my analysis. On the basis of the sequences I can find out who takes the initiative in the sequence and who is closing it, who structures the sequence and who makes the follow-up move. Besides, I can study the role of the teacher compared to that of the pupils. That way, I hope to get a better understanding of the influence of the language use of the teacher in practice within classroom conversations.

In the original study, a total of 10 sequences were analysed. Within the scope of this chapter, I will present the analysis of two examples of these sequences. The conclusion relates to the analysis of all sequences.

Outcomes

At this point I would like to introduce two sequences of discourse from a conversational activity in an elementary classroom. This activity occurred in a combined Year-3/Year-4 class within a unit about Indians the class had been working on for several days. One morning after recess the teacher returned the conversation to this unit. The text is a translation from the original Dutch transcripts.

Table 11.1: Closed question sequence:
T = Teacher; S = Simon
I = Initiation; R = Response; F = Follow up

1. T	Well, who can tell us now; we are working for two or eh more than one week on a certain unit. What unit do we work on then, Simon?	closed question; structuring	I
2. S	Indians	short answer	R
3. T	(nod yes) We work on Indians, very well.	responsive tone	F

The teacher starts the discussion by asking a closed question What unit do we work on then? and takes the initiative to this sequence (initiation). The result of this closed question is a short answer from the pupil in the second move (response): Indians. In the third move (follow-up) the teacher evaluates the response of the pupil in terms of right and wrong: we work on Indians, very well. The teacher controls the sequence.

The teacher's personal educational view or own thinking defines the classroom culture to a great extent. The teacher of this class told me that she attaches great importance to the presence of structure in the classroom. For example, she believes that it is necessary that the pupils focus on the subject the class is talking about or working at, that they do not talk out of turn and raise hands before speaking. This sequence can be seen as a reflection of this striving. What we see here is the influence of the teacher's own view on the course of the conversational activity. We can also say that the 'theory' from which the teacher starts (microgenetic dimension of the institutional level) influences the conversation. Here we descend to the classroom level and observe that a complex dialectical relation exists between the institutional and classroom level. Not only the teacher, but also the pupils react to the characteristics of the culture of their classroom, the educational system or the educational concept of the school. Pupils have their own views and ideas, for example on how they are supposed to react in a certain situation in the classroom setting. Subsequently, those views affect the interaction patterns between teacher and pupils. Here the dialectical relation can be observed between the individual and the classroom level as well as between the individual and institutional level.

Further, the educational concept of the school influences the activity. The conversational activity and the classroom itself are embedded within the institutional context (organised according to the concept of Educational Development and as part of the language-oriented project). Within the scope of promoting the pupils' language development, emphasis is laid on the importance of the teacher's understandable language input to students. One of the requirements for understandable language input in conversational activities is that it should be quite clear what the discussion is about. Pupils can follow a conversation better when they know and understand the topic of conversation. This can also be seen as a part of structuring the activity. With an eye on creating understandable language input at the beginning of a conversation, the above-described structured sequence might be a logical reaction.

And finally, the educational system plays a role. Developmental Education schools and the National Centre for Language Education try to find alternatives for the traditional way of organising classroom conversations. Traditionally, conversations are mostly forms of monologues by the teachers. The teachers ask the questions to find out if the pupils have learned something from the lessons given. Interaction is an important aspect of the educational practices in Developmental Education schools, and teachers and educators try to find ways to establish a balance between the input of the pupils and that of the teachers during classroom conversations.

In short, other factors than simply a starting question from the teacher influence the course of a classroom conversation. The closed question of the teacher in the beginning of the conversation results in a short answer from the pupil, but this effect can not only be explained by referring to the conversational strategy used by the teacher. The next fragment shows more clearly that a classroom conversation is influenced by several aspects of the institutional context.

Table 11.2: Open question sequence
T = Teacher; S = Simon; D = Dave; E = Eric
I = Initiation; R = Response; F = Follow-up

4. T	Eh, there we have a book (points to the edge of the blackboard). We are talking about Indians. What do we already know about Indians?	a sort of open question	I
5. S	A lot.	short answer	R
6. T	(to Simon) you say: "a lot". What do we for example know about the Indians, Simon?	revoicing and open question	F
7. S	Eh, ehm, that they in the, in the tent in the middle, ehh, have a campfire.	elaborated answer	R
8. T	Yes, very well. (T gives time for discussion)	responsive tone	F
9. S	And to, and to, and with the skin the, eh the, from the house...	elaborated answer	R
10.D	(interrupts) to close the inside.	'assistance' form another pupil; short contribution	I
11. S	Yeah.	responsive tone	R
12. T	Yes, help him a moment, Dave, why?	responsive tone; open question	F
13. D	Those buffalo, eh, eh, skins they are cut off and then they make clothes from it and put it on the inside of the tents when it is very cold.	elaborated answer	R
14. E	And then they are going to eat them.	initiative	I
15. T	Yes thus, that buffalo is very important for the Indians, very good. Thus we know [...] about the Indians on which animals they live and why.	revoicing move 14	F

In the fourth move the teacher takes again the initiative to the sequence. This time the teacher asks a more open question *(initiation)*: *what do we already know about the Indians?* The pupil's response is very short *(response): a lot.* The follow-up move (move 6) from the teacher consists of two strategies: 'revoicing' and 'questioning'. First, the teacher repeats and rebroadcasts the pupil's response to reach a wider audience than the pupil did: *you say 'a lot'.* Then, the teacher goes on asking a question to give this pupil the opportunity to solidify and concretise his contribution and to elaborate it: *what do we for example know about the Indians?* After the more elaborated response from the pupil, the teacher evaluates this with a responsive tone to give the pupil more time and space to tell more: *yes very well...*followed by a long pause. This follow-up move (move 8) again consists of more than a simple evaluation of the pupil's answer. The pupil understands the teacher's reaction and elaborates his contribution (move 9). In the first sequence (see table 11.1) we saw that a closed question resulted in a short answer from the pupil. We are analysing on the microgenetic dimension. In the second sequence (see table 11.2) the teacher starts with a more open question. In view of the teacher's assumption that open questions lead to active language involvement of the pupils in the conversation, we might expect more elaborated answers from the pupils in the second move. However, we see that the pupil in this case gives a (unexpected) short response here. Thus we can see that it is not only the form of the question that influences the conversation. To what else can we refer to explain this?

An activity itself – and also a classroom conversation- is embedded in a sociocultural context, and the rules that hold for that context influence the activities within that context. Therefore we wonder which rules here (probably without being aware of it) influence the course of the conversation. Maybe the pupils are used to traditional classroom conversations in which the teacher asks the questions. Questions that anticipate only one right answer, the answer the teacher already knows. A possible explanation here might be that this pupil is used to these questions and that he therefore gives short answers. It is probably a consolidated style of questioning and answering.
This conversation takes place in a school where the teachers work on improving the classroom conversations and interaction patterns during those conversations and the teacher knows about the importance of stimulating active language use of the pupils. Therefore she uses consciously a conversation strategy to enhance the pupil's active contributions. However, as we can see in the second fragment, active language use on the pupils' part can not always be stimulated only by using such strategies: sometimes pupils continue giving relatively short and closed answers, without any tendency to elaborate, or to use exploratory talk. Other factors, like the social rules that hold for the classroom, seem to influence the conversation.

Until the tenth move it seems that the teacher structures and controls the conversation. In the tenth move we see that one of the pupils, Dave, completes the contribution of the other pupil, Simon (who seems to stammer despite the fact that the teacher gives him enough time). Dave knows that he is not allowed to speak without raising his hand first and his contribution is short. He has the opportunity to speak (there is silence), but the rules that hold for the classroom (do not speak out of turn, raise your hand when you want to say something) prevent him from saying much. However, this contribution does influence the course of the conversation, because the teacher encourages Dave to help his peer. Instead of rendering assistance herself, it is the pupil who does this. Dave takes over the role of the teacher. In the first instance, Dave gives a short reaction, because he actually breaks the communication rules of the classroom. Only when the teacher herself encourages this peer assistance explicitly and gives time to Dave to react, a more elaborated reaction follows.
On the one hand, social rules in the classroom might explain to a great extent the short answers and short contributions of the pupils. On the other, the course of the conversation in this classroom is also defined by the principles of the Vygotsky-based approach / Developmental Education and the language-oriented project. Besides, we can

see that the teacher not only stimulates the language use of the pupils, but also the course of the classroom conversation. Pupils take the opportunity to react to each other's contributions and to explicate them. The teacher gives priority to stimulating the contributions of the pupils over maintaining the social communication rules that hold for the classroom. The pupil's interruption and consequently his breaking of the rules do not interfere with the intentions of the teacher or the conversation, and probably therefore, the teacher stimulates the pupil to elaborate his contribution. The teacher still seems to structure the activity. Thus, the language used by the teacher not only influences the pupils' language use, but also the course of the conversation.

Conclusion

In view of the results of the analysis presented here, the narrative summarised in the beginning of this chapter, *'conversational strategies like questioning (e.g. open questions) and revoicing should stimulate pupils' active language use during whole classroom conversations'* seems to be too narrow and just a part of the teachers' theoretical assumptions. The results of my study show clearly that pupils' active language use during classroom conversations is not only determined by the conversational strategies deliberately applied by the teacher. Other strategies that arise unconsciously from rules, norms, values and views influence the conversational activities. The same applies to the way pupils react during classroom conversations, which is also defined to a great extent by the social rules that hold for the classroom. Using open questions is no guarantee for optimal verbal interaction processes during the classroom conversations. Also, the situations that have to do with the agreements (implicit and explicit) within the educational context, must give space for such interaction patterns. Besides, an area of tension often exists between advisable consensus (based on the official teaching plan) and 'free' interaction processes in the classroom. When the teacher is more aware of the implicit rules that hold for his or her classroom and when he or she pays attention to the institutional context more deliberately, conversational activities that do not seem to be running optimally can be analysed from a different angle. That is, in my view, the next step in the direction of creating optimal interaction processes in the classroom in which the pupils will use language actively and abundantly to develop their language potentials. Until that time, I would like to formulate the following new narrative: *'Despite teachers' efforts language development of pupils is not always successful. Conversational strategies like questioning (e.g. open questions) and revoicing influence the course of classroom conversations, but the effects in terms of more or less active language use from the part of the pupils must be studied within the institutional context'.*

References

Cole. M. (1998). Cognitive development and formal schooling - the evidence from cross-cultural research. In: D. Faulkner, K. Littleton, & M. Woodhead, (Eds.), *Learning relationships in the classroom* (pp. 31-53). London: Routledge.

Edwards, D. & Mercer, N. (1987). *Common knowledge -the development of understanding in the classroom*. London: Routledge.

Gauvain, M. (1998). Thinking in niches: sociocultural influences on cognitive development. In: D. Faulkner, K. Littleton, & M. Woodhead, (Eds.), *Learning relationships in the classroom* (pp. 111-130). London: Routledge.

Janssen-Vos, F. (1997). *Basisontwikkeling in de onderbouw* [Basic Development in the early grades]. Assen: Van Gorcum.

O'Connor, M.C. & Michaels, S. (1996). Shifting participant frameworks: Orchestrating thinking practices in group discussion. In: D. Hicks, (Ed.), *Discourse, learning, and schooling* (pp. 63-103). Cambridge, M.A.: Cambridge University Press.

Oers, B. van (1997). Ontwikkelingsgericht onderwijs in de onderbouw: contouren van een cultuurhistorische onderwijsvisie [Developmental Education in the early grades: outlines of a cultural historical perspective on education]. In: B. van Oers, & F. Janssen-Vos, (Eds.), *Visies op onderwijs aan jonge kinderen* [Perspectives on education for young children] (pp.53-71). Assen: Van Gorcum.

Oers, B. van (1999). Education for the improvement of cultural participation. In: G. Brougère, & S.Rayna, (Eds.), *Culture, Childhood and Preschool Education* (pp. 217-238). Paris: Unesco.

Vygotsky, L.S. (1978). *Mind in Society: the development of higher psychological processes*. Cambridge, MA: Harvard University Press.

Wells, G. (1999). *Dialogic Inquiry. Toward a Sociocultural Practice and Theory of Education*. Cambridge: Cambridge University Press.

Wertsch, J.V., Tulviste, P. & Hagstrom, F. (1993). A sociocultural approach to agency. In: E.A. Forman, N. Minick, & C.A Stone, (Eds.), *Contexts for learning* (pp. 336-356). New York, Oxford: Oxford University Press.

Wertsch, J.V. & Tulviste, P. (1998). L.S. Vygotsky and contemporary developmental psychology. In: D. Faulkner, K. Littleton, & M. Woodhead, (Eds.), *Learning relationships in the classroom* (pp. 13-30). London: Routledge.

[12]

The roles of the teacher
in a play-based curriculum
in special education

Isabel Peters

Interaction is a powerful educative tool for promoting development. Children's development takes place in and through this interaction. Obviously, the teacher plays an important role in it. She is the one who has to make social-cultural activities available for and accessible to the children. In these activities, a zone of proximal development can be created. This Vygotskian concept refers to the developmental potentials that emerge from interactions with others. Interaction creates the possibility for a child to co-operate with others to benefit from higher intellectual levels and, by means of 'imitation' to make transitions from his actual level of performance to new actions he has not yet mastered. The zone is a product of the interaction between the child and an adult or a more competent peer. The teacher can thereby stimulate the development of her pupils by working in their zones of proximal development. This is important for every child, but especially for children with a handicap and/or learning problems, for they generally show less involvement in activities and have less intellectual interests. They therefore need extra stimulation in order to develop.

During my participatory observations in early special education classrooms, I noticed that teachers can stimulate the children's development by adopting several roles in the interaction with their pupils. For example roles that aim at creating togetherness, alignment of different options in a joint activity, or the role of providing appropriate renditions of the children's utterances ('revoicing'). It is important that teachers are aware of the roles they can adopt. Through the medium of literature I first tried to clarify these teacher roles by describing them and analysing their functions in the context of joint activities with children. In the last stage of this project I made a coupling between theory and practice by elaborating in a theory-driven way upon some examples that I gathered in special education classrooms.

In this chapter, I will describe three of the roles I could identify through my literature study. I start with a description of the two schools at which I did my observations, and the children who were educated there. Both schools ground their education in a Vygotskian-based approach developed in the Netherlands: 'developmental education'. Following this, I will move on to the importance of interaction and the roles that a teacher can adopt.

Developmental education

I did my participatory observations at two schools for special education in the Netherlands. The first school is located in 's-Hertogenbosch, a city in the south of the country. It is a school for children with motorical and multiple developmental handicaps. The school integrates education and rehabilitation care. It strives for the harmonious mobilization of the cognitive, physical, and social potencies of the children. The second school is located in Amsterdam and is a school for hearing-impaired children with learning problems, and for hearing children with severe language and speech problems. The children have difficulties with pronunciation, sentence structure, idea of grammar, word memory, etcetera. I observed 65 children between the age of 3 and 8. In each group there was a teacher and an assistant who took care of the education of the children. There were also several therapists who supported the development of the children.

Both schools ground their education in a Vygotsky-based approach, developed in the Netherlands; known as 'developmental education' (see chapter 7, Janssen-Vos, for a more detailed description). Developmental education assumes that children want to participate in social-cultural activities and to be involved in these activities with peers and adults. At school, teachers stage the social-cultural activities by creating a context in which children are invited to participate and are encouraged to try new actions. On the basis of close observations of her children the teacher selects and designs activity settings that are meaningful situations for them. By participating as a partner in these activities with the pupils, the teacher can create a zone of proximal development through provoking new actions that are significant for the shared activity. This creates opportunities for a child to co-operate with others and to reach a higher intellectual level. By means of such assisted 'imitations' of an activity, the child is stimulated to make transitions from his actual level of performance to new actions he has not yet mastered. It is clear from this that the zone is not a characteristic individual feature of the child. It is a product of the interaction between the child and an adult or a more knowledgeable peer. In this case, 'imitation' definitely does not mean mechanically copying, rather, it means participating in already existing social-cultural activities. For example the way the children play activities where they pretend to be other people, like a doctor or a nurse. In such role plays, children learn how to participate in activities. They learn new specific skills in a meaningful manner, all within a relevant context. It is important to keep the activity as authentic as possible. The teacher should not train individual actions separately and expect that the children in due time can put the actions together into one coherent activity. The teacher takes into account the things the children are not yet able to do, so that the activity continues to be a coherent whole. The exchange between children and adults in the zone of proximal development forms the real foundation of education and pedagogy.

Example:
The children are sitting in a circle. After the teacher has told them what they are going to do today, Carlos (5 years old) points at a book he wants to read to his classmates.

The teacher places a chair next to her, which she calls the 'reading-chair'. Carlos is a bit shy, but the teacher says that she will help him. Carlos sits down and pretends that he is reading to his classmates. He shows the book to the children. The teacher reads the text because Carlos is not able to read yet, but he finishes the sentences of the teacher. Carlos is very proud he had read the story to his classmates.

In this example you see how the teacher tries to create a zone of proximal development. Carlos wants to read a story but he is not able to do so yet. The teacher keeps the activity as authentic as possible. She gives the pupil the special reading-chair, the book, and the opportunity to finish her sentences. She assists the child with accomplishing the reading activity, by taking account of those parts the child hadn't yet mastered by that time.

It is important to involve children in activities by drawing on their actual abilities, rather than starting from their shortcomings. However, people have the tendency to put a label on children with problems and to act accordingly. A teacher who acts like this, most of the time forgets to look at the things a child can do independently by himself; instead, she will only look at the problems a child has. The expectations will not be high, as this teacher will work narrowly from the actual level of achievement of the child. The pupil notices that the teacher does not have high expectations, he gets little challenge and stimulation and consequently he will not be motivated to do his best. This works as a self-fulfilling prophecy, and the problems will only increase (Peters, 2001). This attitude of the teacher is disastrous, as children need challenges. A challenge is created when there is a certain balance between what a child thinks he can do and what the actual difficulty of an activity is. The activity shouldn't be too easy or too difficult, but slightly above the child's actual level of performance. In this way self-confidence can grow and the child can regard himself as the 'owner' of his own development and learning.

Activities have to be meaningful to the children in the first place. The teacher has to select and design these activities in such way that they are motivating and meaningful to the children. The activities have to be connected to the children's world of experiences. For young children it is important to start from their daily actions and routines, which they know from their everyday life. This also applies to children with handicaps and/or learning problems who need safety and recognition.

Children by nature have 'built-in' mechanisms for the development of symbolic behaviour (including language). On the basis of such mechanisms language comes to the fore, if the environment stimulates the children to use language as a means for communication. The children have to be shown what the possibilities of the language are. They will, for example, recognize the words of the adults or older children and start imitating them for their own communicative purposes. In special education, this process needs extra attention. The necessity of elaborated language is very important. For example children who are hearing-impaired catch fewer words from their environment than hearing children do because of their handicap. The school is the place to offer them structured language and appropriate support. If this does not happen, the children's development will get stuck, or worse, may deteriorate.

Roles of the teacher

As I pointed out above, interaction plays a crucial part in the development of children. Learning is based on a continuous exchange of thoughts or negotiation with partners. The teacher has an active, participating role in this. In joint activities the teacher encourages the participation of pupils and mediates between the meanings and motives of the children and the demands of the education.

A teacher will come closer to the meaning and motives of the children when she is able to make contact with the child and win his trust so that he wants to share his feelings, experiences and opinions with her. It is the task of the teacher to get children involved in activities and try to understand what really engages them, what is really important for them, what their motives are, and which meanings they give to activities and contents. It is important that the teacher has an affective relationship with her pupils, so that they feel the teacher's support and experience that the adult is available for them. The attitude of the teacher has to be both sensitive and responsive (Heijkant et al., 2000). Sensitivity implies that the teacher must see the signals that the children give out. She must be able to 'read' the children's expressions, see their attempts at contact and at getting involved in activities; she must find out what they mean with their acts, and what they have in mind. Therefore, sensitivity involves the observation and interpretation of the signals of the pupils and the evaluation of the emotions of the children. Responsiveness implies that the teacher does something with these signals. She lets the child know that he gets her full attention, that she understands the child, or tries to understand him. She makes clear that she is available, that it is her intention to establish a good relationship, offer him protection and all the help that he may need.

A sensitive and responsive attitude is necessary for every child, but especially for children who encounter difficulties in their development and learning. For teachers it is less self-evident and it costs them more effort to be sensitive and responsive to those children who are less open and active, and who do not seem to need much contact (Janssen-Vos, 1997). For example, children with severe language and speech problems find difficulties when expressing themselves. It is easy to feel inclined to react in a friendly way to the child without knowing what he is actually trying to tell. It seems so unkind to repeat the same question over and over, and try to get the child understood, when it is so much easier to just leave it. Instead, what the child needs to experience is that the teacher is really trying to understand him. The pupil wants to notice that he is worth listening to. If the teacher does not succeed in creating this foundation between them, it will be very hard for the children to understand what the teacher wants from them.

When interacting with children, a teacher can adopt several roles and functions. During my investigation in early special education classrooms I described the seven most commonly occurring roles and illustrated them with examples. This is not an exhausted list of commonly occurring roles nor does it mean that these roles are the predominant roles in every school. The examples show the ways in which the teachers can fulfil these roles. In this chapter, I shall discuss three of these roles and their functions: promoter of togetherness, revoicer, and activity organiser.

Togetherness

The first role is creating togetherness. According to Van Oers and Hännikäinen (2001), togetherness can be conceived as a quality of an activity that prevents the activity from breaking down when problems arise and need to be faced. On a personal level, this sense of togetherness is always connected to affective feelings. It creates a bond of solidarity in a group and the feeling that the person wants to stay a member of that group, despite problems that may arise.

The arguments in favour of the relevance of togetherness are getting even stronger when we realize that there is a strong cultural need for cooperative learning that is based on collaborative problem solving and developing a deeper understanding (see Wells, 1999). Collaboration between peers requires reflection on one's individual understanding and comparing this understanding with other pupils through interaction. Collaborative learning calls for revisions of all the knowledge pooled in the interaction. The reason why this leads to improved understandings is that the pupils are willing to share their understandings and keep on doing so despite possible disagreements. This process of collaboration requires a basic feeling of togetherness in the sense that I mentioned before.

It is the teacher who has to rouse this feeling of togetherness among the pupils. It evokes solidarity, with the result that the pupils feel they belong to a group. There is probably no uniform way to create or maintain togetherness. Different strategies can be used for the same purpose of creating or maintaining togetherness, depending on the developmental level of the participants, the situation at hand, and the personal interests of the participants in an activity. For example, this feeling of solidarity can be created by giving a hearty welcome to every child individually, or by sharing one's experience with one another. At the beginning of each activity a teacher has to create a feeling of togetherness among the pupils. This is the foundation from which activities can be built up and expanded.

The goal of creating togetherness is based on rousing a feeling of solidarity, a communal sense provided by the teacher. This is only possible when the children feel confident in this environment and when the teacher has a sensitive and responsive attitude to the children's need. Children feel that the teacher has a genuine interest in what they are saying when she helps them in their thinking process, helps them in putting ideas into words, asks them questions, and elicits a reaction from other pupils. Because the children at the schools where I did my observations usually show less interest in getting involved in shared activities, it would be a priority to stimulate them to become more active participators. They must experience that their contribution is welcomed and crucial. First of all they have to feel safe in the situation in which they are. The teacher has to be sensitive and responsive to the children's outputs and create a positive climate for interactions. When the children feel comfortable they dare to speak and act.

Example:

> *The children (C) and the teacher (T) are sitting in a circle. Florence (F), the speech therapist, is also there (P=pupil):*
> *T: Florence, you were not here for a week, but we have already seen so much, did so much, and the whole classroom is different...*
> *F: Yes, I have seen it already.*
> *C: Yes!!*
> *P: ... sing new songs.*
> *T: And we have sung new songs.*
> *P: There. [points]*
> *F: Oh, the songs hanging over there, you have already sung them? Wonderful. Really good.*
> *P: [walks over there] This one I really like.*
> *T: This one, yes. Shall we sing this one for Florence?*

Florence has been on vacation for a week and the teacher lets her know that they did many things that week. By saying that they saw and did many things, the teacher emphasizes the group's activity ('we') and is contributing to a feeling of togetherness among the pupils: this is what they have done last week, together! One of the pupils says that they have also sung new songs. By doing a song for Florence, the children can show what they did last week.

Revoicing

The next role I want to discuss is revoicing. O'Connor and Michaels (1996) describe revoicing as a particular kind of re-uttering of a pupil's contribution by another participant in the discussion. This can be the teacher, a peer or a therapist. The teacher can use revoicing to relate the pupil's contribution to the ongoing activity or to the utterances of other pupils. The latter is called 'aligning' by O'Connor and Michaels. Aligning describes the act of positioning the pupils relative to one another, by placing their contributions to the discussion alongside or opposite to the other contributions. Such revoicing also creates a slot for the pupils to agree or disagree with the teacher's characterization of the pupils' contributions, thus ultimately crediting the contents of the reformulation to the pupils themselves. Reformulating and recasting of a pupil's contribution can be conceived as an attempt to 'give a bigger voice' to a pupil's contribution. The contribution is necessarily transformed: it can be uttered more succinctly, loudly, completely or in a different register.

A part of revoicing is animation. The teacher can give pupils participant roles and social identities that are relevant to the moment. When the teacher asks a pupil a question, she gives the pupil the role of the person who answers the questions, and herself the role of the one who asks the questions. By using animation, the teacher also puts herself in the role the 'animator'. The animator is the one who appoints the roles. What the pupils have said becomes a 'voice' by animation, a personal perspective related to the role they have taken. By using revoicing, the teacher tries to clarify the pupils' perspective. Instead of using revoicing by herself, the teacher can also let other children give new renditions of another pupil's contribution. In that way the children try to repeat, clarify, and elaborate each other's contributions.

Revoicing can be used for several purposes: more concise formulating of a contribution, reformulation of the contribution in a different register, animation, re-positioning vis-à-vis the other pupils or the content of the conversation, and organizing the social organization in the classroom (for example focusing the attention of pupils). Revoicing is not just repeating a pupil's contribution; by revoicing the teacher puts a surplus in her reformulation and still credits the utterance to the pupils themselves.

For children who need special care and especially children who have hearing and speech problems, it is of great importance that the teacher stimulates their speaking by revoicing. If used in a proper way it gives the children a feeling that it does matter when they say something. And although they may not have said it properly, the teacher was able to understand what they wanted to say and they can confirm the revoicing. It is also an opportunity for them to hear the proper way of speaking.

Example:

> *It is almost Christmas. The teacher (T) and her pupils are pretending they drive in a car to get a Christmas tree. A pupil (P) is driving.*
> *T: Where are we going?*
> *P: Shop, get Christmas tree.*
> *T: Oh, are we going to the shop to get a Christmas tree, that's good!*
> *The pupil nods.*

This is an example of revoicing. The pupil replies to the teacher's question. It is a short sentence; he only uses the necessary words. The teacher repeats the child's contribution and puts it in a better-structured and more complete sentence. By formulating the sentence in this way, she wants to ensure that the pupil will use more extensive language next time. She also gives a 'bigger voice' to this pupil's contribution so all the other pupils can hear and understand more clearly what he has said. After the teacher's contribution the pupil nods. By doing this he approves of the reformulation: this is what he had really said. The pupil, giving out a signal of agreement, credits the content of the teacher's reformulation.

Example:

> *The children have created a supermarket in their classroom. Maarten (M) and Krista (K) are making an advertisement for the sales next week. They try to find a slogan. The teacher (T) takes a look at their work.*
> *K: Cookies cost nothing.*

T: Cookies cost nothing... Does that mean that they are free?
K: No...
T: What do you think Maarten?
M: I don't like it.
T: Why not?
M: They have to cost something.
T: What do you think of... cookies cost almost nothing on Monday? How about that?
The children nod.

This is an example of animation. The teacher likes to know what Krista means with her slogan; does she really mean that the cookies are free? It seems that Krista thinks that the customers still have to pay, although the slogan says that cookies cost nothing. The teacher does not react to this by herself, but asks Maarten what he thinks of it. Here she uses animation so that the other pupil can give his own impression about Krista's contribution. When Maarten does not like the teacher's proposal, the teacher mediates the process by giving an example that both children like. They agree and nod.

Structuring and assisting activities

Structuring is providing arrangement and form to an activity, providing it with a sense of clarity and fluidity. For the teacher, structuring of an activity means that her actions are focused on clarifying actions to and from children, making the activity well organized, and giving coherence. Structuring concerns the handling of the situation, not the handling of the child (Heijkant et al., 2000). This means that the teacher has to clarify, simplify, and organize the activity, so that the situation becomes understandable for the pupil and the teacher. Through this scaffolding the teachers makes the activity more easily accessible for the children. In that sense it has nothing to do with wielding of power, or giving punishment. Meaningfulness and clarity about the way things are organized in an activity makes it easier for the pupils and for the teacher to participate. They know what they can expect from each other and from the activity itself. Moreover, structuring gives the teacher better control of the activity's pace and provides her with a clear overview of the overall situation. It is important to point out here, that the teacher must take care that the process of scaffolding in itself should be a meaningful process for the children, so every step in the structuring must be clear for the children and functional for their shared activity (see Stone, 1993).

By assisting in the activity the teacher lines up as a partner of the children and participates with them in the activity. It is important to pay attention to the content of the activity, the performance, the actions (what everyone is doing and how do they do it), and to the language of the pupils and what they may want to express. The teacher can participate in the children's play. By asking questions and giving them suggestions she can assist the actions of the pupils. Through participation in the children's play a teacher can discover the meanings of the pupils, join in their projects, and from that aid the pupils further in their play and in their development. A goal of the teacher is to let the activity be as authentic as possible.

Assisting an activity starts with closely monitoring the pupils and being attentive and receptive to their messages and meanings. The teacher follows the child but does not take over the initiative of the child. By giving affirmation, she invites the child to think further. In this process, approval for the pupil is very important; with this he gets the confidence that he is able to do things. So, assisting an activity turns out to be more than just being receptive: it has to be a developmental process. The assistance should refer to the actions and thinking of the child.

'Modeling' is an important part of assisting an activity. Tharp and Gallimore (1988) describe modeling as offering behaviour for imitation. Imitation of behaviour is something people have always done. The socialization of children (and also of other new members of a culture) mainly comes about through imitation of the members of their community. Children participate in adults' activities through a process of assisted participation, in which the possibility of learning by means of imitation is interwoven in the structure of daily life. Most of the time this is an unconscious process. Modeling is a powerful tool in the assistance of children. Adults, teachers as well, become a role model for children. Pupils imitate the manner of speech and acting of the teacher and interiorise it in due time .

During the assistance of pupils, the teacher has the possibility to create a zone of proximal development. By participating together in an activity the teacher can see what a pupil is able to do and not yet able to do. Through such collaboration the pupil can be moved a step further in his development. For the time being, the teacher can take responsibility for the actions that a pupil is not able to perform yet. She acts as a model so the pupil gets a chance to imitate her behaviour.

Structuring of activities and assisting children in activities are important roles that teachers can adopt when interacting with children. For children who need special care this is of major importance because such children tend to show less involvement in activities. Assistance has to be refined and more directed to the needs of the child as they engage in the activity. Learning to perform an activity comprehensibly can require that certain actions have to be assisted in a very elaborated and intensive manner. This is possible through making tools available to the pupils. It can also be necessary to structure the activity thoroughly in collaboration with the child and taking more time to give them a chance to work out important details of the activity. For example, when children pretend that the classroom is a supermarket. A teacher has to pay attention to the goal of the activity (buying milk), and the sequence of the actions to attain that goal (put the stuff in the trolley, go to the pay-desk, put the stuff on the counter, pay).

Example:
> A teacher (T) assists a pupil (P) in a shopping-play.
> T: [to a pupil] Shall we go to the shop together?
> P: Yes!
> T: Then we have take along a wallet and a bag with us, right?
> P: Yes.

T: *What shall we buy?*
P: *Milk!*
T: *Milk? Okay. Well, get it. Do you see the milk?*
P: *There!*
T: *Ok, how about putting it in the trolley?*
The pupil puts the milk in it. They walk to the counter.
T: *You can put it on the counter now. Hello sir of the pay-desk. We'd like to pay.*
The pupil puts the milk on the counter.
T: *And now we have to ask: how much is it?*

...
T: *You don't know?*
The 'sir of the pay-desk' (S) mutters something.
T: *Oh, two guilders.*
The pupil goes behind the counter.
T: *Look, here's the wallet. Take a look.*
The pupil is coming back and takes out one coin.
T: *Is that enough?*
P: *Yes.*
T: *Yes? You have to pay two guilders. You just picked out one.*
The pupil takes out another coin. Meanwhile the 'sir of the pay-desk' walks away.
T: *Sir of the pay-desk, where are you going? Look, here's the money. Is it enough?*
S: *(Coming back) Yes. (He takes the money).*

It is difficult for the pupil to participate in activities on his own. That is why the teacher offers to go shopping with him. She assists him in the shopping-activity. First she helps by reminding him to take a bag and a wallet to the shop; thereupon she asks what they shall buy. Step by step she creates a scaffold for the activity. She pays much attention to the performance of the activity, clarifies the actions belonging to doing shopping, and offers these actions within a structural framework to the child. After they are finished with their shopping, they go to the counter. By saying: 'You can put it on the counter now. Hello sir of the pay-desk. We'd like to pay' she assists the pupil in his role as a customer and the other pupil in his role as 'sir of the pay-desk'. In this manner she clarifies both roles for the children and makes clear what they want to do: pay for the things they bought. She assists the pupil by saying that they now have to ask how much it costs and by letting him pay the two guilders. When the 'sir of the pay-desk' walks away the teacher calls him back by asking if the money is enough. Immediately he is back in his role and takes the money.

Conclusion
The roles and functions I described in this chapter are taken from my observations in early special education classrooms that follow the play-based approach. Of course, teachers outside special education can also use this approach. It is in interaction within

the play activity, where young children come to learning new actions and their meanings. That is why it is very important that teachers know which roles they can adopt and what functions these roles have. However, for special education classrooms these roles are of greater importance. Here the necessity of elaborate language is crucial. If this does not happen the children will get stuck in their development, or even worse, they may not be challenged enough and their development will become 'retroactive', thereby losing what they may have achieved so far.

In conclusion we can say that the theoretically expected roles can indeed be found in current practices. By explicitly describing these examples of good practice I hope to provide meaningful models for the improvement of teaching in a play-based curriculum, both in and outside special education.

References

Bodrova, E. & Leong, D.J. (1996). *Tools of the mind. The Vygotskian Approach to Early Childhood Education.* Englewood Cliffs, New Yersey: Prentice-Hall, Inc.

Janssen-Vos, F. (1997). *Basisontwikkeling in de onderbouw.* [Basic development in the early grades of primary school]. Assen: Van Gorcum.

Heijkant, van den, C. & Wegen, van der, R. (2000). *De klas in beeld. Video Interactie Begeleiding in School.* [The classroom portrayed. Video-interaction coaching in school]. Heeswijk-Dinther: Uitgeverij Esstede.

O'Connor, M.C. & Michaels, S. (1996). Shifting participant frameworks: orchestrating thinking practices in group discussions. In: Hicks, D. (Ed.), *Discourse, learning, and schooling.* (pp. 63-103). Cambridge: Cambridge University Press.

Oers, B. van (1992). Ontwikkelingsgericht onderwijs in de onderbouw: contouren van een cultuurhistorische onderwijsvisie [Developmental education in the early grades of primary school: Outline of a cultural historical view on school]. In B. van Oers & F. Janssen-Vos (red.), *Visies op onderwijs aan jonge kinderen.* (pp. 53-71). Assen: Van Gorcum.

Oers, B. van (1998). In hoofdlijnen. De theorie en praktijk van ontwikkelingsgericht onderwijs. [Main lines: Theory and practice of developmental education] *Vernieuwing, Tijdschrift voor Onderwijs en Opvoeding,* 57, 5/6, 8-10.

Oers, van B. & Hännikäinen, M. (2001). Some Thoughts About Togetherness: an introduction. *The International Journal of Early Years Education,* 9, 2, 101-108.

Peters, I. (2001). Weer samen naar school. Ontwikkelingsgericht onderwijs [Going to school together again. Developmental education]. *De wereld van het jonge kind.* 28, 7, 211-213.

Schiferli, T. & Schoonhoven, E. (1994). De leerkracht als partner in een MLK-klas. Samen met leerlingen werken aan zinvolle activiteiten. [The teacher as a partner in the special education classroom]. *Vernieuwing, Tijdschrift voor Onderwijs en Opvoeding,* 53, 10, 10-12.

Stone, C.A. (1993). What is missing in the metaphor of scaffolding? In: E.A. Forman, N. Minick, & A.C. Stone (Eds.), *Contexts for learning: sociocultural determinants in children's development* (pp. 169 - 184). Oxford: Oxford University Press.

Tharp, R.G. & Gallimore, R. (1988). *Rousing minds to life. Teaching, learning, and schooling in social context.* Cambridge: Cambridge University Press.

Wells, G. (1999). *Dialogic Inquiry. Towards a Sociocultural Practice and Theory of Education.* Cambridge: Cambridge University Press.

List of authors:

BURTON, LEONE,
University of Birmingham,
8 Grange Walk
London SE1 3DT
leone.burton@virgin.net

DIJK, EELJE F.,
Faculty of Psychology and Education,
Department of Education and Curriculum.
Vrije Universiteit Amsterdam.
Van der Boechorststraat 1,
1081 BT Amsterdam, The Netherlands,
ef.dijk@psy.vu.nl

EGAN, KIERAN,
Faculty of Education
Simon Fraser University
Burnaby, B.C. Canada V5A 1S6
email: egan@sfu.ca
http://www.educ.sfu.ca/people/faculty/kegan/
http://www.ierg.net

ENGEL, SUSAN,
Department of Psychology
Williams College
Williamstown MA 01267
Susan.L.Engel@williams.edu

FIJMA, NIKO,
De Activiteit
National Centre for Developmental Education
Kanaalkade 16c, 1811 LP Alkmaar,
The Netherlands
info@de-activiteit.nl

JANSSEN-VOS, FREA
Tureluur 2,
1902 KN Castricum, The Netherlands
janssen-vos@planet.nl

MORSS, JOHN,
m.nichterlein@bigpond.com

VAN OERS, BERT,
Faculty of Psychology and Education,
Department of Education and Curriculum.
Vrije Universiteit Amsterdam.
Van der Boechorststraat 1,
1081 BT Amsterdam, The Netherlands.
hjm.van.oers@psy.vu.nl

PETERS, ISABEL,
Faculty of Psychology and Education,
Department of Education and Curriculum.
Vrije Universiteit Amsterdam.
van der Boechorststraat 1,
1081 BT Amsterdam, The Netherlands.
isabelpeters@wanadoo.nl

POMPERT, BEA,
De Activiteit
National Centre for Developmental Education
Kanaalkade 16c, 1811 LP Alkmaar,
The Netherlands
info@de-activiteit.nl

SCHIFERLI, TRUDY,
Hogeschool Brabant, University of
Professional Education, Faculty of Teacher
Training
Dr.J.Ingenhouszplein 2
P.O Box 90 183
4800 RN Breda The Netherlands
schiferli.g@hsbrabant.nl

SINGER, ELLY,
University of Amsterdam and University of
Utrecht
Department of Developmental Psychology
P.O. 80.140, 3508 TC Utrecht,
The Netherlands
E.Singer@fss.uu.nl

Acknowledgements:

Chapter 2: Kieran Egan's chapter was originally presented as a keynote at the 11th EECERA conference in Alkmaar (2001).

Chapter 3: Susan Engels' chapter was originally presented as a keynote at the 11th EECERA conference in Alkmaar (2001). Some of the material in this chapter is drawn from a forth-coming book on children's thinking, to be published by Harvard University Press, 2004.

Chapter 4: Leone Burton's chapter was originally presented as a keynote at the 11th EECERA conference in Alkmaar (2001); also published in the European Early Childhood Education Journal, 2002, vol. 10, 2, 5 – 18.

Chapter 5: Elly Singer's chapter was originally presented as a keynote at the 11th EECERA conference in Alkmaar (2001); also published in the European Early Childhood Education Journal, 2002, vol. 10, nr 1, 55-67.

Chapter 6: John Morss' chapter was originally presented as a keynote at the 11th EECERA conference in Alkmaar (2001). The author would like to dedicate this chapter to the Noonan family of Dunedin, New Zealand, for their generosity to a nomad.

Chapter 7: This chapter (Frea Janssen-Vos) was originally presented in a preconference workshop of the 11th EECERA conference in Alkmaar (2001). It is partly derived from Janssen-Vos, F. & van Oers, B. (1998). Basic Development: a Vygotskian strategy for development
stimulation.

Chapter 8: This chapter (van Oers, Janssen-Vos, Pompert & Schiferli) was originally written for the 5th EECERA conference in Paris (1995). An abbreviated version is published in French in: S. Rayna, M. Delau, & F. Laevers (eds.), L'education préscolaire: Quels objectifs pédagogiques? (pp. 235-255). Paris: Nathan, 1996.

Chapter 9: This chapter (Pompert & Janssen-Vos) is a revised version of a paper that was originally presented at the 4th EECERA conference in Göteborg (Sweden, 1994).

Chapter 10: This chapter (Fijma) was originally a paper presented at the 10th EECERA conference in London (2000).

Chapter 11: This chapter (Dijk) was originally a paper presented at the 11th EECERA conference in Alkmaar (2001).

Chapter 12: This chapter (Peters) was originally a paper presented at the 11th EECERA conference in Alkmaar (2001).